If *The Church from Every Tribe and Ton*̲ question, "What does it mean to be the church, cannot be divorced from other fundamental matters. *Where* is the church located? How are the people of God to define their identity and mission in *that place*? These creative Majority World voices open up new vistas that can only arise from and in commitment to their contexts. But, these essays are not simply reflections from diverse parts of the globe that can be held at arms-length as an interesting exercise in ecclesiology. They are profound explorations of the inexhaustible riches of the Word that reveal fresh insights into the church as a situated community called to incarnate the presence of God. In sum, they are needful contributions for all Christians to better understand faith and life in the world.

M. Daniel Carroll R., PhD
Blanchard Professor of Old Testament,
Wheaton College and Graduate School, Wheaton, IL, USA

This volume, like its predecessors, aptly captures a plethora of perspectives on what it means to be church. It evokes different emotions as we encounter the familiar and the unfamiliar. The socio-political issues emanating from Latin America and their ecclesiological ramifications are familiar to others elsewhere due to globalization. But we are jolted by the unfamiliar heart-wrenching cry of Palestinian Christians over their land and the strange world of rites, ceremonies, and kinship of Chinese and African families. These contributions should help Christians everywhere not only to broaden their vision of the church but also to feel a kindred spirit with each other.

Rev Simon Chan, PhD
Former Earnest Lau Professor of Systematic Theology,
Trinity Theological College, Singapore

The book presents distinctive theological and biblical features of contextual development. Each study is based on a specific theme close to the social and cultural context of the contributor. The list of contributors reveals a heavy emphasis on Majority World scholars, and on the diversity of church traditions. The authors make a remarkable connection between the theology process and the real-life experience of God's people. This collective contextual theology, however, is also pertinent to the global church. Furthermore, the book succeeds in being both biblically truthful and culturally applicable, emphasizing that the word of God is for the whole of humanity throughout its entire history and various cultures. Each author represents contemporary rationale among an extensive selection of traditional academics. The book will inspire and challenge local and global church leaders and theologians.

Julie Ma, PhD
Associate Professor of Missions and Intercultural Studies,
Undergraduate College of Theology and Ministry,
Oral Roberts University, Tulsa, OK, USA

The Majority World Theology Series has challenged us to remember that all theology is local and contextual and that the global church needs to hear the voices of theologians and leaders from all the churches if it is to effectively fulfill its mission and role in our globalized world. This volume, *The Church from Every Tribe and Tongue: Ecclesiology in the Majority World,* is particularly crucial because our view of the church impacts how we think about our mission in the world.

Globalization offers the promise of hearing more voices and providing platforms for those who have not had one in the past. But globalized markets usually favor theologians from the North and often overwhelm and effectively silence voices from the Global South. The churches from the Majority World lose when the only voices that are published are those translated from the North and the North loses because it ends up in an echo chamber where the voices of the dynamic and growing churches of the Majority World cannot be heard.

This collection of essays reflects the diversity of the churches around the world. Many of these churches trace their roots to the West, but they have taken their specific contexts seriously and are seeking to develop communities of faith that reflect the gospel and address the realities of their social location. They are a reflection of the rich diversity that is the church of Jesus Christ around the world. As we listen to these voices and to each other, we can better learn how to be a part of God's mission in our globalized world.

Juan Francisco Martínez, PhD
Professor of Hispanic Studies and Pastoral Leadership,
Fuller Theological Seminary, Pasadena, CA, USA

MAJORITY WORLD THEOLOGY SERIES

SERIES EDITORS

Gene L. Green, Stephen T. Pardue, and K. K. Yeo

The Majority World Theology series exists because of the seismic shifts in the makeup of world Christianity. At this moment in history, more Christians live in the Majority World than in Europe and North America. However, most theological literature does not reflect the rising tide of Christian reflection coming from these regions. The Majority World authors in this series seek to produce, collaboratively, biblical and theological textbooks that are about, from, and to the Majority World. By assembling scholars from around the globe who share a concern to do theology in light of Christian Scripture and in dialogue with Christian tradition coming from the Western church, this series offers readers the chance to listen in on insightful, productive, and unprecedented in-person conversations. Each volume pursues a specific theological topic and is designed to be accessible to students and scholars alike.

TITLES IN THIS SERIES

Jesus without Borders: Christology in the Majority World
2015 | 9781783689170

The Trinity among the Nations: The Doctrine of God in the Majority World
2015 | 9781783681051

The Spirit over the Earth: Pneumatology in the Majority World
2016 | 978178368256

So Great a Salvation: Soteriology in the Majority World
2017 | 9781783683789

The Church from Every Tribe and Tongue: Ecclesiology in the Majority World
2018 | 9781783684489

Eschatology in the Majority World
forthcoming 2019

The Church from Every Tribe and Tongue

Ecclesiology in the Majority World

Edited by

Gene L. Green, Stephen Pardue, and K. K. Yeo

GLOBAL LIBRARY

© 2018 Gene L. Green, Stephen T. Pardue, and K. K. Yeo

Published 2018 by Langham Global Library
An imprint of Langham Publishing
www.langhampublishing.org

Langham Publishing and its imprints are a ministry of Langham Partnership

Langham Partnership
PO Box 296, Carlisle, Cumbria, CA3 9WZ, UK
www.langham.org

ISBNs:
978-1-78368-448-9 Print
978-1-78368-449-6 ePub
978-1-78368-450-2 Mobi
978-1-78368-451-9 PDF

British Library Cataloguing-in-Publication Data
A catalogue record for this book is available from the British Library
ISBN: 978-1-78368-448-9

Cover art: © The Great Commission by He Qi. www.heqiart.com
Cover & Book Design: projectluz.com

Contents

God's Community in Majority World Theology

GENE L. GREEN

At the 2016 annual meetings of the Evangelical Theological Society and the Institute for Biblical Research, a group of seven international scholars gathered to present papers and discuss the nature of the church. One additional presenter from China submitted her paper but was not able to attend the gathering. Four of the group are specialists in biblical studies and the others are experts in theology. A few participants flew in from their residences in the United States, although their natal homes were Finland, Columbia, and Korea. Others journeyed from Kenya, Uganda, Costa Rica, and Palestine.

All eight of these authors are engaged in developing contextualized biblical studies and theology, and represent the crescendo of voices from the global church who are thinking afresh about the Bible's message and doing theology both from and to their own contexts. All are members of Christ's "one holy, catholic, and apostolic church," as states the Nicene-Constantinopolitan Creed (or the *Symbolum Nicaenum* of AD 381). While they have each reflected on Scripture and theology in relation to the realities and their experiences within their homelands, they present their findings as an offering to Christ's whole church. Throughout the history of the church around the globe, all biblical reflection and theologizing have been carried out with reference to the immediate contexts of the interpreters. As the Peruvian theologian Dr Samuel Escobar once said to me, "Toda la teología es contextual."[1] But that does not mean that these theologies and biblical reflections are simply for a particular time, place, and people. Each contributes to a truly catholic or universal

1. "All theology is contextual."

1

theology just as much as the reflections received from early Christian authors in the first centuries or the Reformers of the sixteenth century. From the beginning the church has sought to understand God and his way of salvation in concert with the daily realities believers faced within their communities and societies. They are not only local expressions of the faith but faithful catholic biblical studies and theology, full stop.

The Majority World Theology Series

The present collection of essays is the fifth in the six-volume Majority World Theology series. The first four volumes covered Christology (*Jesus Without Borders*, 2014), the doctrine of God and the Trinity (*The Trinity among the Nations*, 2015), pneumatology (*The Spirit over the Earth*, 2016), and soteriology (*So Great a Salvation*, 2017).[2] The current volume on ecclesiology (*Christ's Global Church*, 2018) is the penultimate collection, to be followed by eight essays on eschatology (forthcoming, 2019). From the inception of the Majority World Theology series, the editors, K. K. Yeo from Malaysia, Steve Pardue in the Philippines, and Gene Green, who formerly worked in Latin America, have conceived of these volumes as supplemental texts for courses on the respective theological themes or stand-alone volumes for courses on theological developments within the Majority World. We, the editors, have asked each contributor to engage the relevant historic creeds of the church – in this case Nicea-Constantinople – and to survey developments within his or her region. The authors were all invited to contribute their own constructive theological work as well. They were also tasked with pulling together a brief bibliography of additional readings on the topic which represent relevant reflections from their part of the world and elsewhere. In all volumes in the series, we have asked one presenter to survey the Western theological tradition on the topic as we then turn to Majority World developments. Scores of Majority World scholars have expressed their indebtedness to the Western tradition but recognize that it does not always respond adequately to the questions raised within their contexts and has sometimes overlooked important aspects of Scripture's message.

2. Gene L. Green, Stephen T. Pardue, and K. K. Yeo, eds., Majority World Theology series (Grand Rapids/Cambridge: Eerdmans; Carlisle: Langham Global Library, 2014–17).

The design of the Majority World Theology series responds to the repeated questions we have received from colleagues and students who wanted to know what Majority World scholars were saying on a particular topic. While this and other volumes in the series do not present comprehensive surveys of all the biblical reflection and theological developments within Africa, Asia, and Latin America, they are representative of current thinking among a wide sampling of conservative scholars. Some of the names which appear in this and other volumes are well known in the West and elsewhere. Others are younger scholars in the early stages of their own teaching and writing careers. They are all faithful followers of Christ who hold the Bible as God's authoritative Word. Their essays are fresh winds of God's work throughout the world. Reviews of scholarly tomes like this one are always varied and useful, but students' responses ring loudest in our ears. They tell about the delight and deepened faith they have discovered through reading along the grain with Christians elsewhere in the world. They come to understand new dimensions of the faith not previously imagined yet wonderfully relevant.

Ecclesiology in the Majority World: The Authors and Their Essays

This volume on the doctrine of the church, or ecclesiology, vividly demonstrates how reading with a different set of questions and seeing from a non-Western context can broaden our understanding of the gospel. Most trained in the Western academy could not imagine how ecclesiology and a Palestinian Christian theology of the land might intersect, for example. Recently I had the honor of leading a course for the North American Institute for Indigenous Theological Studies (naiits.com) on "Community in the New Testament." Native authors and students pushed out our understanding of God's community to include all creation, as Keetoowah Cherokee scholar Randy Woodley points out in his book *Shalom and the Community of Creation: An Indigenous Vision*.[3] These contextual readings are not a vain syncretism which allows local or traditional values and perspectives to dominate over the gospel.

3. Randy S. Woodley, *Shalom and the Community of Creation: An Indigenous Vision*, Prophetic Christianity Series (Grand Rapids: Eerdmans, 2012).

Rather they seek to be both biblically faithful and culturally relevant, understanding that Scripture is God's Word for all times and cultures. From the beginning God's message has come clothed in culture.

This collection on ecclesiology launches with Veli-Matti Kärkkäinen's essay on "Ecclesiology and the Church in Christian Tradition and Western Theology." Anyone reading about developments in Majority World theology will know Kärkkäinen's interest and publications in this field, especially his five-volume systematic theology entitled *A Constructive Christian Theology for the Pluralistic World* (Eerdmans, 2013–17). The last volume in this series, *Hope and Community*, builds upon his previous work on the church, *An Introduction to Ecclesiology: Ecumenical, Historical and Global Perspectives* (Eerdmans, 2002). Kärkkäinen baptizes us into New Testament teaching on the church, focusing upon its key symbols as the people of God, the body of Christ, and the temple of the Spirit. He moves forward into the creeds which identify the church's unity, holiness, catholicity, and apostolicity. He recalls, however, that the church's existence is instrumental in God's mission. As he states, "God's community on earth (the church) is graciously drawn into the coming of God's kingdom, his righteous reign over all creation. That makes the church missionary by its very nature. The church exists as mission." That the mission has been effective is marked by the church's growth from approximately 10,000 members at the turn of the first century to 2.4 billion members in the first decades of the twenty-first. Moreover, the church has migrated from its center in Europe and North America to the Global South and East. Some readers may not yet realize that Christians living in the North Atlantic region now find themselves on the geographical margins of the church and not at its center. But, Kärkkäinen concludes, the church around the globe faces two great challenges at present: secularism and religious pluralism. "The rise of both secularism and religious pluralism means that the ecclesiologies of the third millennium have to pay attention not only to what is inside the church and within the Christian tradition, but also to the teaching of other religious traditions and the mindset of the secular public." With this observation Kärkkäinen hands off to the other authors in this volume, all of whom are keenly aware of the contextual realities which surround them as they develop this third-millennium ecclesiology.

Ruth Padilla DeBorst is a Latina theologian who resides in Costa Rica where she works with the Comunidad de Estudios Teológicos Interdisciplinarios. Past President of the Latin American Theological Fellowship, Padilla DeBorst has for years been an active participant in the development of Latina/o theological reflection. She possesses the rare ability to present theology lyrically (we could say that she "sings" theology), as readers of her essay will hear. Like many theologians within her context, whether committed to *misión integral* (integral mission) or *las teologías de la liberación* (liberation theologies), Padilla DeBorst traces the relationship between the church and the powers of the day. What does it mean to live as "church" under the imperial power of colonial Christendom or under foreign commercial or educational powers? She notes that the Latin American church sometimes has succumbed to triumphalist metaphors alien to the gospel but she draws hope from developments within the *misión integral* movement which "seeks to engage followers of Jesus in linking the whole gospel to the whole of life under the lordship of Christ in the power of the Holy Spirit so that the reign of God and God's justice may be made visible in particular historical contexts." Padilla DeBorst traces the ecclesial movement "from below" within the base ecclesial communities and surging Pentecostalism in Latin America. But she understands the church as "a school for citizenship," a people drawn together by the Community-of-Love and called to follow Jesus into the world. They are to then go out to the rest of society together. She quotes the late Orlando Costas, who said the church is called to "move into the neighborhood." This, she notes, "entails sacrificial incarnation in the messiness of socio-economic, political, and ecological realities." For Padilla DeBorst, the church is not a community separate and aloof, but a community engaged in all of life's hard realities.

Wonsuk Ma, a Korean theologian who for some time directed the Oxford Centre for Mission Studies and now serves as Distinguished Professor of Global Christianity at Oral Roberts University, is fluent in theological developments in Asia and around the globe. Ma reminds us from the start that "the church was born in Asia" yet today in many parts of Asia it seems like a "foreign religion." K. K. Yeo once said that many in China, for example, believe that one must choose whether to be Christian or Chinese since Christianity is regarded as a Western faith. Despite this, however, Ma recognizes distinct ecclesiological developments within the Asian context. Since the region is so vast, however, he opts for presenting two case studies: the post-Cultural Revolution house church called the Word of Life Church and South Korea's well-known Yoido Full Gospel Church. Both these newer churches actively engage with their contexts and shape the received theological traditions around those realties. In other words, newer churches engage in what Justo González called "self-theologizing" in an attempt to bring the gospel into deep dialogue with their cultural contexts. Ma recognizes the central role of these churches' founders in shaping their theological vision.

Among the theological tenets of the Word of Life Church, developed by its founder Peter Yongze Xu, are "(1) salvation through the cross; (2) the way of the cross; and (3) discerning the adulteress" which they identify as the government-registered Three-Self Patriotic Movement. Given their rejection of the state-sanctioned church, Word of Life members believe that suffering which results from "refusing to submit to atheistic government policies" is a mark of the true church. These realities shape the life of their church since, as Ma observes, "there was no identifiable Western 'mother' church to dictate the shape of the church." Added to these realities is the commitment to personal piety, dependence on the Holy Spirit for miracles and guidance, and a deep commitment to mission. On the other hand, the Yoido Full Gospel Church, the world's largest church, headed by David Yonggi Cho, finds guidance in its founder's theology of a "good God" who is able to heal and do the miraculous. Out of this tenet arises the Five-fold Gospel of Jesus as Savior, Baptizer, Healer, Blesser, and Coming King and the Three-fold Salvation which embraces "spiritual, physical, and circumstantial (which includes material) salvation." Ma reflects elsewhere on the relationship between Cho's emphasis on blessing and Shamanism.[4] The Yoido Full Gospel Church places great emphasis on prayer and presents Jesus as "the answer to all human suffering." In mission the church proclaims "the good God, blessing, healing, and God's intervention on his people's behalf." Both Xu and Cho's churches are born from deep contextualization of the gospel into their respective social contexts without much reflection on the historic traditions of Christian ecclesiology.

Stephanie Lowery was raised in Kenya where she currently serves as lecturer in systematic theology at Scott Theological College. In 2017 Lowery published a text on African ecclesiology[5] and so is well suited to pen an essay entitled "Ecclesiology in Africa: Apprentices on a

---

4. Wonsuk Ma, "David Yonggi Cho's Theology of Blessing: Basis, Legitimacy and Limitations," *Evangelical Review of Theology* 35 (2011): 140–141.

5. Stephanie A. Lowery, *Identity and Ecclesiology: Their Relationship among Select African Theologians* (Eugene, OR: Pickwick, 2017).

Mission." Before embarking on constructive work of her own, Lowery outlines prominent themes emerging within contemporary African ecclesiologies. Is the paradigm for the African church the family, with its extended networks that even reach back to the ancestors who are highly venerated? In a simple observation she captures a compelling reason for embracing this model: "If, then, the idea of 'family' points the church back to the doctrine of the Trinity and humans' inherently relational nature, then we ought to give this model more thought, as so many theologians in Africa . . . have done." She notes the caution, however, raised by Georges Titre Ande who prefers the model of church as a "community of life," life being a key concept within African Christology as well. Lowery also touches on developments within the AICs or African Initiated/Independent/Instituted churches which emphasize biblicism, Africanism, and *philadelphia*, or the church as a community of love marked by *koinonia*. Biblical models which resonate with cultural values are picked up in the AICs, such as the church as a priesthood and leaders as prophets. As Lowery says, "While cultural and Old Testament models abound, other ecclesiologies arise from a mélange of cultural, Old Testament, and New Testament references." She adds that some have taken up corporate models from the business world to outline their understanding of the church. In the midst of the diverse richness of African ecclesiologies, however, Lowery is concerned that some churches are reluctant to see themselves as part of the larger "one, holy, catholic, and apostolic" church given the painful relationship with colonial Christianity. At the end of her essay, Lowery takes a bold step by suggesting that "Those enabled by the Spirit are, I propose, intended to be apprentices." The church is a community of learners who live out God's Word and, as disciples (that's what an apprentice is, she reminds us), they follow their Master and always learn more from him. She notes that apprentices are also involved in praxis, carrying out the *missio Dei* but doing so in the recognition that they are "aliens and sojourners," people "who are in some sense outsiders in their contexts: they seek to be contextual, without losing their holiness and their divinely granted identity."

The first four essays were written by theologians representing the West, Latin America, Asia, and Africa. However, we designed the Majority World Theology series to include biblical scholars alongside them. These participants are well versed in biblical exegesis but also recognize that biblical studies cannot be carried out without reference to one's context. We always read from and to a place, an insight common among Majority World biblical scholars. Their approach to Scripture is not to read it from the balcony, to use the language of John MacKay, but from the road, that place where "life is lived tensely, where thought has its birth in conflict and concern, where choices are made and decisions are carried out."[6] While we expect theologians to ask how the gospel plays out within cultures, some readers may think that biblical interpretation should be done objectively using prescribed methods and the proper tools. But Majority World biblical scholars read in ways akin to what Gadamer describes in his seminal text *Truth and Method*. He states, "In our analysis of the hermeneutical process we say that to acquire a horizon of interpretation requires a fusion of horizons," that is, between the biblical author and the biblical reader. He continues, "Every interpretation has to adapt itself to the hermeneutical situation to which it belongs."[7] Insights abound when these scholars read Scripture while acknowledging their place, knowing that they read from and to that place. Their readings honor the authority of Scripture, the apostolic voice, and the fact that the Bible is truly the Word of God for us.

Carlos Sosa Siliezar is a New Testament scholar from Guatemala. His essay entitled "Ecclesiology in Latin America: A Biblical Perspective" first reads Scripture along the grain of Leonardo Boff's ecclesiogenesis and René Padilla's holistic ecclesiology. Boff, a Brazilian scholar, rejected Roman Catholic hierarchies in the church and favored small base communities which live and read Scripture together. Padilla, an Ecuadorian trained as an exegete, proposed an ecclesiology which supported holistic mission, or *misión integral*. Sosa assesses both their positions. He raises cautions regarding Boff's separation of the ecclesiology of Jesus – if indeed there was one – and that of the early church. Boff believed that "the church was not part of Jesus' intentions" since Jesus taught about the coming of the kingdom of God. The failure to establish God's kingdom resulted in the church becoming "the substitute for the unfulfilled kingdom." Sosa critiques this bifurcation between Jesus and the early church while, at the same time, celebrating Boff's affirmation that laypeople can gather around the Word of God without the interven-

6. John MacKay, *A Preface to Christian Theology* (New York: Macmillan, 1941), 27.

7. Hans-Georg Gadamer, *Truth and Method* (New York: Continuum, 2000), 397. See also Gene L. Green, "The Challenge of Global Hermeneutics," in *Global Theology in Evangelical Perspective*, ed. Jeffrey P. Greenman and Gene L. Green (Downers Grove: IVP Academic, 2012), 9–15.

tion of the church. On both counts Sosa's evangelical commitments are evident. On the other hand, Sosa celebrates Padilla's link between integral mission and ecclesiology. Padilla was one of the founders of the Latin American Theological Fellowship, which roots its theology in the concept of holistic mission, so it is no surprise that he links in ecclesiology here. Sosa is clearly more comfortable with Padilla's view, which coalesces Jesus' teaching with what the Gospel writers wrote.

Sosa's own position builds upon Padilla, however, by appeal to the Gospel of John. Sosa identifies John 13:34–35 as a pointer to Jesus's idea of a new community of disciples but he also sees in the text concerns germane to the Latin American context. He remarks that "churches should see themselves as (1) local communities with global awareness, (2) suffering communities that love the world, and (3) communities where diversity is reconciled." The surprise for many readers outside, and perhaps even inside, the Latin American context is that Sosa views these traits as significant not only for the church in and of itself but also for the wider society. For example, Sosa charges that "Laws that regulate economic agreements between Guatemala and the US and the EU are not based on the Johannine idea of love." He draws the Johannine emphasis on love into realms such as business and international law. Sosa stands with a multitude of Majority World scholars who fully embrace a socially engaged faith.

Xiaxia Xue from China was not able to gather with the other scholars in 2016 but provided a provocative paper entitled "The Community as Union with Christ in the Midst of Conflict: An Ecclesiology of the Pauline Letters from a Chinese Perspective." Xue reflects on the nature of the church from a Chinese perspective and brings her observations into dialogue with Pauline ecclesiology. She reflects deeply on the various ecclesial bodies in China and Hong Kong, including the Three-Self Patriotic Movement, the house churches, local assemblies, registered churches, and the True Church of Jesus Christ. She points out that the Three-Self Church is connected deeply with the Chinese social and political environment, while, on the other hand, house churches are a resistant group which "refused to compromise with the communist government." The local churches started under the leadership of Watchman Nee introduced the concept of one church in one locality, a theological trend that has influenced the thinking of many North American Christians. Churches in China hold varied understandings of their relationship to God, his kingdom, and their socio-political context. Later in her essay she points out the further differences between the churches in China and the Chinese congregations in Hong Kong. In all this she highlights the tensions which exist between the churches. For example, she notes the conflict between the Hong Kong and Mainland churches which "on the one hand, has its roots in divergent political opinions and, on the other hand, is caused by their different value systems."

When considering the divisions she returns to the Creed's confession of one holy, catholic, and apostolic church, but mainly focuses on the varied places within the Pauline letters which address the issue of divisions. In exploring the Paulines she notes that divisions were part of the life of the church from the very beginning and so "tension within the church is not an accidental or alien factor." She points out the tremendous diversity within the early churches, including ethnic diversity, and the attendant problems this caused as evidenced in Galatians. First Corinthians points out the divisions in the church based on varied understandings of leadership which found their roots in the surrounding society's values and the church's economic disparity. While not celebrating division, Xue embraces the idea that division is a natural part of the life of the church, whether in Corinth or in Hong Kong and Mainland China. Indeed, she goes so far as to argue that the very essence of the church is found here: "The Community as Union with Christ in the Midst of Conflict." Paul dealt with the conflicts in the province of Galatia and the city of Corinth, but conflict is natural and, indeed, inevitable in the church. She appeals to Paul, however, in prescribing the solution based upon the sacrificial love of Christ demonstrated on the cross and the recognition that we are one body. The ancient text is brought into dialogue with Chinese realities and addresses them directly.

Peter Nyende is from Kenya but currently teaches New Testament at Uganda Christian University. He appeals to the book of Hebrews in his essay "The Church as an Assembly on Mt Zion: An Ecclesiology from Hebrews for African Christians." Nyende stands in the midst of other African biblical scholars and theologians who recognize, as did the late Kwame Bediako from Ghana, that "Hebrews is our epistle."[8] Nyende begins by outlining various strains of African ecclesiologies: identity ecclesiologies focused upon the interests and perspectives of

---

8. Kwame Bediako, *Jesus and the Gospel in Africa: History and Experience* (Maryknoll, NY: Orbis, 2004), 27.

a particular denomination, ecumenical ecclesiologies which attempt to transcend denominational boundaries, and those emanating from the African Initiated Churches (AICs), those founded by Africans and oriented to African realities. Nyende points out the necessity of ecclesial studies in Africa, since by 2025 "Africa will have the highest population of Christians on any continent, standing at more than 700 million." As he works with the biblical text, Nyende focuses upon the notion of God's dwelling, starting in the garden of Eden and going up through the heavenly Mt Zion (Heb 12:22). Starting with Eden, God's dwelling is accessible to humans. Indeed, the Genesis account shows that "God intended the world to be the place of his dwelling with human beings." Nyende continues the discussion by focusing on the period after the fall when via the tabernacle and temple God restored "his dwelling among humans and his kingdom in the world." The temple is associated with its location on Mt Zion. The prophets Isaiah and Micah predicted that the temple would be restored upon the highest mountain, "symbolic of Mt Zion's superiority over other houses of divinities because YHWH, its resident, is superior to all other gods." Turning to the New Testament, Nyende draws the line between God's dwelling in the Old Testament and the way the ecclesiology in Hebrews conceptualizes the church as God's dwelling where Christ is the high priest and where the community worships him. "In some real sense, then," Nyende concludes, "in Christ this community is in God's heavenly house offering prayers and immaterial sacrifices as they are asked to do in Hebrews 13:15." He understands the relevance of this reality for the African church which, unlike many churches in the West, is keenly aware that the spiritual word interacts with the material world. African ecclesiology lives within the interaction between the material and the spiritual planes. Like all other authors in this and the companion volumes in the Majority World Theology series, Nyende delves deeply into the biblical text without ever letting go of the cultural, and in this case the spiritual, context in which he and other African Christians find themselves.

Munther Isaac is a Palestinian Christian who currently serves as the Academic Dean of Bethlehem Bible College. His essay "Ecclesiology and the Theology of the Land: A Palestinian Christian Perspective" brings together two topics commonly held apart in most Western ecclesiologies. Both Isaac and his colleague Yohanna Katanacho, another author in this series, have written a biblical theology of the land from a Palestinian perspective.[9] More than one reader will register surprise at Isaac's opening line: "The Palestinian church takes its identity and theology from its natural and unbroken relationship with the biblical land." He goes on to quote Mitri Raheb, who states, "My self-understanding as a Christian Palestinian has a *territorial dimension*." Those lands are the home of their ancestors and the interplay between the church and the land shapes their understanding of ecclesiology. Like Katanacho, Isaac points out that the land, known as the promised land, belongs to God. As God declares in Leviticus 25:23, "For the land is mine." Isaac deconstructs some contemporary notions of the promised land, first showing that the boundaries of God's land in the Old Testament were fluid and that Genesis 15:18–21 emphasizes God's universal dominion. As in the Great Commission (Matt 28:18 NRSV), Christ's dominion is universal: "All authority in heaven *and on earth* has been given to me" (emphasis added). The earth is Christ's possession (Ps 2:8). But the church is then tasked to establish new "holy places" in new lands – that is, they "recreate the story of Israel in new lands." In this mission, Jerusalem "no longer has to play a central role in relation to the other new locations, because Jesus is now the cornerstone – the center of the new Christian movement." Isaac wants to show that Christian experience is always rooted in time and space, and, for Palestinian Christians, that place is what many call the Holy Land. Land always matters because it is the place where Christ interacts with the world and his church. As Isaac states, "God is the God of nations and lands, and not just the God of individuals." So for Isaac as a Palestinian Christian, there must be a place for what he terms a "territorial ecclesiology." The church is always rooted in the world and its place is God's place.

The land, then, becomes for Isaac a "Fifth Gospel," a place which acts as a witness to God's presence and work in history. Palestinian Christians, then, continue to bear witness to Christ in the very place where the biblical history began. The land tells the story, not just of the past, but of the presence of God's Palestinian people who reside in that very land. The church then becomes the "Sixth Gospel," the community of faith where God dwells and from which the witness of Christ goes

9. Munther Isaac, *From Land to Lands, From Eden to the Renewed Earth* (Carlisle: Langham Monographs, 2015); Yohanna Katanacho, *The Land of Christ: A Palestinian Cry* (Eugene, OR: Pickwick, 2013); and "Reading the Gospel of John through Palestinian Eyes," in *Jesus Without Borders: Christology in the Majority World*, ed. Gene L. Green, Stephen T. Pardue, and K. K. Yeo (Grand Rapids/Cambridge: Eerdmans, 2014), 103–122.

forth. The land for Isaac and for others from his place is, in Sabbah's words, "a dwelling place for God with humanity, and a homeland for all the children of God."[10] With these words, Isaac opens the door to a deeper understanding of the presence of the church in the world, in any land where Christ is named.

Threads in the Ecclesial Tapestry

In discussing ecclesiology, all of these biblical scholars and theologians affirm that they cannot develop a doctrine of the church without reference to the context in which the church lives out its faith in service to Christ. The opening essay by Kärkkäinen, who is not a Majority World theologian but knows the conversation, says that ecclesiologies must take into account both secularism and pluralism in society. In contrast, Nyende names African awareness of the spiritual world as an important contextual consideration. Ma, Padilla, Sosa, Xue, and Isaac all point to the political context of the church as a factor in the development of ecclesiology. Lowery names the cultural values of the family and community as key contextual considerations, while Xue struggles with ecclesial division rather than unity as a prominent consideration in ecclesiology. If indeed all theology is contextual, each biblical scholar and theologian must be a deep and thoughtful reader of the biblical text, the church's theological traditions, and the cultural contexts in which the church defines its being and mission.

Stemming from these contexts, their reflections on ecclesiology bring us theological insights which are not commonplace in discussions about the nature of the church. Padilla sees the church engaged in a holistic mission, playing its role in society under God's reign. The church, then, becomes a school for citizenship. Others likewise emphasize faithful Christian social praxis as a central piece of their ecclesiology. Lowery talks about the church as a body of apprentices in society engaged in praxis while Sosa sees the church's role in social reconciliation. Isaac's ecclesiology summons us to think about land and place as essential for the church's identity and calling. But both Ma and Sosa remind us that the church is a suffering community and must find its

---

10. M. Sabbah, *Sawtun Sarīkhun Fīl Barriya (A Voice Crying Out in the Wilderness)* (Arabic book; Jerusalem: Latin Seminary, 2008), 28.

self-understanding in relation to the hostility it experiences within society. The church lives along the way of the cross, and Ma reminds us that this includes the deep life of prayer. Xue walks a similar road by working out an ecclesiology which embraces church division as well as unity. These and other living streams bring us all fresh understanding of what it means to be Christ's church in the world. We are all richer and refreshed by their insights.

Conclusion

Read and savor these essays. Each comes from living on the road in faith. Every author in this volume refuses to rest content with constructing theological abstractions. They all long to understand how life and theology intersect. Readers looking for a neatly outlined systematic theology will not find it here. The categories are set within the interplay between the church's context, its Lord, and his Word. The hermeneutical circle runs between context and Scripture in the development of relevant and theological understanding. All the authors offer their reflections as vital air, water, and food for their communities and also as gifts for Christ's church throughout the world. Read and savor, and learn.

This volume, like the others in the Majority World Theology series, was made possible through the generous work of the authors and the faithful support of their respective institutions. We owe them all hearty thanks for their commitment. Bringing together scholars from around the globe is an enormous logistical and financial undertaking which would not have been possible without the underwriting of ScholarLeaders International and John Shen from Beijing. The unwavering commitment of Larry Smith and Evan Hunter, President and Vice President respectively, and of Lynn Simmons, who oversees finances, has meant that this dream could become reality. We cannot adequately express our joy for your partnership. We are also indebted to Langham Publishing for publishing this and all the other volumes in the series. Our gratitude to Pieter Kwant, Director of Langham Literature, is deep. We also want to thank Suzanne Mitchell for her fine editorial work and Jixun Hu for preparing the indices in this volume. Their labor has made this a highly accessible collection.

We stand in awe at what God is doing through his church around the world and, as always, give him the honor and the glory.

CHAPTER 1

Ecclesiology and the Church in Christian Tradition and Western Theology[1]

Veli-Matti Kärkkäinen

ABSTRACT

This essay seeks to provide a concise description of the theology of the church, the Christian community, based on biblical teachings and early Christian intuitions and creedal statements. The missionary nature of the one, holy, catholic, and apostolic church, in the service of the kingdom of God, will be highlighted as well as the church's continual striving for unity in the midst of rampant divisions and splits. The chapter ends with a look at urgent ecclesiological challenges in the religiously pluralistic and secularized global world.

The Evolution and Rise of Ecclesiology

The senior Catholic ecclesiologist Hans Küng opens his now-classic *The Church* by observing that "[t]hough there is much talk nowadays about the Church in the secular world, there is not a corresponding aware-

---

1. I have kept the documentation to a minimum because this essay is based on materials (with full documentation) in "Part II: Church" of my *A Constructive Christian Theology for the Pluralistic World*, vol. 5: *Hope and Community* (Grand Rapids: Eerdmans, 2017). I also glean directly from both my *An Introduction to Ecclesiology: Ecumenical, Historical, and Contextual Perspectives* (Downers Grove: InterVarsity, 2002) and my "Ecclesiology," in *Mapping Modern Theology*, ed. Kelly Kapic and Bruce McCormack (Grand Rapids: Baker Academic, 2012), 345–376.

ness of what the Church is."[2] Whether outside the church or inside, I fear this lack of awareness is even deeper at the beginning of the third millennium!

As important a role as ecclesiology is playing in contemporary theology, we should recall that as a fully developed separate locus, the doctrine of the church did not emerge until the time of the Reformation.[3] This is of course not to ignore the many church-related themes already discussed in the patristic and later doctrinal manuals, particularly sacramentology. It is rather to remind us of the polemical setting of the Reformation theology out of which a full-orbed ecclesiology, an understanding of the "true" church, emerged.[4] Not surprisingly, the construal of first full-scale ecclesiologies at the time advanced slowly and had a somewhat haphazard tone due to circumstances.

In the aftermath of the Protestant Reformation, the church's institutional unity was replaced by an ever-intensifying plurality and multiformity of churches and Christian communities. A couple of centuries later, this diversification got further intensified as the result of the modern missionary movement, which in turn forced the Christian communities to construct viable ecclesiologies. Beginning from the end of the eighteenth century, Christianity rapidly became a world religion with a presence and outposts all over the newly developing inhabited world. The noted late historian of doctrine Jaroslav Pelikan aptly locates the place of the doctrine of the church at the eve of the last century of the second millennium:

> As the twentieth century began, each of the major churches of a divided Christendom was obliged, for reasons of its own, to address anew the doctrine of the church – its place in the mind of Christ, its essential message, its nature and identity, its marks of continuity, its authority and structure, its response to its twofold mission of keeping itself "unspotted from the world" and yet of being "the salt

2. Hans Küng, *The Church* (Garden City: Doubleday, 1976), 11.

3. Happily enough, we are currently served by a most detailed and reliable history of ecclesiology by the senior Catholic theologian Roger Haight, SJ: *Christian Community in History*, vol. 1: *Historical Ecclesiology* (New York: Continuum, 2004); vol. 2: *Comparative Ecclesiology* (2005); vol. 3: *Ecclesial Existence* (2008).

4. A brief detailed outline of the emergence and history of ecclesiology can be found in Wolfhart Pannenberg, *Systematic Theology*, trans. Geoffrey W. Bromiley, vol. 3 (Grand Rapids: Eerdmans, 1998), 21–27.

of the earth," and above all its authentic unity despite and beyond its historic divisions.[5]

Alongside the doctrine of the Trinity and pneumatology, ecclesiology has risen to the center of constructive and ecumenical theological work. As a result, anyone writing on the doctrine of the church at the beginning of the third millennium is fortunate in being able to tap into unprecedented resources and proposals, some of which will be registered below.

In this essay, the following formative themes and topics will be briefly presented. We will begin with a look at the three determinative biblical symbols and metaphors (people, body, and temple) and the four "marks" of the church as described in the Creed (unity, holiness, catholicity, and apostolicity). All Christian churches affirm these. That is followed by a discussion on the lack of unity of the church and the unwillingness of Christian communities to acknowledge each other as true churches. Thereafter, the essay will address the place and role of the church in God's economy – that is, the mission and missionary nature of the Christian community in the trinitarian movement of God's kingdom. The last major topic to be dealt with takes a look at the future of ecclesiology and the new challenges posed by globalization, migration, new forms of ecclesial existence, secularism, and religious pluralism.

A number of essential ecclesiological themes and topics cannot be discussed at all within the constraints of this essay. They include liturgy and worship, sacraments, ministry and ordination, and polity issues.

People, Body, and Temple: Determinative Biblical Symbols and Metaphors

Among numerous metaphors and symbols for the church in the New Testament,[6] the following three have gained particular importance in Christian parlance: namely "people of God" (1 Pet 2:9–10), "body of Christ" (Eph 1:22–23; 1 Cor 12:27; Col 1:18), and "temple of the Spirit"

---

5. Jaroslav Pelikan, *The Christian Tradition: A History of the Development of Doctrine*, vol. 5: *Christian Doctrine and Modern Culture (Since 1700)* (Chicago: Chicago University, 1989), 282.

6. Famously, almost a hundred images are discerned in Paul Minear, *The Images of the Church in the New Testament* (London: Lutterworth, 1960).

(Eph 2:19–22; 1 Pet 2:5).[7] These metaphors obviously reflect the tri-unity of God, whose community on earth the church is. Ecumenically it is of utmost importance that virtually all Christian churches are currently in agreement about the trinitarian basis and nature of the church as well as the anchoring of communion (*koinonia*) in the shared divine life itself. A brief consideration of each of these, beginning with the last one, helps elucidate the ancient self-understanding of the Christian community derived from the Scriptures.

The Spirit's work in the New Testament is not only present in the individual believer's life, it is also community-forming and communally-directed. As the late Lutheran Wolfhart Pannenberg puts it: "The gift of the Spirit is not just for individual believers but aims at the building up of the fellowship of believers, at the founding and constant giving of new life to the church."[8] This was of course evident on the day of Pentecost when a *koinonia* of believers was brought into existence, as beautifully described in Acts 2:42–47.[9] The same Spirit also makes the church charismatic as its members are endowed with various spiritual gifts and capacities for witness and service (Acts 1:8; 1 Cor 12; 14).

As the temple of the Spirit, the church is also the body of the risen Christ who poured out the Pentecostal Spirit. This is to say that there is a dual foundation for the church, christological and pneumatological. The apostolic father Ignatius taught that "wherever Jesus Christ is, there is the Catholic Church," and another early teacher, Irenaeus, made reference to the Spirit's presence: "For where the Church is, there is the Spirit of God; and where the Spirit of God is, there is the Church, and every kind of grace."[10] The balance between the christological and pneumatological basis of the church honors the deep and wide "Spirit-Christology" of the New Testament. In the Gospels and beyond, this "Spirit-Christology" comes to the forefront in that, from the beginning of the history of Jesus Christ to his glorious resurrection, there are references to the work of the Spirit, and conversely, the Spirit's work is

---

7. A massive study of biblical materials is Everett Ferguson, *The Church of Christ: A Biblical Ecclesiology for Today* (Grand Rapids: Eerdmans, 1996).

8. Pannenberg, *Systematic Theology*, vol. 3, 12–13.

9. A massive recent study of all aspects of *koinonia* is Lorelei F. Fuchs, SA, *Koinonia and the Quest for an Ecumenical Ecclesiology: From Foundations through Dialogue to Symbolic Competence for Communionality* (Grand Rapids: Eerdmans, 2008).

10. Ignatius, *To the Smyrnaeans* 8; Irenaeus, *Against Heresies* 3.24.1, respectively.

everywhere associated with that of the Son.[11] Appropriately, the leading communion-theologian of contemporary times, the Eastern Orthodox John Zizioulas, speaks of the church as *instituted* by Christ and *constituted* by the Holy Spirit.[12]

The New Testament contains very few references to the church's status as the "body of Christ," but body terminology abounds, particularly in the form of "one body" or "one body in Christ." Whereas in 1 Corinthians and Romans the individual community is depicted as a body, in Ephesians and Colossians it is the whole church. In Pauline teaching the main point of employing the body metaphor with regard to individual communities has to do with interrelated virtues and the qualities of love, unity, and working for the common good; just study 1 Corinthians 12–14 to that effect.[13] In the context of the whole church as the body, to the fore is a cosmological Christology and the cosmic work of the triune God working out his eternal purposes towards the reconciliation of all peoples and all of creation.

The widest and most comprehensive biblical image of the church is the people of God. In the Bible, peoplehood is based on divine election, as first presented with regard to Yahweh's choosing of Israel as his people. That election, however, should not lead to separation (as happened at times with Israel); rather, membership in the community is towards the goal of the gathering of the people of God in the new Jerusalem, as the programmatic vision of the seer of Revelation testifies to (Rev 21:3–4). The people metaphor is also critical in its link with Israel, the "first" people of God. While affirmed by all Christian communities from the beginning, over the centuries there have been immeasurable difficulties in trying to hold together the distinction of the two peoples, "old" and "new," without a harmful separation. Paul's most extensive exposition in Romans 9–11, understandably, has been the focus of millennia-long debates.

These three guiding metaphors of the church, as mentioned, have also been rightly linked with the foundational Christian confession of

---

11. See my *A Constructive Christian Theology for the Pluralistic World*, vol. 1: *Christ and Reconciliation* (Grand Rapids: Eerdmans, 2013), ch. 8, for the Spirit's role in Christology; and vol. 4: *Spirit and Salvation* (Grand Rapids: Eerdmans, 2016), ch. 2, for Christ's role in pneumatology.

12. John D. Zizioulas, *Being As Communion: Studies in Personhood and the Church*, trans. John Meyendorff (Crestwood, NY: St. Vladimir's Seminary Press, 1997 [1985]), 22.

13. See also Küng, *The Church*, 186–189.

one God as triune. Hence, already in patristic theology the church was envisioned as an image of the Trinity. Just as each person is made according to the image of the Trinity, so the church as a whole is an icon of the Trinity. This teaching has been particularly pronounced in the Eastern Orthodox tradition.

This trinitarian vision of the church based on the eternal Trinity has also helped the church to foster a robust vision of *communion*, that is, a communion ecclesiology. The triune God is the eternal communion of Father, Son, and Spirit. Consequently, the church as the communion of human persons may be said to echo that communal, relational existence.

One, Holy, Catholic, and Apostolic: The "Marks" of the Church

In the Nicene-Constantinopolitan Creed (381), confessed by (virtually) all Christian traditions throughout history, the church is believed to be one, holy, catholic, and apostolic. It is to be noted that in the Creed, unlike often in later tradition, these four classical "marks" (also called "notes" or "signs") were not used in any apologetic sense. Furthermore, it is worth noting that rather than carefully formulated, fixed definitions, the marks were most probably added to the Creed somewhat haphazardly.

It is important to realize that rather than abstract definitions of the church, the marks are first and foremost an object of faith. Whereas in the creeds we believe *in* the triune God as Father, Son, and Spirit, when it comes to the third article, an accurate rendering of the original text states that we believe the church. As a result, the marks are as much also "statements of hope." Eventually, the four marks become "statements of action," because they urge us to realize what is believed and hoped for.[14] It is usual and useful to consider the marks as "gifts" and "tasks." On the one hand, they are gifts from God. We do not make the church one, holy, apostolic, and catholic; only God can. On the other hand, we see too clearly that any church in the world, including our own, is far from those markers. Hence, each description is also a matter of hope, which leads to action for attaining its realization more closely.

14. Jürgen Moltmann, *The Church in the Power of the Spirit: A Contribution to Messianic Ecclesiology*, trans. Margaret Kohl (London: SCM, 1977), 339–340.

Although the oneness or unity of the church has been a spiritual and theological conviction from the beginning of history,[15] we notice that already in the biblical era the church began to encounter splits and has been divided since. Not for nothing are there a number of biblical exhortations to restore and help retain the oneness and unity as the one body of Christ under one head. Repentance is needed as a condition for seeking lost unity (John 10:16; 17:20–26; Acts 2:42; Rom 12:3–8; 1 Cor 1:10–30; 12:12–27; Gal 3:27–28; Eph 4:1–6).[16] This same desire to restore unity was also present in early patristic theology, as is evident in ecumenical tracts such as the early third-century *On the Unity of the Church* by Cyprian.[17]

In keeping with the non-apologetic employment of the marks of the church in early Christianity, the meaning of the term "catholic" – literally in Greek, "directed towards the whole" – in Ignatius of Antioch, in whom we find it for the very first time, simply meant the "whole" church in distinction from local communities.[18] There is no indication yet of the later meaning attached to catholicity of "fullness" and "perfection," that is, not lacking in anything; nor is that meaning present in secular Greek. The linking of "catholic" with the *pleroma* ("fullness") of Ephesians 1:23 came later, beginning from the third century, due to polemics and apologetics. Then the term's meaning first came to match materially with "orthodox" and by derivation to mean something like "valid." This came to its zenith with the establishment of Christianity as the only legitimate state religion in Christendom. Quite naturally, the further layers of the term also took on geographical and numerical connotations as the church extended to new territories and grew in membership. By the fifth century, Vincent of Lérins's celebrated formula speaks of "that faith which has been believed everywhere, always, by all."[19] The contemporary understanding needs to remember the original New Testament meaning of the term "catholic" (notwithstanding the lack of the term therein): it simply means the whole church as that which consists of all local churches, which in themselves are full

---

15. For examples, see J. N. D. Kelly, *Early Christian Doctrines*, rev. ed. (New York: Harper & Row, 1978), 200–201.

16. For details, see Küng, *The Church*, 352–353.

17. See Kelly, *Early Christian Doctrines*, 204–207.

18. Ignatius, *To the Smyrnaeans* 8.

19. Vincent of Lérins, *A Commonitory* 2.6. For details of this development, see Küng, *The Church*, 385–386.

churches insofar as they are in communion with other similar communities. "While the individual local Church is *an* entire Church, it is not *the* entire Church." By derivation, each such local church is truly catholic. In other words, the plurality of local churches does not make either them or the whole church un-catholic; what strips the church(es) off from catholicity is only separation from others, self-sufficiency, and isolation.[20] Furthermore, we have to say that, although spatial extension, numerical quantity, and temporal continuity are not irrelevant to catholicity, they do not alone – or even primarily – constitute it.

The celebrated ecumenical document *The Nature and Mission of the Church* reminds us of the obvious dilemma facing each and every church: "[t]he essential holiness of the Church stands in contrast to sin, individual as well as communal" (#54).[21] Not surprisingly, various tactics have been tried in order to ensure the church's holiness. An early dispute between the followers of Augustine and the Donatists illustrates this. The latter party sought to ensure holiness by not receiving back into membership the leaders and members who had lapsed under persecution. The Donatists, rather, wanted to cultivate the idea of a "pure church," a principle later followed by Free Churches throughout their existence. On the other hand, for Augustine and the mainline party, the principle of love and unity of the body was the determining principle and he advocated for the idea of a "mixed body," the rule adopted later by Protestant, Anglican, and Roman Catholic communities. Therein, the holiness of the church is located in its head, Jesus Christ, rather than in the members (even if the pursuit of holiness in the Christian walk is not unimportant in itself either). Be that as it may, all churches have to live in the dynamic tension between belief in holiness and acknowledgment of the presence of sin and sinful members.

An elusive and pluriform concept both in the New Testament and in later ecclesiastical usage, beginning from the early fathers, "apostolicity" became a commonplace in Christian usage, whether in relation to the church, a bishop, or Christ. Although the adjective "apostolic" never occurs in the Bible (and hardly in other contemporaneous sources), as a

---

20. Küng, *The Church*, 387–388.

21. World Council of Churches, *The Nature and Mission of the Church: A Stage on the Way to a Common Statement.* Faith and Order Paper no. 198, 15 December 2005; available at https://www.oikoumene.org/en/resources/documents/commissions/faith-and-order/i-unity-the-church-and-its-mission/the-nature-and-mission-of-the-church-a-stage-on-the-way-to-a-common-statement, accessed 14 October 2016.

noun, the term is of course frequent in the New Testament, most often in Luke and Paul, where its meaning resembles that of "ambassador" (for Christ). The term is not limited to the Twelve, as is often popularly assumed. It can also refer to various persons and groups; Paul himself is of course often its object, and he also mentions "false apostles."

Despite complex debates in later history, it is undisputed that the original meaning of the term "apostolic" simply had to do with the linkage to apostles. Apostolicity, then, essentially involves the continuity of life and faith of the apostles and the apostolic church of the New Testament. That much all ecclesiastical traditions affirm. Differences coming to the surface have to do with the way the linkage with the church of the apostles should be determined. Broadly speaking, two main approaches have been tried without a final consensus having yet been reached. For Orthodox and Catholic traditions, episcopal succession (somewhat differently conceived in each church) serves as the needed evidence. With the laying on of hands, each new generation of bishops is guaranteed to be standing in the line of the apostles. Although Protestant Reformers did not totally do away with the office of bishop, theirs was the claim to the primacy of the apostolic Word, the Scriptures. Where Scripture is preached and followed (alongside the right celebration of sacraments), apostolicity can be assumed. While among the Free Churches no defined opinion of apostolicity is to be found, recently some Pentecostal theologians have proposed that the presence of the Spirit's charismatic vitality and obedience to Christ's command to evangelize and serve all people should qualify as an indication of apostolicity. The reason for that claim is simple: according to the New Testament testimonies, that is what seemed to be happening everywhere among the communities established and led by the apostles.

As mentioned, the one church of Christ on earth is deeply and painfully divided. The continuing divisions, splits, and conflicts between the churches and their unwillingness to acknowledge each other's ecclesiality is the most critical issue facing the church of the past and tomorrow.

The Unity of the Divided Church: The Ecumenical Challenge

The Question of Ecclesiality: What Makes the Church, Church

The ecumenical challenge, namely the issue of restoring the unity of the church, has to do with two major challenges. First of all, there is the lack of willingness among various church traditions to acknowledge and embrace the full "churchliness" (ecclesiality) of other Christian communities. Let us name that the question of ecclesiality. The second, related, issue has to do with the pursuit of restoring unity among communities that are separated. That is the wider ecumenical challenge. Let us begin with the first one.

Notwithstanding the general consensus about the trinitarian basis of the church based on biblical testimonies and the universally confessed nature of that community as one, holy, apostolic, and catholic, there is a lack of willingness among churches to fully acknowledge other communities' full ecclesiality. The term "ecclesiality" simply refers to what makes the church, church. In other words, some churches do not consider others as churches but as something "less" or "defective." This wound is particularly deep between the "older" (Roman Catholic and Orthodox) and "younger" churches (Free Churches and various types of Independents), but it also relates to Protestant and Anglican communities, which in this respect stand somewhere in the middle of the debate.

The key debate has to do with the role of sacraments, episcopacy, and personal confession of faith in relation to what makes the church, church. There are three main positions. First, for Orthodox and Catholic ecclesiology, not only does the church carry out the sacraments, but the sacraments first and foremost make the church. This means that only where there is the celebration of the sacrament of the Eucharist (whose attendance requires water baptism), there is the Christian church. And for that celebration to be ecclesiologically valid, there needs to be a bishop whose standing is considered to be linked with the first apostles, as noted above. In sum, this is the "sacramental" and "episcopal"[22] definition of the ecclesiality of the church.

Second, for the youngest Christian family, the Free Churches, decisive is the presence of a personal confession of faith of the men and

---

22. Hence in the following, the word *episcopal* (as distinct from the proper name Episcopal, i.e. Anglican, Church) is used in that technical theological sense.

women who then gather together as the church. That faith is mediated directly, as it were, and does not necessarily require mediation by the sacraments or office. The celebration of the sacraments of water baptism and the Lord's Supper is an important part of the church's life, but these are not considered ecclesiologically constitutive and, in the case where personal faith is missing, might even be taken as something formal and useless. Furthermore, while among those Free Churches some have an ecclesiastical office by the name of "bishop,"[23] this does not have any ecclesiologically determinative function.

Third, there is the Protestant mainline definition of the church's "foundation" in terms of the administration of the sacraments (baptism and the Eucharist) and the preaching of the gospel, as famously defined in the Lutheran Augsburg Confession (#7). Although for Anglicans and many Protestants (all Lutherans and some Reformed) the theology (of salvation) is sacramental in the sense that one becomes and is sustained as Christian by the sacraments (when integrally linked with the Word), neither sacraments nor ministerial patterns are considered ecclesiologically constitutive after the manner of Orthodox and Catholic theology. As a result, even if they have a bishop (as a large number of Lutherans do), that office is not constitutive for the being of the church and can also be otherwise.[24]

Now, the ecumenical and ecclesiastical implications are simply these: for Orthodox and Catholics, neither Protestants and Anglicans, regardless of their sacramentality, nor Free Churches qualify as churches because they lack episcopal and sacramental validity for the reasons explained above. Even the Anglican and Protestant celebration of the sacraments (particularly the Eucharist) is invalid because of the episcopal deficit. On the other hand, for Free Churches, particularly in the early years of the movements, no amount of appeal to episcopacy or sacraments had any church-constitutive meaning; indeed, putting them at the forefront often elicited a response against mere formal religion! The mainline Protestants (and Anglicans, I suppose) come closest to not having binding reasons for non-recognition of either Free Churches

---

23. This is common among most African-American churches in the US, as well as in a large number of Pentecostal and other Free Churches all over the world, particularly in Africa but also in the former Soviet Union, and so forth.

24. A materially similar presentation (limited to Orthodox or Catholic and Free Churches) can be found in Miroslav Volf, *After Our Likeness: The Church as the Image of the Trinity* (Grand Rapids: Eerdmans, 1997), 130–135.

(as long as they also honor the sacraments, and they do appreciate the preaching of the Word, after all) or Orthodox and Catholic churches (without endorsing their exclusive appeal to episcopal succession). It is here that the complex and demanding work of the ecumenical movement begins.

The Ecumenical Movement: The Striving for the Unity of the Church

Nearly everybody would agree that "[e]cumenicity was the great new fact in the history of the church."[25] A number of initiatives and developments prepared for the coming into existence of the contemporary ecumenical movement, including important ecclesiastical unions and agreements in Europe, North America, India, and elsewhere, with the establishment of the World Council of Churches (WCC) in 1948 as the most visible sign. A significant early twentieth-century push towards concerted efforts for unity came from the Edinburgh Missionary Conference whose centennial was celebrated in 2010 in Edinburgh. Ecumenical platforms to deal with social issues (Life and Work) and doctrine (Faith and Order) further helped bring the WCC to existence.

The Roman Catholic Church and most evangelicals are not officially members of the WCC. It is not a church but rather a "fellowship of churches," currently about 350 churches from all continents. Its self-understanding was established in the 1961 New Delhi basis statement: "a fellowship of churches which confess the Lord Jesus Christ as God and Saviour according to the scriptures, and therefore seek to fulfill together their common calling to the glory of the one God, Father, Son and Holy Spirit."[26] Its purpose is:

> not to build a global "super-church," nor to standardize styles of worship, but rather to deepen the fellowship of Christian churches and communities so they may see in one another authentic expres-

25. Pelikan, *Christian Doctrine and Modern Culture*, 282. The most comprehensive and accessible resource on various facets of ecumenism and the ecumenical movement, including the WCC, is the *Dictionary of the Ecumenical Movement*, ed. Nicholas Lossky et al. (Geneva: WCC, 1991). For key texts, see Michael Kinnamon and Brian E. Cope, eds., *The Ecumenical Movement: An Anthology of Key Texts and Voices* (Grand Rapids: Eerdmans, 1997).

26. "The Basis of the WCC," World Council of Churches, https://www.oikoumene.org/en/about-us/self-understanding-vision/basis, accessed 13 October 2016.

sions of the "one holy, catholic and apostolic church." This becomes the basis for joining in a common confession of the apostolic faith, cooperating in mission and human service endeavours and, where possible, sharing in the sacraments. All these acts of fellowship bear testimony to the foundational declaration of the WCC that the Lord Jesus Christ is "God and Saviour according to the Scriptures."[27]

An important part of the ecumenical work happens constantly in the form of bilateral and multilateral dialogue between Christian churches. In most countries there is a national council of churches (such as the NCC, USA) which works in close cooperation with Faith and Order, facilitating ecumenical conversations, events, and projects at national, regional, and local levels. There are also a number of informal ecumenical contacts between leaders as well as laypeople at various levels, making a significant contribution to the search for unity. In other words, the term "ecumenical" has to be understood most inclusively and should in no way be limited to what might be called the "official" or "formal" ecumenism (that is, the work done by the WCC and other such agencies). Recall that the two biggest players in the Majority World, namely Roman Catholics and Pentecostal-charismatics (as well as the majority of evangelicals), are not affiliated with the WCC (although Catholics collaborate in many projects).

While there is no agreement about the form and shape of "visible unity," the ecumenical movement at large has adopted that as the main goal. There are also a number of dividing issues with regard to ministry, sacraments, and, say, the issues of evangelism and proselytism, which call for patient, long-term consideration and mutual understanding.

"Church as Mission"

The Church as the Sign of the Kingdom of God

The one, holy, catholic, and apostolic church does not exist for itself, but, rather, as the image of the triune God – the people of God, the body of Christ, and the temple of the Spirit – it participates in the

---

27. "The WCC and the Ecumenical Movement," World Council of Churches, http:// archived.oikoumene.org/en/who-are-we/background.html, accessed 13 October 2016.

wider salvific purposes of God. This forges an integral link between God's community (church) and God's kingdom. This is to say that God's community on earth (the church) is graciously drawn into the coming of God's kingdom, his righteous reign over all creation. That makes the church missionary by its very nature. The church exists as mission.

At the heart of Jesus's proclamation was the announcement of the dawning reign of God that he came to usher in. A shorthand for the divine rule was the term "kingdom of God." Not only as individuals responding to Jesus's message, but as a community – people, body, and temple – Christians are graciously invited to participate in the coming of this righteous rule. This means that the church serves as the sign of the kingdom of God.

The church in itself is not to be equated with God's rule, as has happened at times during Christian history, particularly at the height of Christendom – to which development the sad history of colonialism in South America tragically testifies, as discussed in Ruth Padilla DeBorst's essay. God's reign, his kingdom, is much wider and more comprehensive than the church or even human society. What the church is, is a preceding sign pointing to the coming righteous rule of God in the eschaton, an anticipation of the coming consummation and gathering of all God's people under one God (Rev 21:3–4). The distinction between the sign and the "thing" to be signified sets the church and its function in relation to God's rule in their proper place, as Pannenberg puts it succinctly:

> A sign points beyond itself to the thing signified. It is thus essential to the function of the sign that we should distinguish them. We must not equate the thing with the sign in its weakness. Only by this distinction can the thing signified be, in a certain sense, present by way of the sign . . . If the church fails to make this distinction clearly, then it arrogates to itself the finality and glory of the kingdom, but by the poverty and all too human character of its own life it also makes the Christian hope incredible.[28]

Acknowledging the anticipatory and preparatory nature of the church's existence helps avoid uncritical alignment with any political or ideological order. So what is important to note is that as far as the church faithfully functions as the sign, it "has its end not in itself but in the

---

28. Pannenberg, *Systematic Theology*, vol. 3, 32.

future of a humanity that is reconciled to God and united by common praise of God in his kingdom."[29] Exactly as an imperfect, often failing sign and instrument, the church shows to the world that it points to something more perfect and permanent.

The Missionary Nature of the Church

This integral relation of the church to the movement of the kingdom of the triune God is aptly described in the Roman Catholic Vatican II's (1862–65) ecclesiological document, *Lumen Gentium*: "The pilgrim Church is missionary by her very nature" (#2). Importantly, several streams of missiological thinking coalesced in this new acknowledgment of the church's missionary nature. Highly influential was the untiring call from the late United Reformed Bishop Lesslie Newbigin, a long-term missionary to India, for considering the West (Europe and the USA) as a "mission field" and thus the need for all churches everywhere to adopt a missional approach and existence.[30] One of the offshoots from that call was the establishment of an ecumenical network and research initiative by the name of "Gospel and Culture";[31] soon it was followed by similar networks in the United States[32] and beyond. In the American context, the 1998 book entitled *Missional Church: A Vision for the Sending of the Church in North America*,[33] a collection of essays by representatives of the Gospel and Our Culture Network, made an effort to bring WCC discussions of *missio Dei* ("the mission of God") and Lesslie Newbigin's missionary insights to bear on North America. The book urges the church to move away from a Christendom model that focuses on maintenance to a missional way of life based on outreach and expansion.

The American Presbyterian theologian Darrell Guder reminds us that embracing the missional understanding of the church helps con-

---

29. Pannenberg, 45–46 (45).

30. The best resource to get into basic ideas is Lesslie Newbigin, *The Gospel in a Pluralist Society* (Grand Rapids: Eerdmans, 1989).

31. Introduction, activities, and resources can be found at The Gospel and Our Culture, http://www.gospel-culture.org.uk/index.htm, accessed 13 October 2016.

32. See e.g. the Gospel and Our Culture Network at http://www.gocn.org/, accessed 13 October 2016.

33. Darrell Guder, ed., *Missional Church: A Vision for the Sending of the Church in North America* (Grand Rapids: Eerdmans, 1998).

ceive of ecclesiality and the marks of the church in the same dynamic manner: "By 'apostolicity,' we do not merely mean 'the church descended from the apostles,' as important as that is. We mean 'apostolicity' in the active sense of the New Testament verb, meaning 'to be sent out,' and the noun 'apostle' as the 'sent-out' one. The community formed by the Holy Spirit through the initial apostolic witness is called to be sent."[34] The second mark, catholicity, would remind the church of "the message . . . to be made known to the ends of the earth, . . . [to be] translatable into the life and experience of every ethnicity, as concretely demonstrated at the first Pentecost."[35]

Typically in Christian tradition, the tasks of the missionary church in the world include worship, liturgy, and sacramental celebration, proclamation of the gospel, cultivating mutual fellowship (*koinonia*), and engaging in *diaconia* (meeting the various needs of men and women). When placed in the wider context of God's universal purposes over creation, it is appropriate to add to these important tasks and dimensions of ministry the following: working towards equality and justice, whether with regard to gender, economy, or socio-political issues; participating in efforts to restore peace and reconciliation at various levels of human communities, from the local to regional to global levels; and helping care for nature and the environment.

In Lieu of Conclusions: New Challenges and New Opportunities in the Third Millennium

The Christian Church Goes Global

From what is estimated to have been fewer than 10,000 Christians in 100 CE,[36] Christianity has grown to be the largest religion, with over 2.4 billion adherents. Not only that, but the rapid growth of the church in the Global South (Africa, Asia, and Latin America) has helped shift the center of the church away from the Global North (Europe, North America). The Majority World now houses more than two-thirds of all

34. Darrell Guder, "The Nicene Marks in a Post-Christendom Church," https://www.pcusa.org/site_media/media/uploads/reformingministry/pdfs/nicene_marks.pdf, 9–10, accessed 13 October 2016.

35. Guder, "Nicene Marks," 9–10.

36. Rodney Stark, *The Rise of Christianity* (San Francisco: Harper Collins, 1997), 57–61.

Christians. By 2050, only about one-fifth of the world's three billion Christians will be non-Hispanic whites.

At the same time, the composition of the church worldwide is changing dramatically. As of now, one-half of all Christians are Roman Catholics, another quarter is composed of Pentecostals and charismatics, and the rest are Eastern Orthodox Christians (by far the largest segment in this section), as well as Anglicans, mainline Protestants, and Free Churches.[37] This means that Roman Catholics, Pentecostals, and charismatics together constitute three-fourths of the global membership. As a result, conservative and traditional mindsets will be strengthened even as theological liberalism and pluralism reign in Western academia. The "Pentecostalization" of the Christian church in terms of Pentecostal and charismatic spirituality and worship patterns infiltrating all churches is yet another implication of the transformation.

Particularly significant to the future of the Christian church is the rapid and steady growth of Christianity in Africa[38] – which also has become an important exporter of migrant and diaspora Christianity to the Global North.[39] Indeed, as part of the globalization process underway, migration and diaspora have caught the attention of some ecclesiologists and missiologists. According to the 2013 Pew Research Center data, of over 200 million migrants (which constitutes 3 percent of the world's population), about one-half are Christians; the United States houses most of them. The next largest number are Muslims (about one-fourth), followed by smaller groupings of other religious affiliations.

37. The basic statistical sources are David B. Barrett, George T. Kurian, and Todd M. Johnson, eds., *World Christian Encyclopedia*, 2 vols., 2nd ed. (New York: Oxford University, 2001; pages 12–15 contain a useful global summary); and the more recent Todd M. Johnson and Brian J. Grim, *The World's Religions in Figures* (Oxford: Wiley-Blackwell, 2013).

38. For the currents in African ecclesiology, see the two informative essays in this volume by Stephanie Lowery and Peter Nyende.

39. Among a number of reports and studies on the influence of diaspora Christianity in the West, informative are, for example, the following: Frieder Ludwig and J. Kwabena Asamoah-Gyadu, eds., *African Christian Presence in the West: New Immigrant Congregations and Transnational Networks in North America and Europe* (Trenton, NJ: Africa World, 2011); Mark R. Gornik, *Word Made Global: Stories of African Christianity in New York City* (Grand Rapids: Eerdmans, 2011).

New Forms of Ecclesial Existence

An important aspect of the re-formation of the global church has to do with the rise of new forms of ecclesial existence. Regrettably, theologians are still slow to discern and acknowledge the significance of these changes. By and large, doctrines of the church – similarly to ecumenical documents – are still written as if a Christendom model were in place and "mainline" churches were the only players on the field. Similarly, denominational markers stay intact for theologians and ecumenists although they have become fluid and at times almost nonexistent among a growing number of church members. Yet in many cases, traditional churches are rapidly losing their former status in both society and Christian imagination – even if the Roman Catholic Church, differently from all counterparts, continues to constitute a majority in many locations. At the same time, new forms of the Christian church are mushrooming and flourishing. Wonsuk Ma's essay on two emerging Free Church-type ecclesiologies wonderfully illustrates this trend.

Many specialists hold the opinion that the Free Church congregational model might well be the major paradigm in the third millennium alongside the Catholic one. Owing to the heritage of the Radical Reformation, Christian communities such as the Anabaptists and (later) Mennonites, Baptists, Congregationalists, Quakers, Pentecostals, some Methodist and Holiness movements, as well as a growing number of independent movements, are usually included under the somewhat elusive concept of "Free Churches."

Many younger-generation Christian leaders drawn to and influenced by postmodernity have been engaged in ecclesiological experiments known under elusive names such as ChurchNext (2000)[40] and The Liquid Church (2002).[41] The most widely researched among these new forms of ecclesiality are "Emerging/Emergent Churches," as they are called in the USA, and "Fresh Expressions of the Church," as they are known in the UK. Highly active in virtual networks and ways of connecting, their ecclesiologies are fluid. They do not always meet in sanctuaries, but may instead rent comedy clubs or pubs. Deeply missional in orientation with the focus on praxis and everyday Christian service, they do not typically

---

40. Eddie Gibbs, *ChurchNext* (Downers Grove: InterVarsity, 2000).
41. Pete Ward, *The Liquid Church* (Peabody: Hendrickson, 2002).

bother to delve into theological debates about ecclesiology, although many of their leaders may have solid academic training in religion.[42]

Facing Religious Plurality and Secularism

Alongside globalization and the rise of new forms of ecclesial existence, two other major challenges to the church and ecclesiology have been recently identified. They have to do with the simultaneous rise of secularism and religious pluralism. In contrast to the (in)famous "secularization thesis" revived in the secular 1960s, which built on the foundation laid by the great atheists of the nineteenth century (Feuerbach, Marx, Freud, and others) and predicted the death of religion as a result of a scientifically based "enlightened" worldview, the world of the third millennium is even more religious than before. At the global level, religions are not only holding their own but are flourishing and (at least in some cases) growing in numbers. Religious plurality is no longer a matter of certain locations and continents, but also a reality over the whole globe, including the Global North.

The rise of both secularism and religious pluralism means that the ecclesiologies of the third millennium have to pay attention not only to what is inside the church and within the Christian tradition, but also to the teaching of other religious traditions and the mindset of the secular public. Just think of a topic such as "land," a deeply biblical issue but so far largely ignored by theologians; Munther Isaac's essay from a Palestinian perspective makes a significant contribution in this regard. Similarly, questions of power and identity, among others, loom large in the contemporary globalized world.

Regarding religious pluralism, two theological sub-disciplines provide wonderful help, namely Christian theology of religions and comparative theology. Theology of religions seeks to investigate the theological value of religions and Christianity's place and function among

---

42. So far the most thorough study – ethnographic as well as theological – on both sides of the Atlantic Ocean suggests that emerging churches (1) identify with the life of Jesus, (2) transform the secular realm, and (3) live highly communal lives. Because of these three activities, they (4) welcome the stranger, (5) serve with generosity, (6) participate as producers, (7) create as created beings, (8) lead as a body, and (9) take part in spiritual activities (Eddie Gibbs and Ryan Bolger, *The Emerging Churches: Creating Christian Community in Postmodern Cultures* [Grand Rapids: Baker Academic, 2005]).

other religions.[43] Comparative theology builds on that work, as well as the accumulated results of comparative religion – which, as the name indicates, compares religious beliefs and rites without stated theological-philosophical presuppositions in order to accomplish specific and detailed comparisons among religions.

Further Reading

Gaillardetz, Richard R. *Ecclesiology for a Global Church: A People Called and Sent.* Theology in Global Perspectives. Maryknoll, NY: Orbis, 2008.

Gibbs, Eddie, and Ryan Bolger. *The Emerging Churches: Creating Christian Community in Postmodern Cultures.* Grand Rapids: Baker Academic, 2005.

Haight, Roger, SJ. *Christian Community in History.* Vol. 1, *Historical Ecclesiology.* Vol. 2, *Comparative Ecclesiology.* Vol. 3, *Ecclesial Existence.* New York: Continuum, 2004, 2005, 2008.

Harper, Brad, and Paul Louis Metzger. *Exploring Ecclesiology: An Evangelical and Ecumenical Introduction.* Grand Rapids: Brazos, 2009.

Kärkkäinen, Veli-Matti. *A Constructive Christian Theology for the Pluralistic World.* Vol. 5, *Hope and Community.* Grand Rapids: Eerdmans, 2017.

———. *An Introduction to Ecclesiology: Ecumenical, Historical, and Contextual Perspectives.* Downers Grove: InterVarsity, 2002.

Küng, Hans. *The Church.* Translated by Ray and Rosaleen Ockenden. London: Burnes and Oates, 1967. Reprint, Garden City, NY: Doubleday, 1976.

Mannion, Gerard. *Ecclesiology and Postmodernity: Questions for the Church in Our Time.* Collegeville, MN: Liturgical, 2007.

Moltmann, Jürgen. *The Church in the Power of the Spirit: A Contribution to Messianic Ecclesiology.* Translated by Margaret Kohl. London: SCM, 1977.

Pannenberg, Wolfhart. *Systematic Theology,* vol. 3. Translated by Geoffrey W. Bromiley. Grand Rapids: Eerdmans, 1998.

---

43. For details, see Paul F. Knitter, *Introducing Theologies of Religions* (Maryknoll, NY: Orbis, 2002); Veli-Matti Kärkkäinen, *An Introduction to the Theology of Religions: Biblical, Historical and Contemporary Perspectives* (Downers Grove: InterVarsity, 2003).

CHAPTER 2

Church, Power, and Transformation in Latin America: A Different Citizenship is Possible

RUTH PADILLA DEBORST

ABSTRACT

This chapter invites readers to trek through the centuries, looking through theological and historical lenses at the various expressions of church in Latin America. It pays particular attention to diverging practices and understandings regarding church and power, and to the relationship between the church and the powers of the day. Echoing mainly two ingredients of the ancient creed, it explores the double movement experienced by the people of the triune Community-of-Love as it lives out the reign of God, following Jesus in the power and gifting of the Spirit while, at the same time, never making itself fully at home in the world. It posits that it is precisely the *holy* and *apostolic* calling of the church which constitutes it as a school of citizenship.

The country was worn down by hyper-inflation and a military dictatorship. People who dared question the government's repressive policies were deemed disloyal citizens and made to "disappear." Even so, excitement rippled through the small congregation that sunny March morning at the beginning of the school year. It was ordination day in the Baptist church on the outskirts of Buenos Aires. Young children were first: they raced to the front, and sat on the floor. The ministry team, composed of women and men, laid their hands on them. "To learning, growing, being good friends, and following Jesus at home, school, and neighborhood, we ordain you." A resounding "Amen" issued from the rest of the congregation. Next were the high-schoolers, who, in a colorful circle, received their charge. They were followed by college students, who were ordained to explore their vocation and hone their skills for service. Employees, business people, stay-at-home parents, manual workers, professionals in diverse fields, people in full-time Christian ministry, all were ordained, group by group, to live as citizens of God's kingdom, following Jesus with the gifts and the power of the Spirit in their particular occupations.

The occasion was celebrated with a classic Argentine lunch, *empanadas* and *asado*,[1] in the back yard of the *templo*.[2] Once the meal was over, the chairs were drawn into a circle and a community consultation began. The question of the day was: Should there be wine or grape juice for communion? Historically, the church had always had wine for the Lord's Supper. However, a recently arrived missionary had explained to the ministry team that he was unable to participate in communion because he did not believe Christians should drink alcohol. A frank conversation ensued: "Why should we change simply because a US-American missionary doesn't like our way of doing things?" resisted several young people. "Yet we must find ways to preserve our unity as a church body; we cannot have people excluded from communion." "Additionally, what about the people who are wrestling with drug addiction and alcoholism?" questioned others. "Would it not favor them to *not* have alcohol in church?" People, younger and older, women and men, freely expressed their perspectives. The discussion proceeded to include volunteers for the after-school program and recruitment of a social worker to work in the rehabilitation center sponsored by the church. And, from that day forward, half the communion cups were filled with white grape juice and half with red wine.

This paper does not propose to prescribe the proper content of communion cups nor to discuss the benefits and drawbacks of congregational modes of church order. Neither does it intend to present an exhaustive review of ecclesiologies generated within Latin America.[3] Instead, it invites readers to trek through the centuries, looking through theological and historical lenses at the various expressions of church in

1. Argentine-style barbecue.
2. The term *templo* is frequently employed to name church buildings in Latin America and allows for a helpful distinction between place (*templo*) and people (*iglesia*).
3. The resources cited at the end of the paper could prove useful for such a study.

Latin America and paying particular attention to diverging practices and understandings regarding church, power, and the relationship between the church and the powers of the day. It then posits the church as a school of citizenship in light of its identity as the people of the triune Community-of-Love and its calling to follow Jesus into the world while never making itself fully at home in it. These theological reflections on church, power, and transformation in Latin America and beyond are born out of the dialogue between Scripture, historical analysis, personal experience as a member of the *Iglesia Evangélica Bautista de La Lucila*, and involvement in a variety of Christian faith communities since then.

Church and Power in Latin America: A Historical Trek

The question regarding *what*, or rather *who*, is the church has received divergent responses and concrete outworkings throughout the history of Latin America. Each of these conceptual and embodied responses rests on theological understandings regarding the nature of God, of humankind, of the relationship between them, and of the relationship between gospel and power. We will note these as we walk through the centuries, after a few clarifications are made. First, a word on power. No realm of creation or human existence is devoid of it. Crucial questions in the analysis of all relationships include: Who exercises power and who is deprived of it? What is the source and nature of power? How, for what, and for whom is that power employed? Although a comprehensive response to these questions is beyond the scope of this paper, the issues themselves are inextricably woven through the entire account and mark the contrasting faces of the Christian church in the subcontinent.

Second, the story of Christianity in Latin America is as complex and diverse as the people, cultures, ethnicities, and traditions of the people that compose this vast region that spans from North America, through Central America, and all the way south till Fire Land. Our walk today, then, is necessarily riddled with generalizations and omissions.[4]

---

4. See Ondina González and Justo L. González, *Christianity in Latin America: A History* (New York: Cambridge University, 2008), for a valuable overview. Also find primary sources in Klaus Koschorke, Frieder Ludwig, and Mariano Delgado, eds., *A History of Christianity in Asia, Africa and Latin America, 1450–1990: A Sourcebook* (Grand Rapids: Eerdmans, 2007), 277–418.

Ruth Padilla DeBorst

The Church under Imperial Power, and Followers of "The Other Spanish Christ"

On the wall of the cathedral of Quito, Ecuador, two plaques register the names of the city founders. Among them is Juan Padilla, my ancestor. I do not share this with pride, however, because Catholic churches like this one were built upon the ransacked ruins of ancient Inca, Aztec, and Maya temples. Colonial Christendom was erected upon the pillage and plunder of the native population, who were also my ancestors. The original inhabitants of Abya Yala received the Christian gospel on the blade of a sword when the Spanish and Portuguese *conquistadores* "discovered" them at the end of the fifteenth century.[5] In the words of John Mackay, "The sword and the cross entered into partnership. It was this partnership, formed in the name of evangelism, in which the sword opened the way for the cross, and the cross sanctified the work of the sword, that constituted the originality of Spanish Christianity."[6]

The god of imperial power blessed military conquest and thirst for wealth, and brought with him unintelligible languages, intractable illnesses, and alien cultural traditions. Says Mackay, "While their religious message was entirely devoid of ethical content and their own lives of Christian attractiveness and consistency, the *conquistadores* had a passion for the external rites of Catholicism."[7] The *conquistadores* could piously attend mass on Sunday morning, beat an indigenous slave to death in the afternoon, and rape several indigenous women at night. Deprived of agency and dignity, with no access to the Bible, and simply deriving their understanding of Christianity from the behavior of the Europeans, the people called into being by this imperial god learned to superimpose foreign ritualistic religious practices onto their traditional ways,

5. Abya Yala is a compound term coined by the Guna (or Kuna) people who live in present-day Panama and Colombia. It means "land of plenitude and maturity," and has been employed by autochthonous groups to refer to what Europeans named America. The usage of the term is customary now in decolonization circles which affirm the rights of indigenous peoples. It is also increasingly being used more broadly as a more felicitous term than "Latin America" since it focuses on the land shared by peoples from many ethnic backgrounds, a continent that is not merely Latin or European, but also indigenous, African, and Asian in makeup. This is the sense in which the term is employed in this chapter, interchangeably with the more traditional one, Latin America.

6. John Alexander Mackay, *The Other Spanish Christ: A Study in the Spiritual History of Spain and South America* (New York: Macmillan, 1933), 26.

7. Mackay, *The Other Spanish Christ*, 37.

intermingling them into forms acceptable to the ruling authorities in varying expressions of religious patriotism. Yet they often lacked a deep-seated passion for God, and the consequent ethical commitment that would make itself visible in day-to-day life, their values, their priorities, and their relationships.

A few notable exceptions did make known the "other Spanish Christ," the Christ of the Gospels. Catholic priests like Antonio Montesinos, and Bartolomé de Las Casas advocated for the life and dignity of the original inhabitants of the Americas. Jesuit Pedro Claver served for many years in the Colombian port city of Cartagena as a self-appointed "slave to the slaves." As missionaries like these gave their lives away in compassionate pastoral work, selfless service, and the defense of the dignity of all people, they made God known as the loving one, who protects the weak, affirms diverse cultural values, and builds a faithful community from the bottom up.

During colonial Christendom, the Roman Catholic Church was not only the hegemonic religious power. It was also the keeper of the keys to citizenship. No person was officially born, married, educated, recognized as dead, or buried unless he or she was Roman Catholic. Since the only registry was the Roman Catholic Church, Protestants, Jews, and people who claimed no faith had no legal personhood and no recourse in the face of abuse. Church and civil power were inextricably bound.

The Church under Commercial Power, and Education and the Bible among the People

As the Latin American colonies fought and gained independence from Spain, towards the beginning of the nineteenth century, they began organizing into national entities and sought to gain a place in the "modern" world of progress, technology, and education. In order for the young nations to open commercial relations with the Protestant European nations, they had to break the hegemony of the Roman Catholic Church; otherwise Protestant Christians would not be welcome. Consequently, in many instances, commercial agreements included clauses on freedom of worship.

Immigrant Protestant churches which were formed during the commercial expansion of the British and Dutch powers were often uncritical of the business interests of their nations in the new world, even when the pursuit of those interests demanded the exploitation of indigenous people or involvement in the slave trade. The double ethic of proper religiosity on the one hand and self-interested business practices on the other marked the people who rallied around the god of commercial prosperity. There are fascinating stories of British pirates who read the Bible and prayed before plundering Spanish ships and paying dues to the newly forming countries.[8]

In contrast, there were women and men who sacrificially lived the good news of the reign of God not only in their private lives but also in the public arena, serving especially the more relegated sectors of society and validating their inclusion as full citizens. Their most significant contribution was making the Bible and education accessible to people who had been deprived of them for centuries. Among them, English missionary Allen Gardiner worked among indigenous populations. Scottish missionary James "Diego" Thompson, with the support of the British Bible Society and the Lancasterian Society, distributed Bibles, began a teachers' training college in Peru, and opened schools in the poorest areas for indigenous and black children. He advocated for the education of women, saying, "Female education in my opinion is the thing most wanted in every country; and when it shall be properly attended to, the renovation of the world will go on rapidly."[9]

Along with Francisco Penzotti, known as the first great Latin American promoter of Protestantism, Thompson introduced the New Testament as a school textbook. He also translated the New Testament into the Quechua language so the indigenous people of the Andes and the jungle could read it. For the translation, he collaborated with willing Roman Catholic priests, who also helped distribute Bibles. This ecumenical and holistic model of mission not only marked many church communities at the time but also opened a track on which future generations were able to tread.

Moving into the early twentieth century, we encounter Latin American Christian intellectuals and activists like Erasmo Braga and Baez Camargo, and missionaries like John Mackay and William Morris, who took on roles in public education and in the shaping of public policy

8. See papers published in *Journal of Latin American Theology* 6, no. 2 (2011), and the work of Mexican historian Lourdes de Ita Rubio.

9. Tomás Gutierrez, "James Thompson in Perú: Protestant Influence in the Beginning of the Republic," *Journal of Latin American Theology: Christian Reflections from the Latino South* 6, no. 2 (2011): 140.

for the common good out of their Christian convictions. Through education and new access to Scriptures, "Oppressed sectors like African slaves, freed slaves, and indigenous people heard in the non-conformist Protestant message a call to faith and hope in their fight for freedom."[10]

The church called into being through access to the Bible and education were women and men who knew their dignity as people made in God's image, and for whom faith was not merely a Sunday matter but one that infused the whole of their lives, attitudes, relationships, priorities, values, and transformative presence in the broader society.

The Church under Global Capitalism, and the Power of Radical Discipleship

As geopolitics shifted toward the end of the nineteenth century, and the United States gained ascendancy, mission and empire took a new turn. Latin America continued to feel the impact of foreign mission work, but the origin of the missionaries and the funding for church life and work shifted significantly from Europe, with its Protestant ethos, to North America, with its more independent, "faith-based" evangelical and Pentecostal denominational paradigms. In a century marked by world wars, the Cold War, military dictatorships, revolutions, and growing exploitation, Latin American nations and all sectors of society were wooed or compelled to follow the suit of their powerful northern neighbor. So-called free-trade agreements drew them into the global market, in which everything and everyone is susceptible to being bought and sold. To this day, while US farmers are paid for dumping their crops, Central American farmers watch their corn rot because prices bottomed out, thanks to the surplus shipped from the US. While US consumers dispose of clothes outdated by the latest fashion, Central Americans slave away in sweatshops with no labor laws to protect them. While capital is free to travel, invested and divested at will and for the benefit of big business, only wealthy people – with passports or visas of the empire – are truly free to come and go. The other millions are held down, deprived of any right to hope for a way out of poverty, free

10. Jaime Adrián Prieto Valladares, "Historical Antecedents of Protestantism, the Beginnings of the Spread of the Bible in Independent Central America . . . ," *Journal of Latin American Theology* 6, no. 2 (2011): 186.

only to be victimized by gangs, die in the desert, or become rejected nobodies in the wealthy north.

As the self-identified evangelical and Pentecostal population grew in the region, and particularly in Central America, churches were not immune to the shining neon lights of consumerism and the illusion that bigger is always better. With a triumphalist spirit, many entered the race for the largest *templo*, the furthest-reaching radio, the record number of members. Many scrambled to mix in with the governing elites and establish business connections that would favor evangelicals' interests. Contemporary "apostles" began to wear, drive, and exude the symbols of success. Massive growth, alliances with state and financial leaders, and the impact of positive images all crowded out any need for suffering. In the understanding of many, the days of being persecuted or excluded for one's faith were buried in the past, when evangelicals were a minority with no say in the makings of their countries.

In stark contrast to these religious expressions were two movements of radical discipleship which sprouted from the seeds of public education and the Bible in the hands of the people which had been planted in Abya Yala during the nineteenth century. Earlier in the twentieth century, these seeds had matured into small but growing local churches, the members of which were known as the "Bible people" and *evangelistas*, and were often persecuted by the Roman Catholic majority. The two indigenous and transnational movements of the mid-twentieth century which generated alternative Christian communities that engaged with the social realities of the context were the *misión integral* movement among radical *evangélicos* and the Roman Catholic *comunidades de base*. As the last stop in our historical trek we turn briefly to these movements, which have been more thoroughly described in other publications.[11] Mention is also made of the Pentecostal movement, which, as such, cuts across the boundaries of traditional church denominations.

11. See, for example, Samuel Escobar, "Doing Theology on Christ's Road," in *Global Theology in Evangelical Perspective: Exploring the Contextual Nature of Theology and Mission*, ed. Jeffrey P. Greenman and Gene L. Green (Downers Grove: IVP Academic, 2012), 67–85.

The Misión Integral *Movement*

The seeds of the radical *evangélico* movement were sown by early twentieth-century Protestant-evangelical pioneers like those already mentioned. The first shoots became visible when several Latin American Christian student movements came together in Cochabamba, Bolivia, in 1958 to form the *Comunidad Internacional de Estudiantes Evangélicos*. And the plant struck root more broadly with the formation and growth of the *Fraternidad Teológica Latinoamericana*, from 1970 onwards.[12] At the core of both movements was a group of friends, principally three couples – Lilly and Samuel Escobar, Emma and Pedro Arana, and Caty and René Padilla – who built theologically both on their transnational belonging – each was formed in part in Europe and in the US – as well as on their Latin American evangelical matrix.[13] They intentionally situated themselves within the Latin American context, which was marked by revolutionary fervor on the one hand and by a lack of solid biblical teaching in churches on the other. They were committed to responding to the issues of that context and strengthening the capacity of the church to contribute out of the stores of their faith to the transformation of society. Together they developed what has come to be known as *misión integral*, a theological-missiological articulation and practice that seeks to engage followers of Jesus in linking the whole gospel to the whole of life under the lordship of Christ in the power of the Holy Spirit so that the reign of God and God's justice may be made visible in particular historical contexts.

For these friends, the vocation of theology was to nourish the mission of the church, so their academic work was pastorally and missiologically directed. The radical, socially all-encompassing perspective earned this movement and its adherents the rejection of more conserva-

---

12. See Daniel Salinas, *Latin American Evangelical Theology in the 1970s: The Golden Decade* (Leiden: Brill, 2009); Carlos Mondragón, "Los movimientos estudiantiles como precursores de movimientos teológicos: el caso de la FTL. Consulta 2014: La FTL: Su Identidad y Misión Hacia el Siglo XXI" (paper presented at FTL Consultation, San José, Costa Rica, 22 September 2014).

13. See Ruth Padilla DeBorst, "Latin American Communities I: *Comunidad Internacional de Estudiantes Evangélicos* and the *Fraternidad Teológica Latinoamericana*," in "Integral Mission Formation in *Abya Yala* (Latin America): A Study of the Centro de Studios Teológicos Interdisciplinarios (1982–2002) and Radical *evangélicos*" (PhD diss., Boston University, 2016), 94–142.

tive sectors of the Latin American church, who to this day write them off as communists. Meanwhile, their respect for Scripture as the Word of God caused more liberal sectors to judge them as far too conservative. Even so, through speaking, teaching, preaching, publishing, and dialoguing in homes, churches, campuses, seminaries, and conferences across Latin America and beyond, and through their own engagement in the life and ministry of local congregations, they influenced the understanding and practice of church for hundreds of church leaders and lay professionals.

The Comunidades de Base *Movement*

The Vatican II process (1962–65) catalyzed renewal in the Roman Catholic Church, and suddenly millions of people who had never had access to Scripture were able to purchase Bibles in their language. The Bible Societies began selling Bibles across Abya Yala as never before. While previously the Roman Catholic mass had always been led in Latin, priests were finally allowed to minister it in Spanish. God's Word reached God's people, and in cities, villages, and rural settings, women and men began gathering in circles of Bible study and prayer. So began the *Comunidades Eclesiales de Base*, gatherings of believers who explored the Bible in light of their context and their context in light of Scripture. Father Armando Márquez Ochoa, head of the CEBES (El Salvador), explained: "We gathered as a believing community around God's Word, and so we gained a vision of God's kingdom. Out of that vision grew our commitment to the transformation of our context and service in the community."[14] As was the case with the *misión integral* movement, undergirding the theological articulations of many liberationists was the living, breathing, suffering, and thriving reality of local communities of believers who sought to live into the already inaugurated reign of God.[15]

14. Father Armando Márquez, personal conversation with author, San Salvador, 12 August 2005.

15. See Carlos Sosa Siliezar, "Ecclesiology in Latin America: A Biblical Perspective" in this volume for further details on this process.

The Pentecostal and Neo-Pentecostal Movement

The Pentecostal movement was born early in the twentieth century at the margins of Christian life, among the lower classes; but it grew exponentially in the second half of the century to occupy center stage. It struck a chord of popular religiosity in ways not achieved by the established Catholic Church nor the illumined Protestant circles. Central to Pentecostal teaching is the baptism of the Holy Spirit; a focus on emotion, freedom, and spontaneity in worship; a search for holiness; an apocalyptic eschatology; direct access to biblical revelation; and the empowerment of laypeople, including women, many of whom lead churches and freely exposit Scripture.

Over the last forty years, Pentecostal growth became explosive and has resulted in many new denominations, churches, and church members. It has also had a noticeable impact on all denominations, including the Roman Catholic Church. Although initially many Pentecostal preachers rejected education, including theological education, and some considered the Bible to be merely a legalistic compendium of "dos" and "don'ts," many have more recently begun deepening their theological formation, their appreciation for responsible Bible study, their involvement in social matters, and their cross-cultural mission initiatives.[16]

Contrasting postures regarding power are also present in this movement. Native and imported neo-Pentecostal churches and neo-apostolic churches began to consolidate during the last decades of the twentieth century, many of them with strong elements of prosperity gospel, ostentatious buildings, and weak processes of financial accountability. Plenty of megachurch leaders in Latin America today claim their inheritance as children of the sovereign King, and feed off their congregations in order to wrap themselves in the trappings of power and prestige of our consumer society. Some see the rapid growth of Pentecostal and evangelical churches as a sure sign that "our time" has come: after centuries of Catholic hegemony, it is now *our* turn to assert political ascendency and benefit from the privileges of power. In contrast, other Pentecostal pastors and congregations have sacrificially moved into some of the most violence-ridden neighborhoods, befriended gang members, and

16. For an example, see Ruth Padilla DeBorst, "The Social-Ethical Impact of CETI: Formation Nourishing Transformation," in "Integral Mission Formation in *Abya Yala*," 313–333.

opened opportunities for them to find livelihoods. As did the Lord they follow, they are making God's love tangible through their embrace of the rejects of society.[17] As a result of his study of Pentecostalism in El Salvador, researcher Timothy Wadkins attributed much of the credit for the "social consciousness" of the *Misión Cristiana Elim* and the way its leaders "prophetically apply the gospel to El Salvador's crushing social reality" to "a careful reading of the gospels and the somewhat quiet influence of the . . . *Latin American Theological Fraternity*," and to the Center for Interdisciplinary Theological Studies (CETI), generated in Argentina by radical *evangélicos*: "In their two-year training program they emphasize what they call integral ministry – an emphasis on God's comprehensive, incarnational intention of not leaving any human and any corner of the earth untouched by his love."[18]

As we have trekked through the centuries, while the eyes of faith reveal the work of the triune God calling God's people into full life as citizens of God's reign and promoters of God's love and justice in the world, they also lay bare the glory and dust proper to any human venture. This jumbled and paradoxical portrayal points to the ambiguity of the church, a people riddled by the very same challenges as any other human gathering, yet drawn together by the divine Community-of-Love with the highest of purposes: being the dwelling place of that Community – the palpable, historical expression of reconciling love – and living in the world as citizens of a realm governed by the eternal life-giving Creator of all. The following two sections probe the identity and calling of the church, with a special focus on its capacity and potential as a school of citizenship that is critical of any power that conspires against God's life-giving agenda in the world, and that seeks transformation in light of that agenda.

The Church: A School for Citizenship

The people gathered that March Sunday in La Lucila included the unlikely combination of home-making women, students, recovering drug

---

17. A powerful example is the life, ministry, and writing of Church of God pastor Darío Lopez in Perú.

18. Timothy Wadkins, letter to Eliberto Juárez, Canisius College, Buffalo, New York, 1 July 2011.

addicts, long-term Christians, professionals from many fields, young people, manual laborers, newly converted Christians, immigrants, high-powered business people, unemployed people, elderly people, foreigners, and native Argentines. After a long week of work and the shared burden of an oppressive government and the climbing cost of living, worship services constituted an opportunity to rest, to celebrate life with music and fellowship, to take personal and national burdens to God in prayer, to regain hope through reflection on God's Word in community, to grapple with ethical dilemmas, and to muster courage for living faithfully throughout the new week. Yet further, for most of the people gathered, church services and assemblies were the only places where they had a voice, their opinion was welcome, and their perspective was respectfully received. The annual "ordination service" affirmed the lordship of Christ over every dimension of life, as well as the value of each person and every occupation; none of them was more worthy or more sacred than any other. Everyone was recognized as an active member of the community and a responsible citizen in God's economy. Within the faith community, women and men, young and old, gained a clear sense of their identity as members of God's people, of the gifts granted by the Spirit, and of their calling to follow Jesus in the world without belonging fully to it. Theirs was a lived definition of church, experienced less as a static condition and more as the constant double movement Jesus referred to in his prayers and words to his disciples.[19] They were being called out of the world into one body and granted a distinctive identity, and they were being sent into the world in radical followership of Jesus for the sake of God's life-giving, transformative purposes. Without necessarily articulating it in the very words of the Nicene Creed, this double movement experienced by the members of that local congregation echoed that ancient affirmation: they were *holy*, called out, separate; they were *one* in spite of their significant social differences; and they were *apostolic*, grounded in the ministry of the apostles and sent out, as they had been, into the world as witnesses of the good news.[20]

---

19. See Jesus's prayers and words to his disciples in John 17:15–18 and John 20:21.
20. See Veli-Matti Kärkkäinen's chapter in this volume.

Called Out to Be the People of the Community-of-Love

Not a place and not an institutional structure, the Greek *ekklesia* was an assembly of citizens called out from their homes and gathered in some public place. The testimonies and letters compiled in the New Testament depict the *iglesia* (church) as a body-politic composed of women and men who are called out of their particularity to integrate into a distinct community. In contrast to the biddings in the *polis*, however, the call is not issued by some passing political authority, but by their sovereign Creator, who in the past had already called a people together to serve as a living, loving witness of God's good purposes in the world.[21] In contrast to the unity enforced by Roman armies and deterring crucifixions, the church is drawn together by the love of the incarnate, crucified, risen, and ruling Christ. Rather than being held together by crippling fear and grueling taxation, the church is granted unity by the life-giving Spirit, who extends bridges across linguistic, ethnic, and social differences. In sum, through God's gracious action, Christians become the people of the Community-of-Love and citizens of a new realm.[22] Citizenship under the rule of this loving community is not purchased or earned; it is not subject to migratory eligibility or dependent on skin color or ethnicity. Belonging, in God's new humanity, is a condition freely granted to all who admit to their created condition, acknowledge Jesus Christ as Savior and Lord, recognize that their very breath depends on the living Spirit, look forward to God's complete restoration of the entire creation, and live in light of these confessions in the world.

Citizenship under the rule of the Community-of-Love is not some otherworldly, extra-terrestrial, or imagined condition, but a concrete belonging embodied in the church. That real-existing community is portrayed in the unburnished New Testament accounts of the early church as it grew, spread out, and grappled with cultural differences, human greed, power contestations, and external persecution in light of the ultimate leveling and reconciling work of Jesus. They nourished hopeful perseverance by singing their faith, writing letters, and visiting one another. Notable in spite of their growing pains and expressions of fallen human nature is the extra-biblical historical testimony of their contemporaries who attest to the integrity of the message taught and

21. See Gen 18:18; 22:18; and 26:4.
22. Eph 2:13–22; 1 Pet 2:9–10.

lived out by these early Christians.[23] In contrast to many churches today, they did not invest in buildings but met in houses. The money gathered from tithes and offerings was then freed up to support the work of missions, to purchase the freedom of slaves, and to care for widows and orphans. Along the way, the church grew because it lived what it preached as an alternative community in which they were tutored in citizenship for life within the church and in society at large.

In like manner today, popular Protestant-evangelical-Pentecostal churches "have become alternative societies that create a closed world where people are accepted and become actors, not on the basis of what gives them status in the world, but of the values that come from their vision of the kingdom of God."[24] The story of that March day in Buenos Aires illustrates this very point. So do the studies of Timothy Wadkins who, having researched a variety of Protestant-evangelical churches in Central America, discovered that, although "individualized rituals of community building such as prayer, Bible reading, and personal testimony" could be considered socially alienating, they actually serve as "micro acts of democracy."[25] "Over time . . . what begins in conversion and is sustained in the context of such deeply rooted communities of faith and personal piety, could lead to the kinds of social organization that have the power to rise up against injustice, overturn the submissive, status quo politics of traditional Christianity, and lay the foundation of democratic participation and social change."[26]

Again, membership in the ecclesial gathering serves as a practice run for citizenship in the broader society, and leads to the second movement of the church in relation to the broader world.

23. A fascinating example is the Epistle to Diognetus. See also Rodney Stark, *The Rise of Christianity: How the Obscure Marginal Jesus Movement Became the Dominant Religious Force in the Western World in a Few Centuries* (San Francisco: Harper, 1997).

24. Samuel Escobar, "A Missiological Approach to Latin American Protestantism," *International Review of Mission* 87, no. 345 (April 1998): 170.

25. Timothy Wadkins, "Getting Saved in El Salvador: The Preferential Option for the Poor," *International Review of Mission* 97, no. 384/385 (2008): 46.

26. Wadkins, "Getting Saved in El Salvador," 46. Wadkins's work is representative of what Samuel Escobar denominates "a new generation of social scientists working at the micro level [who] have brought to light the transforming nature of the spiritual experience offered by these churches" (Escobar, "Missiological Approach," 170).

Called to Follow Jesus into the World

While God's people are called out of the world to become an alternative community, they are simultaneously called to enter the world. Says René Padilla, "To speak of the Kingdom of God is to speak of God's redemptive purpose for the whole creation and of the historical vocation that the church has with regard to that purpose here and now, 'between the times.'"[27]

Recognition that the whole created order belongs to God compels the people who live under God's rule to engage with all dimensions of human experience. The crucial issue is from where and in what manner this engagement takes place. The pattern of the church's involvement must follow that of the King it represents. The amazingly subversive good news is that God, the Creator and Sustainer of all that is, in Christ squeezed into time-limited, earth-bound, suffering human form. God could have remedied all the world's maladies in one grand swoop of life-giving power. But that's not the God of the gospel. God could have spoken justice into our unequal world. But that is not the God of the gospel. God could have decreed sustenance for all that lives – from above, from outside, without getting God's hands dirty. But that is not the God of the gospel. God could have extended a compassionate hand from a distance. But that is not the God of the gospel. Instead, consistent with the relational nature of the Community-of-Love, God chose to enter the world God so loves and, in this way, to bridge the greatest divide of all, the one that separates a broken, fumbling, wandering humanity from its Source of Life, from itself, and from the rest of the creation of which it is a part. Further yet, far from entering through the splendorous gates of a Roman imperial family, with all its trappings of grandeur and dominion, God approached a poor Palestinian woman to become a working-class boy in an occupied territory and was first visited by simple shepherd folk. God became a fearful refugee in a foreign land. God became an anonymous worker, carving stone and wood for wealthy folk. God became an itinerant teacher, with no place to rest his head. God befriended women and despised imperial lackeys. God knelt and washed the dusty feet of bewildered and treacherous fishermen. God became a criminal, executed to demonstrate the fate of anyone who

27. René Padilla, *Mission Between the Times: Essays on the Kingdom* (Carlisle: Langham Monographs, 2010), 186.

dared disturb the deathly *Pax Romana*. And it was from there, from the bottom up, from inside, from underneath, that God sovereignly effected the most astounding reversal of all times. By entering the darkest darkness, the abyss of death and alienation and sheer aloneness – "Father, Father, why have you abandoned me?!" – God broke those chains of death and alienation and sheer aloneness. God, the Community-of-Love, worked a true peace into the dough of a fractured society, not one precariously pounded together by iron nails and grueling taxation. In Christ, the Creator continued the work of creation. God began fashioning a new humanity by effecting peace, *Pax Christi*, weaving together the unlikeliest assortment of women and men – slaves, slave-owners, freed slaves, manual workers, wealthy home-owners, Jews and Greeks – into a new humanity.

For the church today, following Christ's choice to set aside his power and "move into the neighborhood" (John 1:14 MSG) entails sacrificial incarnation in the messiness of socio-economic, political, and ecological realities. Following Christ's life-choices entails making similar ones: befriending the people who are marginalized by systems of power and exclusion, recruiting them for active ministry, and reinstating them to their rightful place in society. Following the King who chose the way of the cross and rejected violence entails abandoning "Christendom projects," which confuse the kingdom of God with the institutional church, the gospel with culture, and the power of the cross with the power of the sword.[28] Following the King who rose from the dead and rules sovereignly today entails resisting every form of imperialism, relativizing the authority of all rulers, nations and powers, pledging ultimate allegiance only to the Kingdom of God, and "bearing witness to God's purpose of love and justice revealed in Jesus Christ, in the power of the Holy Spirit."[29]

---

28. Orlando E. Costas, *Christ Outside the Gate: Mission Beyond Christendom* (Maryknoll, NY: Orbis, 1992), 181. See also José Míguez Bonino, *Toward a Christian Political Ethics* (Minneapolis: Fortress, 2007), 98; and Paul John Davies, "Faith Seeking Effectiveness: The Missionary Theology of José Míguez Bonino" (PhD diss., Utrecht University, 2006).

29. René Padilla, "The Ebb and Flow of Kingdom Theology and Its Implications for Mission," in *Evangelical and Frontier Mission Perspectives on the Global Progress of the Gospel*, ed. Beth Snodderly and A. Scott Moreau (Oxford: Regnum, 2011), 285.

Conclusion

Necessary questions in light of these reflections are: Is the evangelical church in Latin America, in the US, and around the world living into its calling as a people called out of the world into another primary belonging as the people of the Community-of-Love? Is its life as a community such that all members participate as active citizens and are ordained to contribute as Christians to the broader society? Is the presence and witness of the church in the world distinctive, not thanks to some religious veneer but by virtue of its ethical embodiment of God's reign? Does the church pay ultimate allegiance to the powers of the day or to the Lord of life, the God of History?

The people gathered in La Lucila that March morning were being schooled in these matters. And as they faced the world in light of the Word, and vice versa, they grew in their capacity to live out a different citizenship as active members under the reign of the Community-of-Love in the world.

Further Reading

Arias, Mortimer. *Announcing the Reign of God.* Philadelphia: Fortress, 1984.

Cook, Guillermo. *New Face of the Church in Latin America: Between Tradition and Change.* Maryknoll, NY: Orbis, 1994.

González, Ondina E., and Justo L. González. *Christianity in Latin America: A History.* New York: Cambridge University, 2008.

Journal of Latin American Theology Special Issue on 19th-Century Protestantism 6, no. 2 (2011).

Míguez Bonino, José. *Faces of Latin American Protestantism.* Grand Rapids: Eerdmans, 1997.

Mondragón, Carlos. *Like Leaven in the Dough: Protestant Social Thought in Latin America 1920–1950.* Madison: Fairleigh Dickinson, 2011.

Padilla, René. "La Nueva Eclesiología en América Latina." *Boletín Teológico FTL* 18, no. 24 (Diciembre 1986): 201–226.

Yamamori, Tetsunao, and C. René Padilla. *The Local Church, Agent of Transformation: An Ecclesiology for Integral Mission.* Buenos Aires: Ediciones Kairós, 2004.

Yoder, John H., Lilia Solano, and C. René Padilla. *Iglesia, Ética y Poder.* Buenos Aires: Ediciones Kairós, 1998.

CHAPTER 3

Two Tales of Emerging Ecclesiology in Asia: An Inquiry into Theological Shaping

WONSUK MA

ABSTRACT

Ecclesiology in Asia, especially in evangelical and Pentecostal and charismatic circles, has not been adequately articulated. This study examines the shaping of ecclesiology in two "Free Churches": the Word of Life group in China and the Yoido Full Gospel Church in Korea. The study illustrates the need for theological construction and articulation in Asia, as the former has no ties with churches outside of the country, while the latter has developed its own unique understanding of the church. The study also demonstrates that, in these two particular cases, the founders and the social contexts play a significant role in the theological shaping of each community. Hence, their ecclesiologies have been functional in nature, and their sense of a relationship to the historic tradition of ecclesiology is minimal. The urgency is further felt as these two communities represent a thriving and fast-growing segment of Asian Christianity.

Ecclesiology in Asia

The Christian presence on this continent is ancient. In fact, the church was born in Asia. And yet, today, in many parts of Asia, Christianity remains a foreign religion. This directly affects how Christians as well as society understand the community of followers of Christ that is called the "church," especially its nature and function.

The historic churches have shown encouraging efforts in reflecting on the engagement between the Christian gospel and socio-cultural contexts. The Roman Catholic Church has done impressive theological work, especially after Vatican II. The Federation of Asian Bishops' Conferences has been shaping a new participatory model of the church for decades, particularly paying close attention to a dialogue between church hierarchy and women.[1] Equally active is the publication program of Christian Conference of Asia (CCA), which is the regional arm of the World Council of Churches. Again, it has consciously engaged with Asian contexts and issues.[2] Mainline Protestant churches also seem to have been paying attention to this theologizing process. With their theological identities relatively well established, the natural next step will be to become relevant in the Asian setting. One CCA publication, although dated, is devoted specifically to the diverse nature of the church and its life in several Asian countries, primarily in response to the historical, cultural, and social context of each church.[3]

When it comes to the evangelical and "Free Churches," including Pentecostal ones, studies of the nature and function of the church are relatively rare, especially ones which take Asian contexts into account. Only recently have some efforts begun to appear among evangelicals.[4] For indigenous churches with little or no affiliation with Western

1. An extensive study is found in Thao Nguyen, "A New Way of Being Church for Mission: Asian Catholic Bishops and Asian Catholic Women in Dialogue: A Study of the Documents of the Federation of Asian Bishops' Conference (FABC)" (PhD diss., Graduate Theological Union, Berkeley, 2013). For other Catholic resources, see Federation of Asian Bishops' Conferences, www.fabc.org/pub_p8.html.

2. "CCA Publications," Christian Conference of Asia, www.cca.org.hk/home/publications, accessed 10 October 2016. Although dated, a ten-year process of developing Asian theology with Asian resources is a fine example: John C. England and Archie C. C. Lee, *Doing Theology with Asian Resources: Ten Years in the Formation of Living Theology in Asia* (Auckland: Programme for Theology and Cultures in Asia, 1993).

3. Kwok Nai Wang, *The Local Church* (Hong Kong: Christian Conference of Asia, 2005).

4. In the Philippines, for example, Asian Theological Seminary has held a very successful annual theological conference dealing with theological and missional themes. Its proceedings have been published, serving as valuable resources: see "ATS Theological Forum Books," Asian Theological Seminary, http://www.ats.ph/ats-theological-forum-books/, accessed 4 October 2016. Its first publication was E. Acoba et al., *Doing Theology in the Philippines* (Quezon City, Philippines: OMF, 2005).

churches, theological reflection is even more scarce. Of course, these churches will have different theologizing processes from historic ones, which received their theology from the Western mother churches. Free Churches, unlike the historic churches, tend to be more autonomous, without a mother church or its accompanying well-developed theology. Moreover, even Asian churches that have Western mother churches may exercise relative autonomy in their ecclesial structure and theology.

Two Case Studies

This study is an initial attempt to address the immense need presently in the new churches in Asia. The approach is to select two church groups in East Asia and trace the development of their ecclesiologies. The first is a house church network in China called the Word of Life Church in Henan Province, a post-Cultural Revolution-era indigenous house church. The second is Yoido Full Gospel Church in Seoul, Korea, a Pentecostal congregation with a network of sister and daughter churches. Both are representative of the "newer" churches in Asia.

These two cases are selected for several reasons. Both are extremely influential churches and both claim a large membership. The Word of Life Church is estimated to have three million followers throughout China, while Yoido Church and its network form the world's single largest congregation, with more than 700,000 members. The rise and growth of the Word of Life Church provides a model for, and its influence on, house church movements in China. Its recent decline also reveals the structural vulnerability of rural house church networks, which rely heavily on their leader-founders. Yoido Church and its founder David Yonggi Cho have established a unique Korean interpretation of Pentecostal theology and spirituality. Its "full gospel" theology has had a far-reaching impact on Korean Christianity and beyond. Most importantly, however, my choice of these two was motivated by their active engagement with their contexts, their own reading of the Scriptures, their adaptation or modification of any "received" theology (especially in the case of the full gospel theology), and the processes of their own theology-shaping. This creativity has resulted in some controversies, and yet their theologizing processes are noteworthy.

Approaching the Subject

My focus is on the shaping of local theologies, preferably those perceived among members of the churches. The focus of observation is on the process through which each community has been shaped, and how it is understood to function and operate. On the one hand, it negotiates and interacts with, and sometimes reacts to, the context. On the other hand, it reads and interprets the Bible and draws from Christian traditions. This theology, often unarticulated, is lived out in church and daily life. As I began observing these two churches, I soon realized that traditional theological categories would not be adequate for analyzing the living process of theologization.

This is primarily due to the fact that the received theology and its categories are shaped and sustained in a Western Christendom setting. In such a religious context, the church existed predominantly to provide pastoral care to the parishioners. The "world" was perceived to be a fully Christian empire, to some degree. In contrast, the Asian church today exists in constant engagement with the world, which is sometimes even hostile to Christianity. The place and function of the church, therefore, is heavily shaped by this context and experience.

I have been immensely aided by several creative inquiries on contemporary ecclesiology. The first is a work by Veli-Matti Kärkkäinen. Well exposed to Asian realities through his missionary work, he characterizes each of the six major ecclesiological traditions with their theological foci. His exploration of several new and emerging churches and their ecclesiologies (for example, African Independent Churches) is particularly enlightening.[5] The present study is focused on the category of "Free Church" in Kärkkäinen's categories.[6] Equally refreshing are the ecclesiological categories which Gerald Bray has proposed through his historical study. In his survey of the New Testament church, and subsequent persecuted and imperial churches, he ultimately raises the question of what the fundamental tenets of the church might be, in light of diverse traditions and forms.[7] If this question is posed to believers in the Global South, whose population corresponds to two-thirds

5. Veli-Matti Kärkkäinen, *An Introduction to Ecclesiology: Ecumenical, Historical and Global Perspectives* (Downers Grove: IVP Academic, 2002), 194–201.

6. Kärkkäinen, *Introduction to Ecclesiology*, 59–67.

7. Gerald Bray, *The Church: A Theological and Historical Account* (Grand Rapids: Baker Academic, 2016), viii.

of the world's Christians, I suspect the responses will be challengingly different from those one gets from the North.

Because of my interest in the construction of ecclesiologies, Simon Chan's book on grassroots theology in Asia has a strong appeal.[8] It is particularly helpful in the case of the Word of Life Church, due to the scarcity of any "magisterial" theology. As Chan proposes, this study will assess each church with regard to both (1) the stories of its members, often expressed in the church's testimonies, sermons, programs, and leaders, as well as (2) ancient theological traditions, specifically the Nicene-Constantinopolitan Creed.

There are several foci to which I will pay particular attention: the theological formation of the founding leader of each church, the self-understanding of the nature of the church, and the perception of the mission of the church. Relying on empirical evidence is pertinent in observing the Word of Life Church, as I have had few encounters with founder Peter Xu. For the Yoido Church, I have maintained a reasonable degree of contact with both the clergy and the laity. More published materials are available for this case, which I intend to utilize.

Peter Xu and the Word of Life Church

Peter Yongze Xu (1940–)

David Aikman categorizes Xu as one of the three "uncles" who served as the founders of three large house church networks in the post-Cultural Revolution era.[9] They were responsible for the miraculous resurrection of Chinese Christianity after the Communist takeover of this vast nation. Xu is also linked to today's Chinese Christianity through the previous or "Patriarch" generation. Prayed over by his Christian grandfather, he grew up in a Christian family. It is even recorded that he saw visions at the age of five.[10] His first house arrest took place in 1967, and during the Cultural Revolution he was targeted for his "counter-revolutionary" offenses. In 1978, he emerged as a significant house church leader. His

---

8. Simon Chan, *Grassroots Asian Theology: Thinking the Faith from the Ground Up* (Downers Grove: InterVarsity, 2014).

9. David Aikman, *Jesus in Beijing: How Christianity Is Transforming China and Changing the Global Balance of Power* (Washington DC: Regnery, 2003), 73–74.

10. Aikman, *Jesus in Beijing*, 87.

evangelistic teams spread beyond Henan Province to various other parts of China. After his imprisonment in 1982, a state persecution began, and many full-time evangelists were sent out for evangelism and church planting. This resulted in the establishment of more than three thousand churches by 1988.

However, Xu was concerned by the widespread emphasis on healing and miracles among many house church networks. Perhaps in reaction to this, his ministry stressed genuine regeneration and discipleship. With an increasing number of house churches and leaders joining Xu, the "Born-Again Movement" was born and grew to become perhaps the most controversial house church network in the country. The emphasis on a genuine experience of regeneration has also led this network to develop a heavy focus on evangelism.

Xu spent more than two decades of ministry as a fugitive hiding among the "floating population" during this turbulent time. This was also a time when he actively ministered to them, as he kept discovering hidden believers, both active and inactive. It is not unreasonable to suspect that his theology and ministry practices were affected by this experience and shaped through his reflection. The ever-mobile nature of his life must have been particularly significant in the understanding of the nature and purpose of the church (that is, ecclesiology) within his particular historical and social setting. There are two notable aspects of his ecclesiology: (1) how the nature of the church is understood, and (2) what is perceived to be the mission of the church. They are "assumed" as their theology is practiced, especially in the absence of any articulate theology.

The Nature of the Church

First, because they often gathered secretly for worship, Bible study, prayer, and fellowship, the marker of the church was not a visible building or an established organizational structure. The church was, and still is to a certain extent, identified primarily as the community of believers regardless of location. The first three points of the seven-point theology of the church concern the purity of the church through genuine conversion. They are: (1) salvation through the cross; (2) the way of the cross; and (3) discerning the adulteress (i.e. the Three-Self

Patriotic Movement).[11] This important characteristic of the Word of Life Church, as with most other unregistered churches, has been shaped by three contextual realities. The first is that there was no identifiable Western "mother" church to dictate the shape of the church. The second is the newness of its existence, without a historical link. The third is the social context, which prohibits any open gathering of people for religious activities, unless registered. In addition to these contextual factors, it is notable that a reading of the book of Acts likely encouraged and reinforced this understanding of the church.

Second, its given socio-political context has kept this unregistered church illegal. Xu developed his serious ministry-consciousness through his (Christian) reading club in his vocational school years. Then, his Christian faith was seriously questioned by the authorities "for a non-stop period of forty days," even "forcing him to remain standing for seventeen hours."[12] Subsequently, during the Cultural Revolution, he was in self-exile to hide from the authorities, and mostly separated from his family. Through his life, he experienced several imprisonments and house arrests. Details of how he was treated are not readily available, but I had a glimpse of such a persecuted life. In light of all this, it is not surprising to find in the seven-point theology of the church a "theology of the cross." The second point reads: "Take the way of the cross to persevere in faith during suffering." Xin interprets such a period as a theologically formative process for becoming a "missionary."[13]

Two junior women leaders from the Word of Life Church studied theology in the seminary where I served as the academic dean. Upon becoming Christian, they offered themselves to the service of the Lord. They participated in different forms of training and were sent to various parts of Henan Province for evangelism and church planting. Eventually, they were arrested by the authorities and sentenced to prison terms. They openly shared about the harsh treatment they had received during their incarceration, including utter humiliation before male prison guards as part of their punishment. They implied that most of their colleagues and leaders went through similar experiences. It was claimed that among ordinary believers, a popular perception was formed that

---

11. Yalin Xin, *Inside China's House Church Network: The Word of Life Movement and Its Renewing Dynamic* (Lexington, KY: Emeth, 2009), 80–81.

12. Aikman, *Jesus in Beijing*, 87.

13. For the whole seven points, see Xin, *Inside China's House Church Network*, 89–90.

imprisonment was a mark of one's devotion, thus preferable, if not necessary, for a leadership appointment.

The hostility of the world has kept the identity and mission of Christians and the church clear. Christianity is never viewed as a means to upward social mobility, as observed in some Christian sectors. Indeed, being Christian results in a voluntary downward social mobility. At a seminary chapel session, one of the women leaders shared her prayer after she was physically exposed for humiliation: "Thank you, Lord, for considering me worthy of participating in your suffering." As Gerald Bray has noted, the persecution was a critical aspect of the early church, and some of the characteristics of this era are very similar to the experience of the Word of Life Church.[14] The seven-point doctrine of the Word of Life Church includes a statement affirming that the official Three-Self Patriotic Movement (TSPM) "embraces worldly authority."[15] The TSPM "registered" churches have lawful status, are visibly organized, but operate under government guidance. A distinct mark of the true church in the minds of most house church members, therefore, is suffering for refusing to submit to atheistic government policies.

The third characteristic of the Word of Life Church is that it understands itself to be a community of regenerated people of God. Following the Free Church model of ecclesiology, each member is expected to have repented of his or her sins, been forgiven by God, and become incorporated into the community of faith, and that is the church. Xu and the church have consistently stressed the necessity of discipleship, for which a genuine experience of regeneration is essential. Aikman contends that this was a reaction to the increasing Pentecostal faith among the house church networks.[16] To foster such a lifestyle, the church encouraged its members to participate in spiritual retreats where repentance was emphasized and exhorted. Soon, it became common or even "normative . . . for everyone to weep," often for a prolonged period, as evidence of genuine repentance.[17] In spite of repeated denials by Xu and the leaders, many members, including local-level leaders, believe that weeping has obtained a significant theological meaning.

14. For example, the ascetic tendency and the decisive role of episcopacy (or leadership), the spread of the gospel, and an adverse social context largely resonate with the Word of Life Church. See Bray, *The Church*, 61–89.

15. Xin, *Inside China's House Church Network*, 89.

16. Aikman, *Jesus in Beijing*, 88.

17. Aikman, 88.

The church soon became known as the Born-Again Movement or simply "the Weepers." By the mid-1990s, the security authorities and the TSPM labeled the church as a cult and Xu as a cultic leader. This controversial issue led various house church networks to come together to work out theological and personality differences, and set criteria for orthodox Christianity. This was further developed in 1998 to create a unified front against the government's persecution by adopting a common statement called "United Appeal of the Various Branches of the Chinese House Church."[18]

The strong emphasis on regeneration and Christian discipleship attracted many Christian groups, especially in the 1980s. The 1998 issue of *Christianity Today* rejected the claim of heresy and estimated that the church had reached about three million members.[19] Like most house church networks, Xu and his church often pray for healing and God's miraculous intervention. The work of the Holy Spirit in evangelism is particularly stressed. However, they do not encourage other spiritual gifts that are common among Pentecostals, such as speaking in tongues or prophecy. Luke Wesley, a Pentecostal academic working in China, concludes the group is evangelical in nature, but not Pentecostal: "the Word of Life Church represents an interesting mixture of conservative theology and experiential piety. They expect to see miracles, pray for healing, and look to the Holy Spirit for supernatural guidance and deliverance. At the same time, they are generally quite closed to some manifestations of the gifts of the Spirit, such as prophecy and tongues . . . I would classify this group as non-charismatic."[20]

The Mission of the Church

Based on the strong emphasis on genuine regeneration, the church has set evangelism as its foremost and primary mission. Xin points out that Xu had a deep appreciation for Christian leaders of previous eras, and recalls how Xu drew much inspiration from Charles Finney's

18. For the full text, see Aikman, 293–294.

19. Timothy C. Morgan, "A Tale of China's Two Churches," *Christianity Today* 42 (13 July 1998): 30–39. Similarly, Daniel H. Bays, *A New History of Christianity in China* (Chichester/Malden, MA: Wiley-Blackwell, 2012), 195.

20. Luke Wesley, *The Church in China: Persecuted, Pentecostal, and Powerful* (Baguio, Philippines: AJPS Books), 2004, 48.

books that had been hand-copied during a difficult period.[21] In 1983, the church's most important theological process took place when the church's theological position was articulated in the seven points (or "Seven Principles"). They begin with "salvation through the cross" and end with "frontier evangelism." New life in Christ is the absolute foundation for Christian discipleship and mission. The description of the last point is worth quoting, as this is the only one with a specific action plan prescribed: "This is the Great Commission of Christ to the Church for the fulfillment of God's eternal salvation scheme. As Chinese Christians, we are burdened with the one hundred million souls that need salvation. In order that the gospel be preached to all the people in China, frontier evangelistic teams should be organized and sent to the unreached areas."[22]

In the same year, 1983, with the government crackdown renewed, the church's top seventeen itinerant evangelists, called "Messengers of the Gospel," scattered, hiding themselves. The circumstances effectively pushed them into full-time ministry. The authority's persecution and opposition were instrumental in the creation of the powerful evangelistic program of the church, called the "Gospel Band."[23]

More intentionally, the church evolved to create a massive training program to serve the entire process of Christian discipleship, from conversion to evangelism and church planting. And each congregation implemented various levels of training programs, often mobile in location. The completion and publication of the two-volume training manual in 1987 enhanced the development of the training programs. The "missiological cycle" illustrates the life of an evangelist of the church: from short-term training and theological education (called "Seminary of the Field") to leading a member to join the Gospel Band. Eventually, teams of evangelists are sent out to frontier regions to establish house churches.[24]

Within the given social context, the development of house churches drew a large number of women, and thus young women have had a prominent role in leadership. Wesley describes eight leaders of the Word of Life Church, seven of whom were women, while most, if not

21. Xin, *Inside China's House Church Network*, 88–89.
22. Xin, 90.
23. Xin, 91. See pp. 102–105 for details of the training, activities, and fruits of this program.
24. Xin, 99.

all, of the leaders which the Philippines seminary trained, were women. Xin, who participated in a number of congregations, estimates that about 70 percent of the church's members are women. He also believes that women make up about the same proportion of the Messengers of the Gospel, the backbone of the church's leadership structure.[25] This is common with other house church networks, reflecting the social circumstances in which they exist. In a number of places, Xin stresses the important leadership role of Xu Yongling, Peter's younger sister, especially when he was imprisoned. She may have served as a good role model for women in leadership within the church. However, the recent drastic decline of the Word of Life Church raises a serious question about the very nature and shape of this church, and particularly about the role of leadership. In the absence of strong leadership, the entire church network is now in danger of disintegration. The next case demonstrates a more stable structure.

David Yonggi Cho and Yoido Full Gospel Church

The development of this largest single congregation under Cho's leadership has been studied extensively. A brief overview of its half-century history highlights the development of its ecclesiology. Due to the decisive role of Cho in this process, his own theological formation is integral to the church's "full gospel" ecclesiology.

David Yonggi Cho (1936–) and the "Full Gospel"

The development of this largest single congregation in the world is traced in three geographically oriented stages. David Yonggi Cho grew up through the turbulent changes of Korea: Japanese colonialism (1910–45), independence (1945), the Korean War (1950–53), military dictatorship (1970s and 1980s), and economic development (from the 1990s on). His conversion took place in his youth as he was dying of tuberculosis: he was healed at the same time as his spiritual birth. This brought a radical transformation to his life and to his attitude towards daily life in this post-war society.

25. Xin, 105.

His first tent church, called Full Gospel Church, was established in 1958 on the outskirts of the war-torn capital city of Seoul. Ministering to the urban poor, at the center of Cho's "full gospel" was the gift of healing and miracles. His church always expected the sick to be present, and the ministry of healing has been an integral part of almost all the gatherings of the church. The tent church was looked down upon by the general population and by churches in the vicinity. Many objected to the makeshift state of the church building, and even more so to the internal makeup of the church. At the same time, the power of God attracted those who were marginalized and helpless. True to the Pentecostal tradition, this was a church *of* the poor, not one *for* the poor. In fact, Cho himself *was* sick and poor.

When Cho took his congregation to the downtown Sudaemun area in 1961, the venue had been secured by American missionaries as a Central Revival Hall. Cho had regularly served as their interpreter, when the main message was hope and healing. The new congregation, therefore, represented a convergence between Cho's "full gospel" message and mainstream Pentecostal theology. The church in this urban setting began a new phenomenon which has characterized Korean Christianity until today: the megachurch movement. His passion for church growth is understandable in the context where Christianity was still around 10 percent of the national population at the beginning of the 1960s. While continuing his message of God's power in healing and miracles, he presented a theological notion of a "good God." The exponential growth of his church began to attract the world's attention.

In 1973, he moved the church to Yoido Island, the newly emerging financial center of the capital. During this era, his congregation reached the unprecedented height of claiming 750,000 members. He also theologized his concept of "a good God" into a Five-fold Gospel and Three-fold Salvation. The Five-fold Gospel was an adaptation of the traditional christological formula of the Assemblies of God: he added "Jesus the Blesser" to "Jesus the Savior, Baptizer, Healer, and the Coming King."[26] Based on 3 John 2, his Three-fold Salvation includes spiritual, physical, and circumstantial (which includes material) salvation. His emphasis on God's blessing triggered a theological controversy, with many alleging that his ministry had Shamanistic tendencies or advo-

---

26. Wonsuk Ma, "David Yonggi Cho's Theology of Blessing: Basis, Legitimacy, and Limitations," *Evangelical Review of Theology* 35, no. 2 (April 2011): 140–141.

cated the prosperity gospel. Cho's ministry has expanded globally,[27] and he has become perhaps the best-known Korean in the world. At the same time, the church has increased its mission program. Before his formal retirement, Cho began to strengthen the church's ministry to the socially marginalized. His successor, Younghoon Lee, has taken the social responsibility of the church even further.[28]

"Full Gospel" Faith as Lived Out

Why are people attracted to Yoido Full Gospel Church and its massive Jashil Choi Fasting and Prayer Mountain? Their expectations are a valuable window through which the popular perception of Yoido Full Gospel Church can be deduced.

First, Yoido Church has been a popular haven for those who have nowhere to turn. The unique character of the church was defined from the very beginning, and it has continued. Myung Soo Park's analysis of selected published testimonies in the *Shinang-gye* (*World of Faith*), the monthly magazine of the church, points to this. He lists "the last hope for solving problems of life" as the "starting point of Pentecostal spirituality."[29] Almost every teaching opportunity, from Sunday sermons to cell group Bible studies, contains the message of God's power to solve life's problems. These often include physical and mental illness, family problems such as in marriage and parent–children relationships, financial difficulties, business issues, addiction to gambling and substance abuse, suicidal tendencies, and many more.

To provide various spaces for people to come and experience God's power, the church has developed many prayer programs in addition to the traditional daily dawn prayer and Wednesday evening prayer.

---

27. Myung Soo Park, "Globalization of the Korean Pentecostal Movement: The International Ministry of Dr Yonggi Cho," in *Korean Church, God's Mission, Global Christianity*, ed. Wonsuk Ma and Kyo Seong Ahn (Oxford: Regnum, 2015), 228–241.

28. See Younghoon Lee, "Yoido Full Gospel Church: A Case Study in Expanding Mission and Fellowship," in *Called to Unity for the Sake of Mission*, ed. John Gibaut and Knud Jorgensen (Oxford: Regnum, 2014), 275–284.

29. Myung Soo Park, "Korean Pentecostal Spirituality as Manifested in the Testimonies of Believers of the Yoido Full Gospel Church," in *David Yonggi Cho: A Close Look at His Theology and Ministry*, ed. Wonsuk Ma, William W. Menzies, and Hyeon-sung Bae (Baguio, Philippines: APTS, 2004), 47.

The church began a Friday overnight prayer meeting, which spread to almost all the churches in Korea and extended to all the weekdays in the church. It has instituted a special series of prayers, such as Daniel Prayer (for twenty-one days) and 40-Day Dawn Prayer. Members are encouraged to dedicate a designated time frame to pray for a specific need, and fasting prayer was uniquely promoted and encouraged by Rev. Choi, the long-time ministry partner of Cho. The massive Jashil Choi Fasting Prayer Mountain draws thousands of people from different churches in Korea and far beyond. Praying for healing and life's problems is a regular feature of all services in the church.

Second, accordingly, every gathering of the church is a space and time where God's power and love is expected and experienced. Every part of the service is designed to help the worshippers to experience an encounter with God, through the Holy Spirit. The lively and contemporary pre-worship music and prayer welcome the worshippers who fill the auditorium, which was emptied minutes prior by the worshippers of the previous service. The post-sermon session of ministry is rather extended. Normally it begins with a corporate prayer time when each member is encouraged to put his or her problems into the Lord's care, based on the sermon just heard. The famous three shouts of "Juyo!" ("Lord!") at the beginning of this corporate prayer powerfully transform thousands of individuals into a spiritual community. The auditorium-filling prayers and shouts are followed by a prayer led by the preacher. Each member is asked to lay his or her hand on the part that is ailing, or on the heart if there is a problem other than physical. The prayer is a mixture of petition to God and a command to the force(s) responsible for the problem. This is the real climax of the service, when shouts of "Amen" and "Hallelujah" continue. This ministry session ends with the eruption of praise and thanksgiving.

This modern scene of Yoido Church's worship has its historical roots in the very beginning of the tent church. Cho repeatedly declared that Jesus is the answer to all human suffering,[30] which overwhelmed his life and the tent church. His church was regularly filled by more

---

30. For example, in his own words, "Pastoring is preaching the gospel of Jesus Christ, leading them to salvation through faith in Jesus, and helping them to serve the Lord as God's people, and to love their neighbors." David Yonggi Cho, "An Interview: Pastoring with the Holy Spirit" [in Korean] in *Charis and Charisma: Church Growth of Yoido Full Gospel Church*, ed. Sung-hoon Myung and Yong Hong (Seoul: Institute for Church Growth, 2003), 14.

sick people than healthy ones. The former often included the pastor himself! His radical conversion experience is well documented. On his deathbed, with no hope of recovery from tuberculosis, he experienced not only spiritual rebirth, but also physical restoration. The church, by design, is a sacred space where God's reality is encountered and his gracious power is experienced.

Third, this type of spirituality engenders countless narratives of who God is and what God has done. In a typical Pentecostal worship service in the early years, and still today in many parts of the world, sharing of testimonies is a major part of any worship. Normally, the participants are not prearranged: anyone can stand up or come forward to tell his or her story of an encounter with God. And the exchange of such life stories is practiced very regularly. Although the sheer size of Yoido Church prohibits a formal service from providing sufficient space for sharing of testimonies, sermons utilize such experiences as a powerful illustration of God's love and power. Moreover, the most active place where such sharing takes place is the weekly cell group meetings, often in a member's home.

This is the unique and powerful process of grassroots theologization. True to the Pentecostal theological process, the members actively contribute to the construction of theology, either by sharing, appropriating, adjusting, or discerning. Also, by articulating their experiences, they often reflect on the teachings of the Bible and the church. This helps the members to build confidence and contents for evangelism. Theologically, this is an example of the "prophethood of all believers," and practically this theological and spiritual orientation is responsible for the numerical growth of the church.

Mission of the Church

Closely related to the above, there are three areas the Yoido Full Gospel Church has taken as its unique mission. The first is the spreading of full gospel faith. At the core is the message of the good God, blessing, healing, and God's intervention on his people's behalf. This was radically opposite to the prevailing other-worldly orientation of Korean Christianity. Coupled with his healing and exorcism, Cho and his church were looked at suspiciously by the mainstream church in Korea. In fact, he was either included in the watch list of doctrinally "questionable" groups, or condemned outright as a heretic. He and the church were cleared from the "heresy" list not long ago.[31] His belief and practice were also linked to shamanism by two well-known Western scholars. Both Hovey Cox and Walter Hollenweger made this link as a positive and successful attempt at connecting Christian faith with the widespread indigenous religious tradition. In this way, they applauded that Cho had successfully made Christianity relevant to the Korean cultural and contemporary context. Hollenweger regarded him as a "Pentecostal Shaman *par excellence.*"[32] Understandably, the church emphatically denied such allegations, and, in fact, the church brought Cox to its pulpit a number of times, so that he could have a firsthand experience. However, Cho is still viewed by many as a prosperity gospel preacher.

These controversies prove that Cho's full gospel faith and ethos has radically challenged normatively practiced Christian beliefs and practices. In the end, he has succeeded in convincing the Korean church of his full gospel faith, and this can be argued on at least two fronts. First, the worship and songs of his church and various prayer programs were adopted by churches across all denominations. They were particularly popular among pastors, who saw that people were attracted to such worship and messages. Through this powerful influence, Cho's Pentecostal spirituality has become a common feature of the Korean church.[33] Second, the growth of his church served as a sure and visible proof of the validity and impact of his full gospel faith. At the height of the church growth movement (for example, at the School of World Mission of Fuller Theological Seminary), the Yoido Full Gospel Church was a favorite illustration. There was a practical side to this as well. His prayer mountain and overnight prayer sessions drew people regardless of their church's theological standing. "Sheep stealing" was a common

31. For example, the Presbyterian Church of Korea (known as the Tonghap Group) formally classified Cho as a heretic in its 1983 General Assembly and withdrew this decision in 1994.

32. Walter J. Hollenweger, *Pentecostalism: Origins and Developments Worldwide* (Peabody: Hendrickson, 1977), 100, n. 2; Harvey Cox, *Fire From Heaven: The Rise of Pentecostal Spirituality and the Reshaping of Religion in the Twenty-First Century* (Reading, MA: Addison-Wesley, 1995), 100.

33. For example, the Pentecostalization of Korean Presbyterianism was pointed out by a concerned theologian: Chang-sup Shin, "Assessing the Impact of Pentecostalism on the Korean Presbyterian Church in Light of Calvin's Theology," *Chongshin Theological Journal* 3, no. 1 (1998): 115–131.

charge lodged against Yoido Church and its branch worship centers in various parts of the metropolis.

Second, Cho and his church have served as the best advocates of church growth. It began with his strong desire for his church to grow in numbers and influence. This could have been, at least in the early years, a reaction to his dilapidated tent church, which symbolized the downcast status of his members. In the 1960s, the icon of a decent church was Youngnak Presbyterian Church. In many ways, it served as a symbol of Christian glory. Many founding members of the church were land and business owners in the northwestern part of North Korea who had fled the communist regime before the Korean War.[34] It is well known that in the early days of his tent church, Cho and his partner Mrs Jashil Choi (who later became his mother-in-law) were returning from a disappointing trip downtown after his lottery ticket did not win. As the bus passed a large cinema, which was close to the location of his future downtown church, he said he heard the Holy Spirit say, "Do you see the cinema? I will give you a church which is larger than that."[35]

In 1976, Cho organized Church Growth International (CGI) to systematically spread the experience and principles of Yoido Church's growth. Its board members have been senior pastors of megachurches throughout the world. The annual meetings bring a large number of pastors from around the world to hear the experiences of leaders of large churches and cell group leaders of the church, and to participate in church life.

Third, the church has been widely known for its active mobilization of the laity for ministry, particularly women. Logically this is a natural development: the church has helped to enable its members to have life-changing encounters with God and provided spaces for them to share their stories with people. At the beginning of the exponential growth of his church, Cho decided to organize the church according to the administrative districts of the capital. When he announced to the church that he would select and train lay women to lead the small groups ("cells" in the church language), resistance was strong, both

34. Sebastian C. H. Kim and Kirsteen Kim, *A History of Korean Christianity* (New York: Cambridge University, 2015), 173.

35. David Yonggi Cho, *Dr. David Yonggi Cho: Ministering Hope for 50 Years* (Alachua, FL: Bridge-Logos, 2008), 51.

within and without the church, and from both men and women! Soon, however, this empowered women and laity to undertake ministries.

Christianity in Korea has a long tradition of promoting the welfare and education of women. Early Protestant missionaries began many schools, some of which were exclusively for girls and women. Pentecostalism took this Christian contribution to another level. The Korean Assemblies of God, to which the church is affiliated, was one of a few denominations which ordained women ministers. The first women ministers were ordained in 1979.[36] This is extremely significant given the male-privileged social culture in Korea. Cho's cell group system took this even further by radically sharing ministerial responsibilities with laity (and mostly women)! This is an important contextual and practical expression of the Pentecostal theology which promotes the democratization of ministry to every believer.

Free Church Ecclesiology in Asia: A Preliminary Picture

A close look at the two churches in East Asia raises more questions than when the study began. These two may not be typical enough to represent the incredible variety of "Free Church" types in Asia. For example, in India, a recently published study presents the transformation of "Every Home Crusade," a mission operation, into "Christ Groups" through the adaptation of rural Indian culture.[37] Its ecclesiological shaping is quite different from the two cases above.

Notwithstanding this deficiency, this study indicates a close interplay between the social context, church tradition that was transmitted or lack thereof, and the way the gospel is understood. The nature of the church in both networks is defined by their function within their given contexts, perhaps with little or no consciousness of ancient ecclesiological formulae. Because this study used "ground evidence" to understand the nature and function of the church widely understood in each circle, the present ecclesiological description has the advantage of a close connection to actual ecclesial realities in these communities.

36. The church's bylaws were amended to allow women to be ordained in 1972. Publication Committee of the 60-Year History, *With the Holy Spirit: A 60-Year History of the Korean Assemblies of God* [in Korean] (Seoul: Assemblies of God Korea, 2013), 103, 108.

37. Saheb John Borgall, *The Emergence of Christ Groups in India: The Case of Karnataka State* (Oxford: Regnum, 2016).

Also noticeable in both cases is the decisive role of the leaders in theological shaping. In a Free Church setting, where each congregation exercises a sufficient degree of autonomy, the leader's role is substantial in shaping the culture, ethos, life, and theology of the congregation. In the case of Yoido Full Gospel Church, Cho "revised" the fourfold gospel of the (US) Assemblies of God. His experience of healing had a substantial influence on the construction of full gospel theology. For him, this is part of the recovery of the apostolic ministry as spiritual gifts are restored. The leader's role is especially prominent in independent churches, as in the Word of Life Church. Xu's encounter with hidden Christians during the Cultural Revolution caused him to prioritize genuine repentance and regeneration as the most foundational aspect of Christian faith. Although the "apostolic" aspect of the Nicene-Constantinopolitan Creed has been interpreted variously, the strong leadership and authority of Xu and Cho are reminiscent in some ways of the apostolic succession in ancient churches. As in some house church networks, Xu's family still holds the church's leadership in Xu's physical absence. Theological controversies notwithstanding, both have been subject to moral, ethical and legal charges, and they are certainly disturbing.

The recognition of other Christian communities, of the "one" and "catholic" dimensions of the Nicene-Constantinopolitan Creed, is least manifest. The "survival" experiences of both communities have affected their attitudes. The Word of Life Church was and still is unlawful and subject to various restrictions. The negative attitude towards registered churches in China among house church networks has been caused by and resulted in a narrow definition of the true church. As a Pentecostal congregation, Yoido Church also experienced marginalization among Korean churches. Only lately, partly due to its massive growth and influence, has the church been able to join the National Council of Churches. Today, its ecumenical participation and leadership are significant.

The role of the social context is undoubtedly critical in the formation of church life. It is expected that an average member of the Word of Life Church would not consider the presence of a building, church structure, or clergy to be essential for a gathering to be a church. The church's status of lacking legal sanction or recognition has forced them to develop the notion of a church as the gathering of God's people. On the other hand, Cho's Yoido Full Gospel Church has existed in a social setting where religious activities and entities are legally provided for and protected. Nonetheless, it struggled with allegations of unorthodoxy.

It is not unexpected that both groups were caught in theological controversies. This may be seen as an indication of their theological and spiritual creativity, exploring what the church is and what it does beyond the normal boundaries. Their Free Church state affords this uninhibited freedom. At the same time, it points to a need for a historic framework of Christian orthodoxy to safeguard doctrinal and practical integrity. This is where the ancient "catholic" nature of the church can be particularly relevant.

How the church is understood to be, and the process through which it is shaped, have direct implications for its mission. The two churches have remarkably stark contrasts in their missions. Both communities uphold the "holy" nature of the church, set apart as God's people for his mission in the world. But how they understand and try to fulfill it is radically different. The core of Cho's message is blessing, while Xu's is the cross. Their growth is symbolized by a massive auditorium (Cho) or an extensive network of congregations (Xu). Their mission is spreading the message of blessing and church growth (Cho), or evangelism and church planting (Xu). Both invoke the work of the Holy Spirit, to baptize in the Spirit (Cho), or to bring continual cleansing (Xu).

In Asia, more models of the church are expected to appear both in the historic and the Free Churches. Many historic churches have remained theologically evangelical, while seeking to integrate cultural elements into church life. Free Churches will proliferate as some of these churches are now actively sending their missionaries to many parts of the continent and reproducing themselves. The growing passion of the Chinese house churches for the Back to Jerusalem movement is an example.[38] Varying and rapidly changing social contexts, especially in those areas hostile to Christianity, will play a decisive role in the shaping of the church and its understanding of its nature and mission. The two communities, with their leadership now in the hands of a younger generation, face formidable challenges. The population of Korea and China is aging rapidly, and the rise of urban house churches in China is significantly impacting how churches operate. How the *de facto* de-

---

38. A textbook for this movement was recently published by a prominent urban house church leader: Mingri Jin, *Back to Jerusalem with All Nations: A Biblical Foundation* (Oxford: Regnum, 2016).

nominational function of the Word of Life will respond to the trend among urban churches towards the formation of denomination-like organizations will decisively affect their ecclesiological orientation.[39] It is therefore essential for churches and mission communities around the world to extend their theological hospitality, to "watch each other's back," while encouraging creativity that is a gift of the Holy Spirit. This hospitality, as long as it remains an offer rather than an imposition, will give birth to varying dynamic and creative ecclesiologies that are lived out, reflected, and articulated, from both the newer and the older churches in Asia.

Further Reading

Chan, Simon. *Grassroots Asian Theology: Thinking the Faith from the Ground Up.* Downers Grove: InterVarsity, 2014.

Kärkkäinen, Veli-Matti. *An Introduction to Ecclesiology: Ecumenical, Historical, and Global Perspectives.* Downers Grove: IVP Academic, 2002.

Phan, Peter C. *Christianity with an Asian Face: Asian American Theology in the Making.* Maryknoll, NY: Orbis, 2003.

Wang, Kwok Nai. *The Local Church.* Hong Kong: Christian Conference of Asia, 2005.

39. For example, Brent Fulton, *China's Urban Christians: A Light That Cannot Be Hidden* (Eugene, OR: Wipf and Stock, 2015).

CHAPTER 4

Ecclesiology in Africa: Apprentices on a Mission

STEPHANIE A. LOWERY

ABSTRACT

Ecclesiologies on the African continent take many shapes and forms, often drawing on biblical references. Some pattern themselves after Israel, others after angels, and so forth. Many of these models challenge the church worldwide to immerse itself in and tie itself more closely to the Bible. These ecclesiologies also raise challenges with regard to the Nicene affirmation of the church as "one" and "catholic." Finally, a biblical, contextually appropriate model is proposed which links ecclesiology with the *missio Dei*.

Many images may arise in a person's mind when hearing the term "Africa." From ancient churches in Ethiopia, to sprawling metropolises like Nairobi, to the deserts of Namibia and Morocco, Africa teems with life and variety. Given the size and diversity of the continent, I have chosen to offer a brief overview of ecclesiological developments in roughly the last century, discussing how these developments and proposals relate to the Nicene Creed's description of the church as one, holy, catholic, and apostolic, and then proposing a way forward for ecclesiologies in Africa today. From my perspective, the Nicene Creed is a pointed reminder that those in historic or North Atlantic-founded churches in Africa and those outside of Africa need to seriously consider developments on the continent if we want to affirm that the church is "one" and "catholic."[1]

As has been said many times before, Africa is a large continent full of diversity, and such diversity should not be ignored or downplayed. However, I will attempt to offer a general overview with some specific examples, in order to provide a wider perspective on ecclesiologies in Africa.[2]

Historic Ecclesiological Models

For the Roman Catholic churches of Africa, their ecclesiological model is something of a given, though there are modifications within that overall framework. The model of "church as family" has generally been enthusiastically embraced by Catholic theologians across the continent.[3] Protestant theologians too have relied on this imagery of the church, as do African Initiated Churches (AICs are churches begun by and for Africans, and led by Africans, generally speaking; they stand in contrast to historic or mission-founded churches with a North Atlantic bias).[4]

In part, this is because the model finds significant biblical support as well as cultural resonance. This description of the church may seem

1. I am using "Western" and "North Atlantic" interchangeably here to refer to a certain region of the world, as well as the broad cultural traits that persons in that region have in common, such as the Enlightenment heritage.

2. For a more detailed examination of ecclesiologies from historic/mission-founded churches in Africa, please see Stephanie A. Lowery, *Identity and Ecclesiology: Their Relationship among Select African Theologians* (Eugene, OR: Pickwick, 2017).

3. Pope John Paul II endorsed this model in the exhortation "Ecclesia in Africa," 14 September 1995, http://www.vatican.va/holy_father/john_paul_ii/apost_exhortations/documents/hf_jp-ii_exh_14091995_ecclesia-in-africa_en.html#top, accessed 6 June 2017. A few examples of works by Catholic theologians which embrace this model include: Elochukwu E. Uzukwu, *A Listening Church: Autonomy and Communion in African Churches* (Eugene, OR: Wipf and Stock, 2006); Agbonkhianmeghe E. Orobator, *The Church As Family: African Ecclesiology in Its Social Context*, Hekima College Collection (Nairobi: Paulines Publications Africa, 2000); and Augustin Ramazani Bishwende, *Église-famille de Dieu dans la mondialisation: Théologie d'une nouvelle voie africaine d'évangélisation* (Paris: L'Harmattan, 2006).

4. For instance, Paul Mbandi, *A Theology of the Unity of the Church in a Multi-Ethnic Context: Toward a Theological Understanding of the Unity of the Church in Relation to Ethnic Diversity* (Saarbrücken: Verlag Dr. Müller, 2010), explores the biblical imagery of the church as the people of God and the household of God – these images describe family or relatives.

unremarkable to Western ears, but I would suggest that is only because North Atlantic persons may be overly familiar with the terminology, without actually exploring its ramifications in more detail. For one, in African contexts, describing the church as "family" raises issues of ancestors: are non-Christian ancestors included in the church, if church is a form of family? Another concern is just what "family" means. At least in Kenya, "family" carries connotations of blood lines and ethnicity – and ethnic bonds tend to favor insiders. So family notions can consciously and unconsciously reinforce and borrow from the worst of ethnocentrism, and provide justification for treating those who are different or "other" as lesser.

Family models can also be unclear. Amid a ferment of change, what does family mean for Africans today? Old notions have changed in some ways, and it is not necessarily clear just what "family" entails. For example, some theologians have proposed that the church is like a "clan" of African cultures.[5] But which ethnicity's model of "clan"? And given how swiftly Africa is changing, it is valid to ask just how much "clan" means to modern, urbanized Africans who have been impacted by the West through globalization, among other means.

At the same time, the idea of church as "family" is compelling, for equally important reasons. The Bible does use extensive familial imagery to describe God's people, and we would all do well to consider just what responsibilities and implications arise from being part of God's household. Also, as many theologians have pointed out, the ecclesial community should be based on the triune God, and human relationality and the ecclesial community do have the ability to reflect the divine three-in-one in a limited way. If, then, the idea of "family" points the church back to the doctrine of the Trinity and humans' inherently relational nature, then we ought to give this model more thought, as so many theologians in Africa – both Catholic and otherwise – have done.

While many African theologians from various church traditions embrace this model, a few have rejected it outright. For example, Congolese Georges Titre Ande, of the Anglican Church, insists that the family model should not be used to describe the church in an African

---

5. John Mary Waliggo, "The African Clan as the True Model of the African Church," in *The Church in African Christianity: Innovative Essays in Ecclesiology*, ed. J. N. K. Mugambi and Laurenti Magesa, African Challenge (Nairobi: Initiatives, 1990).

context.[6] He goes so far as to claim that the Bible does not use familial language for the church, which contradicts biblical evidence.[7] Yet the stridency with which he opposes this model, and the specific dangers he mentions, should give us pause.

One of his concerns is that familial models are more often rooted in cultural notions of family than in biblical teachings. His own proposal is to root ecclesiology in Christology and the Trinity, describing a "community of life" unified in Christ, an approach designed to give priority to biblical imagery while still contextualizing, taking care that context does not become the determining factor. While I disagree with some of Ande's claims, his work is valuable on several fronts: he contextualizes without idealizing his cultural past and at the same time engaging with issues of globalization and the worldwide, catholic church; he also bases his ecclesiology on biblical study. While Ande is a rare voice for his rejection of familial models, it is worth exploring other ecclesiological developments on the continent.

AIC Ecclesiological Models

As is well known, AICs (African Initiated/Independent/Instituted Churches) have blossomed rapidly, much to the delight of theologians and historians. Omenyo views AICs as a promising "paradigm" for African ecclesiology, and cites the late Kwame Bediako as support for this view. Bediako claims AICs are significant because they manifest the general trends in African responses to Christianity.[8] One excellent source on AICs is Allan H. Anderson, a South African who offers an insider's analysis of the movement. Indeed, Anderson claims that in these AICs, Africa

6. Titre Ande, *Leadership and Authority: Bula Matari and Life-Community Ecclesiology in Congo*, Regnum Studies in Mission (Oxford: Regnum, 2010).

7. See, for example, Gal 6:10; Eph 2:19; 1 Tim 3:15; Heb 3:1–6. Such familial language can be found in the Gospels, Pauline material, and the Catholic Epistles. Christians are those who "belong" to God (John 17:9), who are born by God's Spirit to become God's children and co-heirs with Christ, their elder brother (John 3:1–6; Rom 8:14–17; Gal 4:1–7; Jas 2:5; and 1 Pet 3:7). The OT also is filled with language of Israel as God's child or bride, both terms describing kinship.

8. Cephas N. Omenyo, "Essential Aspects of African Ecclesiology: The Case of the African Independent Churches," *Pneuma* 20, no. 2 (2000): 234; citing Kwame Bediako, *Christianity in Africa: The Renewal of a Non-Western Religion*, Studies in World Christianity (Edinburgh: Edinburgh University, 1995), 66.

has experienced nothing less than a "reformation" which has "revolu-tionized" Christianity.[9] Indeed, even in 1968 David B. Barrett observed that participants in the AIC movement were consciously describing their movement as a "radical mission of renewal and reformation," and noted a "striking number of parallels" between the African scene and the European Reformation.[10] He described three specific areas in which AICS seek reform: biblicism, Africanism, and *philadelphia*.[11] On the final theme, *philadelphia*, he locates one contribution of African theology in AICs: their theology of church as community. Omenyo too emphasizes the importance of *koinonia* in AICs, and views this as an important contribution of African churches to ecumenism in a world which seems to overemphasize the individual.[12] "In short, the move-ment as a whole has introduced onto the African scene and forcibly drawn attention to a new quality of corporate Christian life and respon-sibility, a new *koinonia* (sharing) of warmth, emotion and mutual caring in the Christian community, together with a new philanthropy of all."[13] Ecclesial *koinonia* provides fellowship as well as a sense of belonging.[14] If these scholars are correct, then AIC ecclesiologies (implicit or explicit) deserve closer study.

AICs can be categorized in various ways, but are often divided into three categories: (1) African, Ethiopian, or nationalist churches, which did not claim prophetic roots or special manifestations of the Spirit, and were often secessions from mainline or historic European churches; (2) prophet-healing or spiritual churches, which emphasize the Spirit and his power, often draw on the Pentecostal movement, and tend to embrace many traditional practices and models, such as healers with spiritual powers; and (3) Pentecostal or charismatic AICs which empha-

---

9. Allan H. Anderson, *African Reformation: African Initiated Christianity in the 20th Century* (Trenton, NJ: Africa World, 2001), 4.

10. David B. Barrett, *Schism and Renewal in Africa: An Analysis of Six Thousand Contem-porary Religious Movements* (Nairobi: Oxford University, 1968), 161, 162.

11. Barrett, *Schism and Renewal in Africa*, 164–169.

12. Omenyo, "Essential Aspects of African Ecclesiology," 248.

13. Barrett, *Schism and Renewal in Africa*, 169. He continues, "It is precisely at this point that independency is making its strongest appeal – the emphasis on brotherly love, the innate apprehension that salvation is found only in community, the need to belong met by fellowship as well-being in community," and so forth (170).

14. Omenyo, "Essential Aspects of African Ecclesiology," 237.

size the Spirit, but are usually more critical of traditional practices and roles than spiritual churches would be.[15]

AICs, since they are not constrained by Western influences in the same way that historic/mainline churches are, have more freedom with regard to inculturation and innovation, but there are nevertheless trends which can be seen in this diverse grouping of churches. Some AICs, such as the one founded by Ghanaian Prophet Jemisemiham Jehu-Appiah, pattern the church after cultural communal models. So Jehu-Appiah modeled the church on the traditional Fanti court, making himself the king, and setting up a dynastic succession.[16] Peter Ropo Awoniyi's study of AICs among the Yoruba people in southwest Nigeria notes that AICs in that area give chieftaincy titles "as a mark of honour for distinguished member [sic] of their churches."[17] If ecclesial oneness and catholicity were to require a common model for the church worldwide, these models would be problematic, not least because they are quite contextual and thus less likely to be adopted in other contexts. However, we shall now describe ecclesiological trends on the continent.

Adapting cultural models for Christianity can take many forms. Examining Ghanaian AICs, Dovlo describes instances "such as the Twelve Apostles Church, [where] traditional priests such as John Nankabah and Grace Tanie . . . simply crossed over from traditional priesthood into Christian priesthood and their long experience in the former greatly influenced their new Christian role."[18] Priesthood is not the only cultural model that has been adopted by Ghanaian AICs: the notion of church leader as a "prophet" was also embraced, and this paralleled

---

15. Anderson, *African Reformation*, 15–19. Ayegboyin and Ukah divide churches in Africa into the following categories: mainline, Ethiopian, AIC, or Pentecostal (Deji Ayegboyin and F. K. Asonzeh Ukah, "Taxonomy of Churches in Africa: The Case of Nigeria," *Ogbomoso Journal of Theology*, 13, no. 1 [2008]: 1–21). John Gichimu prefers to categorize AICs as either nationalist/Ethiopian/African, Zionist/Apostolic/Aladura, or African Pentecostal ("Theological Education in African Instituted Churches (AICs)," in *Handbook of Theological Education in World Christianity*, ed. Dietrich Werner et al. [Oxford: Regnum, 2010], 368).

16. Anderson, *African Reformation*, 78–79.

17. Peter Ropo Awoniyi, "Yoruba Cultural Peculiarity and the Making of African Indigenous Churches in Southwest Nigeria," *Ogbomoso Journal of Theology* 17, no. 2 (2012): 127.

18. Elom Dovlo, "African Culture and Emergent Church Forms in Ghana," *Exchange* 33, no. 1 (2004): 35.

"the model of traditional priesthood known in Akan as the *Okomfo*."[19] Dovlo proceeds to note that not just particular roles, but whole structures were adapted, including ecclesiologies. Thus, "the Prophet is in traditional parallel a chief . . . The MDCC and the Ossah Madih Church offer examples of the traditional authority paradigm. They are organised along the lines of the Akan State (*Oman*) which [*sic*; with] the Prophet as the paramount chief and other leaders of appropriate traditional titles, functions and at times regalia."[20]

Jehu-Appiah is certainly not the only one to adopt a monarchical model. Yet some of these monarchical and theocratic models are clearly designed to mirror biblical examples, and not so much cultural paradigms. Interestingly, these models often draw heavily on the Old Testament. For instance, one of the Aladura (praying) churches which arose in Nigeria, breaking off from the Anglican Church, was founded by Garrick Sokari Braide, who renamed his hometown Bakana-Israel, and titled himself Prophet Elijah II.[21]

Such churches often refer to their base as "Jerusalem," "Zion" or "Israel," and the leaders are prophets, prophet-healers, or kings. So in South Africa Zulu Zion leader Daniel Nkonyane established a "Zion City," and leaders were like Moses, except that they found the promised land, and it is in Africa.[22] Others view themselves as lost Jews who must return to Israel.[23] Afolabi's study of Christ Apostolic Church notes many parallels between African and Israelite religious experiences, such as highly valuing sacred sites and elements.[24] Because of the biblical basis and cultural resonances, Afolabi defends the Christ Apostolic Church model against any charges of syncretism: he insists that this church is appropriately contextual and thoroughly evangelical.[25]

While cultural and Old Testament models abound, other ecclesiologies arise from a mélange of cultural, Old Testament, and New Testa-

---

19. Dovlo, "African Culture and Emergent Church Forms in Ghana," 36.

20. Dovlo, 37.

21. Anderson, *African Reformation*, 80.

22. Anderson, 96–97. Ezra Chitando's work on the African Apostolic Church of Zimbabwe provides another example of this: for this church, Zimbabwe becomes Zion ("The Recreation of Africa: A Study of the Ideology of the African Apostolic Church of Zimbabwe," *Exchange* 32, no. 3 [July 2003]: 239–249 [246]).

23. Anderson, *African Reformation*, 118.

24. Stephen Olurotimi Adeola Afolabi, "Yoruba Cultural Reflections in the Christ Apostolic Church," *Ogbomoso Journal of Theology* 17, no. 2 (2012): 149–150.

25. Afolabi, "Yoruba Cultural Reflections," 132, 144, 145.

ment references. So, for instance, the AmaNararetha's leader is a healer, Nazirite rules are followed, and a high place and holy mountain have been established.[26] John Marange, founder of the African Apostolic Church of John Marange (or "Maranke"), claimed to be John the Baptist, and required converts to obey Old Testament laws.[27] Yet other churches describe themselves in none of these earthly terms, but appeal instead to heavenly realities, such as the Eternal Sacred Order of Cherubim and Seraphim, a result of an Anglican prayer group. This church claims to represent angels on earth.

Some AICs frame their leadership and ecclesiology more in New Testament terms, describing their leaders as apostles. One of the better-known AICs was founded by Congolese Simon Kimbangu, a Baptist who preached for approximately half a year before being jailed. Despite his brief ministry as a free man, his church now has approximately 17 million members.[28] Kimbangu is viewed as an instrument of the Holy Spirit who brought a new Pentecost, a prophet, and a miracle worker.[29] Kimbangu's own view of himself was more modest: he denied being a prophet, and instead called himself an "envoy," pointing people to Christ.[30] But to members of his church, he is the "Supreme Authority of the Church and the Guarantor of the unity of the Church and its doctrine."[31] Kimbangu's followers sometimes ascribe divine qualities to him, such as omnipresence, or view him as the personification of the Holy Spirit.[32] Akiele concludes by describing Kimbanguist ecclesiology as a "family," a unity of the faithful whose ecclesial activities "create brotherhood, sisterhood."[33] Given the way in which he emphasizes

26. Anderson, *African Reformation*, 106–107. Unlike Nyende's proposal in this book, this church has designated a literal, physical mountain as its holy place, which reveals a deficient interpretation of the NT, particularly the book of Hebrews.

27. Anderson, *African Reformation*, 116–117.

28. Aurélien Mokoko Gampiot, "Kimbanguism: An African Initiated Church," *Scriptura* 113, no. 1 (2014): 1.

29. Anderson, *African Reformation*, 125–126.

30. Basile Akiele, "Attributes of Simon Kimbangu: Founder of the Kimbanguist Church," *The Journal of the I.T.C.* (Interdenominational Theological Center) 26, no. 2 (1998/1999): 194.

31. Akiele, "Attributes of Simon Kimbangu," 198.

32. Gampiot, "Kimbanguism," 4–5. Regarding his embodiment of the Spirit, Kimbanguists appeal to John 14:15–17, which records the promise to send another comforter, which Kimbanguists identify with their founder.

33. Akiele, "Attributes of Simon Kimbangu," 206.

faith as necessary for inclusion in the church, it would seem that this family model, as least, would not include non-Christian ancestors.[34]

Having mentioned all of these models, there are some churches which seemingly reject any of these paradigms, and choose their models from more pragmatic, modern sources. Ukah suggests that more recently established Pentecostal churches have a "firm-like structural organization," and are run like businesses which produce and sell commodities.[35] The leadership too derives from business world paradigms: the church leader is a combination of a chairman, president, and CEO, with the requisite Board of Trustees. Such a church is led by a person who is a "bank of grace," a "repository of charismata, and a special bridge between his followers and God"; moreover, "his word is law. He is an oracular instrument and initiator of doctrines."[36] However, even such business-oriented churches may still be unconsciously drawing on cultural notions of holy places. Ukah describes a

> tendency to reconstruct religious geography through the construction of religious camps. Particularly in Nigeria and Ghana, these churches buy up large expanses of land, sometimes measuring well over ten square kilometres, and construct a range of facilities such as auditoriums, schools, guesthouses, dormitories, presidential villas (for VIP guests such as politicians), banks, gas stations and hospitals. These camps, which often constitute an "alternative city," function to showcase a Pentecostal leader's charismata, authenticate the claim to divine authorisation, and produce his brand of Pentecostalism.[37]

Then there are churches which seem to defy the "historic or AIC" categorization, such as the Orthodox Church of Africa and the Embassy of God. For the Orthodox Church of Africa, its history in one country – Kenya – is of interest for our purposes in this essay. This church has a

---

34. Akiele also points to the Trinity as one of the foundational principles of the Kimbanguist church ("Attributes of Simon Kimbangu," 200).

35. Asonzeh Ukah, "African Christianities: Features, Promises and Problems," in *Working Papers*, ed. Institut für Ethnologie und Afrikastudien (Mainz: Institut für Ethnologie und Afrikastudien, 2007), 15.

36. Ukah, "African Christianities," 15.

37. Ukah, 17.

large number of members from the Kikuyu ethnic group of Kenya.[38] During the 1950s, British colonialists were struggling to suppress the Mau Mau Uprising; when a state of emergency was declared in 1952, the colonial government banned independent churches and schools as well, assuming they too were hotbeds of rebellion.[39] Though begun as an AIC, the Orthodox Church of Africa had been accepted officially by the Greek Orthodox Patriarchate of Alexandria in 1946, but "no support was offered to its African congregations in Kenya" during this time, and there was but one Kenyan priest – who was detained by the government – in the country for over a decade.[40]

This case study is significant for multiple reasons: (1) it demonstrates that some AICs are seeking out relationships with the church worldwide, even desiring to demonstrate their oneness and catholicity by joining historic or mainline denominations. However, (2) at least for this AIC, the path was not easy and they received little support from their partner organization. It seems that the historic church was not offering meaningful partnership to their newly accepted church in Kenya. Finally, (3) despite being accepted into the Greek Orthodox Church as Africans, "there has been an attempt to impose the sense of a 'Greek-centered' cultural identity that seriously haunts the process of enculturation."[41] For instance, non-African leaders sought to change the church's name to "Greek Orthodox."[42] This indicates that historic churches may not have fully grasped or appreciated the place of contextualization amid catholicity and oneness. Njoroge writes, "Through the transformative energies of the Holy Spirit, the incarnation process brings meaning to the message of the Gospel uniquely to every local context. These energies give balance to the universal meaning of the message and the contextualized interpretation and understanding of the Gospel."[43] But if historic churches do not even respect the necessity of contextualized congregations within their own denomination, there

---

38. John N. Njoroge, "The Orthodox Church in Africa and the Quest for Enculturation: A Challenging Mission Paradigm in Today's Orthodoxy," *St. Vladimir's Theological Quarterly* 55, no. 4 (2011): 409.

39. Njoroge, "Orthodox Church in Africa," 419–421.

40. Njoroge, 423–424.

41. Njoroge, 428; cf. 436–437.

42. Njoroge, 429.

43. Njoroge, 436.

seems little hope of churches from various denominations being able and willing to demonstrate oneness.

There are signs of hope for unity in diversity. Asamoah-Gyadu examines the "Embassy of God" in Ukraine. While AICs are typically churches led by Africans, based in Africa, and targeting Africans, the "Embassy of God," unlike other AICs in diaspora, is not predominantly African in membership.[44] Also, the language of "embassy" is noteworthy with regard to ecclesiology. This model understands God's children as citizens of God's kingdom and his representatives on earth. In other words, this ecclesiology includes missiology: it goes beyond "family" language to include the church's *raison d'être*; it implicitly ties praxis into theology, so that theology does not remain abstract. And given the multiethnic nature of the church, they are succeeding in creating a diverse community, breaking down dividing walls, and demonstrating unity to those around them.[45] This church, then, understands and is manifesting the oneness and catholicity which the Nicene Creed attributes to the church.

Contributions of African Ecclesiologies

What, then, are some of the contributions of African ecclesiologies that churches in other regions need to hear? And what do the AICs offer that mainline churches seemingly do not? As to the first question, ecclesiologies in Africa value solidarity in very practical ways, and in that regard challenge ecclesiologies in other regions to consider how and to what degree they are visibly demonstrating their unity in Christ. The debate over familial language surfaces this concern with solidarity in the ecclesial community, and examines how that solidarity differs from cultural understandings of communal solidarity.

Second, many ecclesiological emphases in African contexts rely quite heavily and directly on biblical models. As Phillip Jenkins has pointed out, the Southward shift of Christianity entails taking the Bi-

---

44. J. Kwabena Asamoah-Gyadu, "African Initiated Christianity in Eastern Europe: Church of the 'Embassy of God' in Ukraine," *International Bulletin of Missionary Research* 30, no. 2 (April 2006): 73.

45. Asamoah-Gyadu, "African Initiated Christianity in Eastern Europe," 74.

ble seriously.[46] Have North Atlantic ecclesiologies, for instance, had a tendency to be too swayed by contextual models and strayed from biblical teachings about unity among God's people? African scholars tend to be more concerned with the biblical text's application than its background, as several scholars have noted.[47] This may be termed a highly pastoral approach, similar to Ellen Charry's argument that theology should ultimately serve pastoral ends. In other words, it is a timely reminder that Christian doctrine is intended to change lives.[48] Stephen C. Barton similarly advocates for an approach he terms "*readerly*," meaning that instead of focusing on reconstructing the world in or behind the text, this approach engages deeply with the historical text itself "*as Spirit-inspired*," with the goal of producing individual and communal transformation.[49] Barton describes this method as "a form of critical reason which is *theological and ecclesial*."

Aside from their more ecclesial, application-oriented approach, ecclesiologies in Africa also raise the issue of the radical nature of following Christ. Many of these churches expect that their members will make great sacrifices for their church, that they will sacrificially care for each other and live in counter-cultural ways. This could be called "costly ecclesiology." Members in these churches may be required to dress differently, give generously, and make pilgrimages – or even move – to a special location which has been designated as a holy place. These responsibilities and burdens are counted as worthwhile for many people if in return they find a community of belonging and an identity as God's people.

Furthermore, it is worth asking what AICs offer that Africans from various backgrounds find so appealing, and what weaknesses in main-

46. See Philip Jenkins, *The Next Christendom: The Coming of Global Christianity* (New York: Oxford University, 2011).

47. Ukachukwu Chris Manus, *Intercultural Hermeneutics in Africa: Methods and Approaches*, Biblical Studies in African Scholarship (Nairobi: Acton, 2003), 59; Grant LeMarquand, *An Issue of Relevance: A Comparative Study of the Story of the Bleeding Woman (Mk. 5:25–34; Mt. 9:20–22; Lk. 8:43–48) in North Atlantic and African Contexts*, Bible and Theology in Africa 5 (New York: Peter Lang, 2004), 3, 219–220.

48. Ellen T. Charry, *By the Renewing of Your Minds: The Pastoral Function of Christian Doctrine* (New York: Oxford University, 1999).

49. Stephen C. Barton, "Christian Community in the Light of the Gospel of John," in *Christology, Controversy and Community: New Testament Essays in Honour of David R. Catchpole*, ed. David G. Horrell and Christopher M. Tuckett, Supplements to Novum Testamentum 99 (Leiden; Boston; Koln: Brill, 2000), 284–285.

line ecclesiology they highlight. First, many provide or are based on divine revelation granted to the founder. These churches value communication from God, and have no doubt that God actively communicates to God's people today. Second, these churches offer a holistic salvation, which means the leaders can heal, cast out spirits, or provide deliverance from oppression, and so forth. In other words, they are convinced that salvation in Christ affects every aspect of life, and they have confidence that God has the power and willingness to address any of their problems. Third, these churches provide freedom and dignity – freedom from Western control and dignity as African Christians. Fourth, often in AICs there is more equality among men and women, and opportunities to lead are open to women, youth, and others who are so gifted. Fifth, many of these churches rely heavily on the Spirit's power, which may indicate that their ecclesiologies are more closely linked to a robust view of pneumatology and the Trinity than other models.

African Ecclesiologies in Light of the Nicene Creed

As we have already noted, ecclesiologies in Africa, whether historic/ mission churches or AICs or varieties in between, offer both contributions and challenges with regard to the Nicene Creed's description of the church as "one, holy, catholic, and apostolic." Some AICs may not be interested in partnering with churches elsewhere in the world, or at least not with Western churches, given the painful history there. In other instances, African churches may be willing to enter cross-cultural partnerships, but Western churches are not interested in such partnership. The fact that AICs are often praxis-oriented may also make Western churches wary, accustomed as they are to doctrinal statements, creeds, and theological literature as a whole. They may ask themselves how they will be able to determine a particular church's apostolicity without formal belief statements. The issue of "holiness" is one which may be more of a concern for African churches as they examine Western churches, whose seeming liberalness can be off-putting. On the other hand, many Western churches would likely be highly wary of churches that permit polygamy. Yet on the whole, unity, catholicity, and apostolicity seem most likely to raise concerns.

A New Model: A Community of Apprentices Continuing Christ's Mission

What is the way forward for African ecclesiologies? It would be well-nigh impossible, and not necessarily desirable, to my mind, to propose an ecclesiological model that would attempt to "solve" or address all issues of a particular church, or be the best choice in every context. So I propose an approach that builds on existing ecclesiological models and is hopefully broad enough to be adapted to various contexts on the continent.

As has been noted, the idea of "family" is a popular model for the church across denominations on the continent, but equally carries significant dangers in a context of ethnocentrism. Therefore, calling the church a "clan" is not a wise route.[50] The Bible does use familial imagery to describe God's people, but makes it clear that the household of God is distinct from and functions differently than biological families. Also, familial imagery describes what the church is to some degree, but does not sufficiently link ecclesiology with the *missio Dei* (though familial metaphors do frequently link ecclesiology with the triune God). AICs have also highlighted that ecclesiology should be more closely related to pneumatology, not just Christology. Thus, I propose that the church be described as *the adoptive children of God, who are a community of Spirit-led apprentices gathered for worship and training to continue Christ's mission in the world.*

The emphasis on adoptive children highlights that being a child of God is not a natural right but a gracious gift, hopefully curbing prideful attitudes and ethnic-like conceptions of the church. The theme of God's free choice of his people runs through the Old and New Testaments. For instance, in Deuteronomy Moses lays out the basis and guidelines for the freed Hebrews who will constitute the nation of Israel. Deuteronomy 7:6–8 emphasizes that God chose the Israelites, not due to their own merit, but because of a promise he had made to their ancestors and because of his gracious love. God's sovereign election of God's people is a source of wonder for the apostle Paul (see Rom 8:15–17; 9:4–26; Gal 4, esp. vv. 4–7; Eph 1:3–12; 2). This theme also arises in John's Gospel (1:12; 15:19) and in 2 Peter (2:4–10).

---

50. Thanks to Rev. Kioko Mwangangi for his input on this matter.

In addition, the call to God's people to realize they are God's children is not a call to be proud, but rather a reminder that God's people are to be marked by humility. Jesus tells his disciples that to enter God's kingdom, one must be like a child: humble and dependent, asking for all that they need (Matt 18:3–4). The disciples did not respect or value children much, or at least saw them as an interference and distraction to Jesus's "true" ministry, and for this they were rebuked. Perhaps this rebuke that the people of God are to be like children before their Father is a reminder Christians need to hear again today. To rely on the Father who chooses and keeps his adopted children safe in God's hand (John 10:28–29) is to trust in God to lead us, and to bring along those who are called to join his people. It is not for God's children to decide whom the Father should adopt into that family.

The emphasis on being Spirit-led is both a call back to Scripture and a reminder that the Spirit unites and guides the church. It also leaves room for the Spirit's present work in manifesting himself to God's people, as well as the Spirit's role in illuminating their minds and grasp of Scripture. This is the same Spirit who empowered Jesus's mission (Isa 61:1–2, quoted by Jesus in Luke 4:18–19) and creates new life in God's people. It is the "Spirit of adoption" (John 3:5–8; Rom 8:14). The Spirit, as Peter preached at Pentecost, has been poured out on "all flesh" (Acts 2:17–18), enabling the people of God.

Those enabled by the Spirit are, I propose, intended to be apprentices. The concept of "apprentices" is one which has echoes of the past but resonance today as well, in both rural and urban contexts. "An apprentice" describes a person who is a learner, and who learns in order to apply her trade. Indeed, if we return to the beginning of Deuteronomy, in chapter 6 God's people are called to actively remember God's acts on their behalf. They are also called to meditate on God's commands, pass them on to their children, and obey them. Thus, they are called to be a community of persons who seek to learn and live out God's words; they are apprentices or disciples (see Sosa's essay in this volume on a holistic church as a community of disciples), following their Master and always needing to learn more of him and from him. Like the seventy-two disciples, after learning from Jesus, Christians are sent out for ministry. Then they return from their work to report to their master, and continue learning from him. This cycle should be ongoing until Christ returns.

Luke 10 unites the concept of being God's children, the call to learning and praxis, and the *missio Dei* being passed on to Jesus's apprentices: Jesus notes that the workers are few, and urges his disciples to pray that God might raise up more harvesters. He then sends the disciples out, after warning them to expect rejection. When the seventy-two return, Jesus warns them not to be delighted about the power they have employed in their ministry; their delight should be in the knowledge that they belong to and are known by Almighty God (Luke 10:17–20). The power they wield on behalf of God and for his mission is not what they should focus on. Jesus continues by referring to his apprentices – or disciples – as "little children," a reminder of their dependency on their heavenly Father. They know God only because he has graciously chosen to reveal God's self to these dependent, humble "children." It is both a gentle encouragement and a sharp reminder that one's position in Christ is more important than the power God bestows upon God's children. They are not to be commended for their insight, as if they had achieved or earned this knowledge, but to realize that their knowledge of God is a blessing from God, as undeserved as the rain that God sends upon the unjust (Luke 10:22–24).

By employing the apprentice imagery and model, the AIC emphasis on praxis can be carried into ecclesiology, and the *missio Dei* can once again be given its due in ecclesiology as the driving force and task of the whole church. Presumably, this outward focus could help the church move beyond its regional boundaries and have a worldwide focus. An ecclesiology which does not have any outward focus is a crippled one, for it fails to consider the purpose of God's people: they are not to be inward-focused, but to go out and represent him in the world and display his love to a world lost in darkness. As Abraham was reminded, he was blessed in order to be a blessing to the world (Gen 12). The *missio Dei* begins with God at creation, as God reaches out to the newly created world, offering to enter into relationship with the creatures made in God's image who will represent God and rule on God's behalf. This mission, driven by the relentless, pursuing love of this God who – aptly described by Francis Thompson as the "Hound of Heaven" – hunts for his people, who are lost in darkness but nevertheless avoiding their holy pursuer, is not frustrated by the intractability of God's people. That mission continues when the Second Person of God enters creation as a human being. Nor does this mission end with Jesus's death. Just as Jesus was sent by the Father into the world, so too the people of God are sent out into the world in the Spirit's power, to be ambassadors of Christ and ministers of reconciliation (John 20:21).

This church, as Petrine language reminds us, is aware of the fact that the ecclesial identity sets people apart. Specifically, Peter describes God's people as aliens and sojourners (1 Pet 2:4–10), those who are in some sense outsiders in their contexts: they seek to be contextual, without losing their holiness and their divinely granted identity. Because they stand out, and because they are following their Lord's way of life, Christians expect suffering. In the two case studies he presented, Wonsuk Ma's work raised the issue of what place suffering plays in ecclesiologies, a timely question in a world facing increasing religious extremism as well as government persecution.

The apostle Peter also describes God's people as sojourners. These sojourners in particular are on a journey toward their heavenly home, as Peter Nyende points out with his ecclesiology based on the book of Hebrews. Nyende's use of Hebrews is a contribution for ecclesiologies in general, in that he employs a book little used in ecclesiologies. For African churches in particular, the basis in Hebrews engages themes of holy places, God's dwelling, Christ's mediatorial role, among others – themes which should resonate with African Christians. Nyende notes that the purpose of God's residence in Israel is to restore his dwelling among humanity. He reads Hebrews as calling God's people to worship, which includes prayer and sacrifices on the one hand, and obedience on the other. However, it is important to expand on just what obedience to God involves, if the church is not to be an insular community focused on itself. Peter describes God's people as a royal priesthood, a holy nation, a people belonging to God. The church is set apart to worship God and to proclaim him in the world, which means they gather for worship and are then sent out into the world as witnesses. An ecclesiology which lacks this "sent out on behalf of the world" aspect is incomplete.

The message of Hebrews – that Christ is best, and that all the Israelite religious aspects foreshadowed him – also links well with Munther Isaac's emphasis that the land is God's. Just as all aspects of religious life were pointing to something else, and were used by God, so too the land of Israel and all the earth belongs to God. God's people tend it for God, but they are not intended to possess or control it for themselves. All of life, from the land to the religious life as mandated by God, to the national and ethnic identities people hold – all of life is to be submitted to Christ, with the reminder that it all belongs to God, who uses it as God deems fit, in order to fulfill the *missio Dei*. Christians are called to hold lightly to the things of this world; their concern is to abide, know their identity as those united with Christ, and look forward to the fulfillment of God's plans on the final day.

With regard to the day of judgment, eschatology too shapes this ecclesiological construct and its understanding of the *missio Dei* in which the church is invited to participate: the church is called to know not only the nature and origin of its mission, but also its goal, as seen in Revelation. The book of Revelation paints a sobering yet hope-filled picture for God's people. They are called to be faithful witnesses amid persecution from both demonic forces and fellow humans. Christians are called to remember they are part of a heavenly battle, one in which Christ is ultimately the supreme victor. As faithful witnesses, God's people are called to speak truthfully, to declare what they know regardless of the consequences. An ecclesiology in Africa – in all parts of the world – needs to address the reality of the spiritual forces attacking the Body, and teach Christians that suffering is a necessary part of taking up their cross and following their Lord. At the same time, God redeems the suffering which God's people endure, and reminds them that regardless of the suffering and evil they face, they can trust and hope in Christ's victory over evil. With these points in mind, it is to be hoped that the church can better negotiate the trials and obstacles it faces, while maintaining its unique identity in Christ, an identity of divine grace that glorifies the triune God. And one day, God's people will rejoice with their Lord and enjoy a feast with him (Rev 19:1–9). May that day hasten!

Further Reading

Ande, Titre. *Leadership and Authority: Bula Matari and Life-Community Ecclesiology in Congo*. Regnum Studies in Mission. Oxford: Regnum, 2010.

Lowery, Stephanie A. *Identity and Ecclesiology: Their Relationship among Select African Theologians*. Eugene, OR: Pickwick, 2017.

Magesa, Laurenti. *Anatomy of Inculturation: Transforming the Church in Africa*. Nairobi: Paulines Publications Africa, 2007.

Mugambi, J. N. K., and Laurenti Magesa, eds. *The Church in African Christianity: Innovative Essays in Ecclesiology*. African Challenge. Nairobi: Initiatives, 1990.

Nthamburi, Zablon. *The Pilgrimage of the African Church: Towards the Twenty-First Century.* Nairobi: Uzima, 2000.

Nyamiti, Charles. "The Church as Organ of Christ's Ancestral Mediation: An Essay on African Ecclesiology." *Revue africaine de théologie* 15, no. 30 (Oct. 1991): 195–212.

Orobator, Agbonkhianmeghe E. *From Crisis to Kairos: The Mission of the Church in the Time of HIV/AIDS, Refugees, and Poverty.* Nairobi: Paulines Publications Africa, 2005.

———. *Theology Brewed in an African Pot.* Maryknoll, NY: Orbis, 2008.

Ukwuegbu, Bernard. "'Neither Jew Nor Greek': The Church in Africa and the Quest for Self-Understanding in the Light of the Pauline Vision and Today's Context of Cultural Pluralism." *International Journal for the Study of the Christian Church* 8 (2008): 305–318.

Uzukwu, Elochukwu E. *A Listening Church: Autonomy and Communion in African Churches.* Eugene, OR: Wipf and Stock, 2006.

CHAPTER 5

Ecclesiology in Latin America: A Biblical Perspective

CARLOS SOSA SILIEZAR

ABSTRACT

Although ecclesiology is still developing in Latin American theology, there are at least two major proposals written from two distinctive angles that use the canonical Gospels as their point of departure: Leonardo Boff's ecclesiogenesis and René Padilla's holistic ecclesiology. After reviewing both proposals, I conclude that Boff's handling of the evidence is not historically accurate and that Padilla's reading of the New Testament can be enhanced by paying attention to the distinctiveness of each Gospel. I then proceed to explore the potential contribution of Johannine thought about community for the articulation of a Latin American ecclesiology.

Protestant Christianity experienced unprecedented growth in Latin America between 1960 and 1990.[1] New denominations and groups were formed and some older ones were "renovated" through the influence of Pentecostalism. Most recently, some Latin American countries have also seen the rise of newer groups called neo-Pentecostal churches. Today, Christianity in Latin America has a diverse and changing face. Not surprisingly José Míguez Bonino, a prominent Argentinian theologian,

---

1. Christian Lalive d'Epinay, "The Pentecostal 'Conquista' in Chile," *Ecumenical Review* 20 (1968): 16–32; Walter J. Hollenweger, *Pentecostalism: Origins and Developments Worldwide* (Peabody: Hendrickson, 1997); Martin Lindhardt, ed., *New Ways of Being Pentecostal in Latin America* (London: Lexington Books, 2016).

analyzed Latin American Protestantism paying attention to its "many faces."[2] However, theological reflections about the nature and purpose of the church in Latin America have not been as copious as its many churches and denominations.[3]

During the 1970s the Roman Catholic Church was dominant in Latin America. They were the first Christians to arrive in this region in the sixteenth century. Priests in Latin America attempted to follow as closely as possible the form, format, and theology of the Roman Catholic Church in Spain and Portugal.[4] For more than three hundred years, there were no formal reflections on the mission and nature of the church produced by Christians born and active in Latin America. The situation of the Protestant churches was similar. They came to Latin America from Europe and, mainly, from the United States during the nineteenth century.[5] However, they too sought to mimic the liturgy and doctrine of their sending churches. Formal reflections on the nature and mission of the church (ecclesiology) by native Latin American leaders are unknown during this period.

Formal reflections on the nature and mission of the church in this region came first from liberation theologians. Liberation theology emphasizes the social liberation of the poor from their oppressors. A foundation for ecclesiological thought is found in Brazilian thinker Leonardo Boff's work. He articulated an innovative way of looking at ecclesiology from within the Roman Catholic tradition. He used the New Testament, especially the Synoptic Gospels (Matthew, Mark, and Luke), as a source for his reflections. In doing that, he employed the methodologies and results of redaction criticism, an approach which aids the

2. José Míguez Bonino, *Faces of Latin American Protestantism* (Grand Rapids: Eerdmans, 1997).

3. Veli-Matti Kärkkäinen's essay in this volume, "Ecclesiology and the Church in Christian Tradition and Western Theology," observes that European ecclesiology advanced slowly and with a somewhat haphazard tone due to circumstances after the Reformation. Similarly, ecclesiology in Latin America is advancing slowly and is being highly influenced by contextual circumstances.

4. John A. Mackay, *The Other Spanish Christ: A Study in the Spiritual History of Spain and South America* (New York: Macmillan, 1933). See also C. René Padilla, "Evangelical Theology in Latin American Contexts," in *The Cambridge Companion to Evangelical Theology*, ed. Timothy Larsen and Daniel J. Treier (Cambridge: Cambridge University, 2007), 259–273, here 259.

5. Sidney Rooy, "Religious Tolerance and the Arrival of Protestantism in Latin America," *Journal of Latin American Theology* 6 (2011): 41–69.

reader to distinguish between received traditions and the theological work of the evangelists in handling such traditions. Boff attempted to provide a theoretical framework to understand base communities, groups of lay Christians living and reading Scripture in community without significant interventions from the hierarchical institution. Boff regarded his proposal as "ecclesiogenesis," that is, the origins (*genesis*) of the church (*ekklesia*). The official Roman Catholic reaction to Boff's proposal was not positive, to say the least. His ideas were rejected by the Church in Rome.[6] However, his proposal is still influential in Latin American theology.

Other voices, past and present, coming from the Roman Catholic Church follow Boff's initial insights.[7] Furthermore, Boff's proposal is unique in that he uses the canonical Gospels (Matthew, Mark, Luke, and John) to articulate ecclesiology. Therefore, we will focus here on his proposal.

The other thinker who has attempted to articulate ecclesiology from a Latin American perspective is Ecuadorian theologian René Padilla. He writes from an evangelical orientation. Padilla uses the canonical Gospels in the form we have them in our New Testament today in order to propose an ecclesiology that can serve a holistic mission. He is well known for proposing that the church's mission should be "integral" or "holistic." That means, in a nutshell, "a mission that maintains the unity between justification by faith and the struggle for justice, between faith

6. Former Cardinal Joseph Ratzinger expressed his disagreements with Boff's ecclesiology in his "notification" *Dominus Iesus*. Boff's vigorous reply is found in his article "¿Quién subvierte el Concilio? Respuesta al Cardenal J. Ratzinger a propósito de la *Dominus Iesus*," *Revista Latinoamericana de Teología* 236 (2001): 33–48. When quoting from works published in languages other than English, I provide my own translation. See also Harvey Cox, *The Silencing of Leonardo Boff: The Vatican and the Future of World Christianity* (London: Collins Religious, 1989).

7. G. Olivieri, *Novas formas de ser Igreja* (Andradina: Novas Formas, 1995); F. L. C. Teixeira, *A gênese das CEBs no Brasil: elementos explicativos* (São Paulo: Paulinas, 1988); J. C. Petrini, *CEBs: um novo sujeito popular* (Río de Janeiro: Paz e Terra, 1984); A. Quiróz Magaña, *Eclesiología en la teología de la liberación* (Salamanca: Sígueme, 1983). More recent work on ecclesiology comes from Latin American thinkers associated with the official Roman Catholic Church. They pursue insights found in the latest Conference of Bishops (Aparecida, Brazil, 2007). See, for example, Fernando Berríos, "Una comunidad de discípulos misioneros: Líneas eclesiológicas de Aparecida," *Teología y Vida* 49 (2008): 685–697. A recent assessment of Latin American ecclesiology is found in Rodrigo Polanco, "Eclesiología en Latinoamérica: Exposición y balance crítico," *Teología y Vida* 50 (2009): 131–152.

and works, between spiritual needs and material and physical needs, and between the personal and the social dimensions of the gospel."[8] His ideas are very influential among Protestant and evangelical churches in Latin America. Although Padilla has shown sympathy for Boff's ecclesiological proposal,[9] a deeper analysis of both ecclesiologies reveals significant differences in the way they handle the biblical texts. Padilla praises Boff for attempting to renew the Roman Catholic Church by going back to the New Testament in order to articulate his "ecclesiogenesis." However, as will be shown shortly, their methodologies for approaching the biblical texts are rather different.

Regrettably, there are not many voices in the Latin American Protestant world that articulate ecclesiology from a biblical perspective. Most of the work has been done as theological articulation[10] or as an "evangelical response" to liberation ecclesiology.[11] Therefore, engaging the foundational work of Padilla seems the best option here.

Since both Boff's and Padilla's proposals are theological articulations, it is difficult to provide a deep engagement with the biblical texts they use for support. In what follows, I will include the biblical citations provided by them, but I won't provide close assessment of their work with the biblical text. Instead, I will assess the methodologies they seem to employ when engaging the New Testament. My overall impression is that general ideas from the canonical Gospels, rather than specific texts from the New Testament, are used by Boff and Padilla to support their views.[12]

8. Padilla, "Evangelical Theology in Latin American Contexts," 269.

9. C. René Padilla, "Introducción: una eclesiología para la misión integral," in *La iglesia local como agente de transformación: Una eclesiología para la misión integral*, ed. C. René Padilla and Tetsunao Yamamori (Buenos Aires: Kairós, 2003), 39–40.

10. For example, Nicolás Panotto, "The Church We Imagine for Latin America: Faith and Identity in Today's Globalized World," *Journal of Latin American Theology* 9 (2014): 139–157.

11. A pioneer and robust evangelical response to liberation theology (including its ecclesiology) is found in Emilio A. Núñez, *Liberation Theology* (Chicago: Moody, 1985). My own essay, Carlos R. Sosa, "Trayectorias de la Nueva Evangelización católica: Un enfoque evangélico," *Kairós* 39 (2006): 61–91, is also an attempt to respond to recent theological developments in Roman Catholic ecclesiology.

12. This is more evident in Boff's proposal. I have been unable to find a single Bible reference in his description of base communities in Leonardo Boff, *Church: Charisma and Power: Liberation Theology and Institutional Church*, trans. John W. Diercksmeier (New

After describing and assessing both proposals, I will attempt to perform an exegetical reading of John 13:34–35 and will try to explore the potential contribution of this passage for the articulation of ecclesiology from a Latin American perspective. By "exegetical reading" I mean paying close attention to a particular text in light of its larger literary context.

Ecclesiogenesis and Christian Origins

The rise and development of "base communities" was truly innovative in Latin American ecclesiology. Leonardo Boff, a former priest within the Roman Catholic tradition, described these communities as "new ecclesiological experiences," "a rebirth of the church," "the emergence of a different way of being church," and "a reinvention of the church."[13] These are *base* communities because laypeople gather together as a church without significant intervention from the hierarchical institution.

Historically, these communities were a response to institutional crises in the Roman Catholic Church. The first General Conference of Latin American Bishops gathered in 1955 in order to find solutions to the lack of clergy in the region. They described the situation as a "distressing problem."[14] Behind their preoccupation lay the idea that a representative of the hierarchical institution was necessary in order for a community to have a legitimate church. Structurally, these communities come close to what observers of the protestant world call "Free Churches."[15]

To the official leaders, base communities seemed an imperfect solution to the problem. Laypeople gathered to read the Bible and to enjoy

---

York: Crossroad, 1985), 125–137, even in those places where he argues that base communities are "Born from the Word of God" (127).

13. These designations are found several times in Leonardo Boff, *Ecclesiogenesis: The Base Communities Reinvent the Church*, 5th ed. (Maryknoll, NY: Orbis, 1986). See also Antonio Alonso, *Comunidades eclesiales de base: Teología-Sociología-Pastoral* (Salamanca: Sígueme, 1970); R. Muñoz, *La Iglesia en el pueblo: Hacia una eclesiología latinoamericana* (Lima: Centro de Estudios y Publicaciones, 1983); J. Galea, *Uma Igreja no povo e pelo povo* (Petrópolis: Vozes, 1983).

14. William T. Cavanaugh, "The Ecclesiologies of Medellin and the Lessons of the Base Communities," *Cross Currents* 44 (1994): 67–84.

15. Interestingly, Kärkkäinen, "Ecclesiology," contrasts the Roman Catholic Church with the Free Church without seemingly noticing the close structural resemblances between Roman Catholic base communities and Protestant Free Churches.

fellowship (*communitas fidelium*) without necessarily being under the authority of a priest. This situation engendered a new ecclesiology, that is, new theological reflections about the meaning, mission, and nature of the church. An important resource for these new reflections was the New Testament. One of the main driving questions for these new reflections was: "Did the historical and prepaschal Jesus want a church?"[16]

Posing the question this way ensures a sharp distinction between the "ecclesiology" of Jesus (if any) and the doctrinal developments of the early Christians, and anticipates giving greater authority to Jesus's own ideas than to the theological thoughts of the New Testament writers. This question also accepts almost without reserve the results of redaction criticism.[17] This methodology focuses on "the unique theological emphases" that the New Testament writers "place upon the materials they used, their specific purposes in writing their works" and the context "out of which they wrote."[18]

Boff asserts that "the church was not part of Jesus' intentions." Jesus was a Jew who announced the coming of God's kingdom. He preached only to Jews because he wanted them to accept his message of the imminent coming of the kingdom.[19] Boff understands this kingdom as a new world order in which God is the supreme ruler, and as the overcoming of all evil that oppresses the world. In this perspective, Jesus's last supper was not a sacrament for the church but the joyous anticipation of the imminent kingdom. However, the Jews rejected Jesus's mission, and therefore he failed in his attempt to set up God's kingdom on earth. This failure was partially resolved in the cross. Since Jesus realized that he was unable to convince people with his message and works, he won people by taking upon himself the sins of the world. Thus, God's king-

---

16. Boff, *Ecclesiogenesis*, 77. In the following paragraphs I will attempt to summarize Boff's arguments.

17. This methodology attempts to distinguish between the putative oral and written traditions about Jesus that the Gospel writers received and their theologically motivated editorial changes and additions to such traditions.

18. Robert H. Stein, "Redaction Criticism (NT)," in *The Anchor Bible Dictionary*, vol. 5, ed. David Noel Freedman (New York: Doubleday, 1992), 647.

19. This idea is still current in historical Jesus research. Cf. Samuel Byrskog and Tobias Hägerland, eds., *The Mission of Jesus*, Wissenschaftliche Untersuchungen zum Neuen Testament 2.391 (Tübingen: Mohr Siebeck, 2015). Historical Jesus research presupposes that the real Jesus of history was different from the Christ portrayed in the four canonical Gospels. Scholars engaged in trying to recover the putative "real" Jesus from the Gospels are said to be part of the "quest of the historical Jesus."

dom was not fulfilled in a universal sense. Jesus himself then became God's kingdom. His message, demands, and self were the kingdom of God in the present time.

The church, then, is the substitute for the unfulfilled kingdom. On the one hand, there is discontinuity between Jesus's preaching about the kingdom and the beginning of the church. This discontinuity is marked by the cross. On the other hand, there is continuity between Jesus and the church. His resurrection ensures his presence among his followers. Since the kingdom is present in Jesus, the presence of the risen Jesus among his followers allows for continuity between Jesus and the church.[20] Notwithstanding this perspective, the disciples did not establish the church immediately after Jesus's resurrection. They still preached the gospel to their fellow Jews and waited for the imminent arrival of God's kingdom. The delay of the parousia, Jesus's second coming to the world, and the wide acceptance of their message among Gentiles drove them to create the church. This they did under the inspiration and guidance of the Holy Spirit.

The disciples started organizing themselves in order to face all the challenges in the world their life without Jesus would imply. This organization was also necessary because their message was being welcomed among Gentiles. Although the historical Jesus did not conceive of a church of Jews and Gentiles, the disciples decided to preach among non-Jews. They received light, illumination, and inspiration from the Spirit in order to transpose eschatology (the things to come with Jesus's second coming to the world) into the time of the church and to translate the doctrine of God's kingdom into the doctrine of the church. Thus, the church is a temporal and imperfect realization of God's kingdom.

Two important components of the newly created church were the apostles and the Eucharist. The group of the twelve selected by Jesus in order to symbolize the twelve Israelite tribes were now sent to preach the gospel to Gentiles. This sending made them apostles of the gospel. An apostle, then, is a post-paschal, post-resurrection, missionary concept.[21] They innovated and preserved traditions according to their own contextual needs. They even wrote Gospels in which their theological

20. Leonardo Boff and Clodovis Boff, *Introducing Liberation Theology* (Maryknoll, NY: Orbis, 1987), 76.

21. Passages such as Luke 6:13 ("Jesus called his disciples . . . whom he named apostles" [ESV]) are not to be attributed to Jesus but to Luke's redaction, according to Leonardo Boff.

perspectives coexisted along with the historical Jesus's own message. Similarly, the Lord's Supper acquires new meanings after Jesus's resurrection. For the church, the Eucharist is not related to the imminent coming of the kingdom but is instead nourishment for the church, a symbol of unity and the permanent presence of Jesus's sacrifice.[22]

Base communities are still current in Latin America, and their ecclesiology is still developing.[23] The designation of Argentinian Bishop Jorge Mario Bergoglio as the 266th pope of the Roman Catholic Church has raised expectations regarding the future shape of the Church.[24] Pope Francis's first apostolic exhortation *Evangelii Gaudium* ("The Joy of the Gospel"), published in 2013, devotes several paragraphs which consider "An ecclesial renewal which cannot be deferred" (§§ 27–33). A remarkable paragraph for our purpose is number 29: "Other Church institutions, basic communities [i.e. base communities] and small communities, movements, and forms of association are a source of enrichment for the Church, raised up by the Spirit for evangelizing different areas and sectors. Frequently they bring a new evangelizing fervour and a new capacity for dialogue with the world whereby the Church is renewed."[25]

A critical evaluation of Boff's ecclesiology should highlight first its positive elements. The most remarkable is the idea that laypeople can gather around God's Word without significant intervention from the "official church." As Pope Francis states, base communities bring renewal to the church. Furthermore, the idea that laypeople should take an active role in the mission of the church comes close to the emphasis on the priesthood of all believers in Protestant theology. Even the early church fathers from the second century AD like Ignatius and Irenaeus highlighted the idea that Jesus's presence through his Spirit legitimizes a community as fully Christian.[26]

---

22. Leonardo Boff, *When Theology Listens to the Poor* (San Francisco: Harper & Row, 1988), 101–115.

23. Stefan Silber, "Los laicos somos la Iglesia: 'Otro modo de ser Iglesia' ya es una realidad," *Alternativas* 30 (2005): 123–146.

24. Pablo Richard, "Otra Iglesia es posible: El papa Francisco nos abre nuevos caminos," *Alternativas* 46 (2013): 185–198.

25. Pope Francis, *The Joy of the Gospel (Evangelii Gaudium)* (New York: Image, 2014), 26.

26. This is shown in Kärkkäinen, "Ecclesiology." He also notices that European ecclesiologies like that of Wolfhart Pannenberg regard the Spirit as "community-forming" and "communally-directed."

Another important positive element is the emphasis on God's kingdom. Since this was a major element in Jesus's preaching according to the Synoptic tradition, any ecclesiology should use this topic as a frame of reference. The kingdom of God is universal and not restricted to a particular faith community or local church. It points, as Boff highlights, to a new world order in which God is the absolute ruler.

However, there are some other elements of Boff's proposal that require further consideration. On the practical side, it is very difficult to imagine that members of base communities in Latin America (many of them with low levels of education and living in rural areas) would make a sharp distinction between the teachings of the historical Jesus and the teaching of the Synoptic Gospels. A plain reading of these texts would certainly point to similarities and differences between them, but it is doubtful that such a reading would lead to the conclusion that Jesus's teachings during his earthly ministry were very different from the disciples' later interpretations of them. It remains possible that someone with knowledge of redaction criticism would lead the discussions of a base community so that its members could reach such conclusions. But then base communities would require a significant intervention from a new kind of "priest," namely, people with a special knowledge about layers of tradition in the final form of the Synoptic Gospels. This new "academic priesthood" goes against the very nature of base communities, in which all the members explore the New Testament without significant intervention from the official Roman Catholic Church.

Boff's claims can also be assessed historically. There is no doubt that Jesus directed his message primarily to Jews. However, not all the evidence supports the contention that the disciples' latter mission to Gentiles was only a later innovation that coexisted along with Jesus's exclusive preaching to Jews. It makes better historical sense to suggest that the disciples' Gentile mission was somehow shaped by Jesus's enduring impact during his earthly ministry.[27]

Judaism during Jesus's time was divided into several groups. On the one hand, some groups such as the Pharisees regarded themselves as "the righteous." This meant that all those who did not fulfill the law in their terms were regarded as "sinners." Thus, the term "sinners" denoted "Jews who practised their Judaism *differently* from the writer's

---

27. James D. G. Dunn, *Jesus, Paul, and the Gospels* (Grand Rapids: Eerdmans, 2011), 97–98.

faction. They were 'sinners' . . . but only from a sectarian viewpoint, and only as judged by the sectarians' interpretation of the law."[28] On the other hand, Jesus was remembered as directing his mission to "sinners" (Mark 2:17) and sharing the table with them. He was seen by his detractors as a "glutton and a drunkard, a friend of tax collectors and sinners" (Matt 11:19; Luke 7:34 NRSV).

Jesus's association with those regarded as "sinners" might suggest that he saw God's grace open to even those deemed to be excluded from the covenant.[29] It is plausible, then, that knowledge of Jesus's mission led the apostles to conclude that God's grace is not restricted to those who fulfill the law.[30] In preaching to the Gentiles, the apostles were not actually innovating and departing from Jesus's mission. They were taking the next natural step in continuity with Jesus's earthly ministry.

Furthermore, it remains possible that Jesus actually had contact with non-Jewish people. There is evidence that Gentiles used to visit Jerusalem during Jesus's time. The existence of two warning inscriptions written in Greek to prevent Gentiles from entering the inner precincts of the Jewish temple would indicate that some non-Jews used to visit Jerusalem.[31] During Jesus's time, Jerusalem was a "metropolis of international, world-wide significance, a great 'attraction.'"[32] The Synoptic tradition "presupposes without further ado" that Jesus was capable of having a conversation in Greek. We find him talking to a captain from Capernaum, Pilate, and the Syro-Phoenician woman.[33] Furthermore, Galilee, a place where Jesus carried out most of his earthly ministry, offered many opportunities to have contact with non-Jews.[34] Therefore, the portrayal of Jesus's contact with Gentiles should be taken as historically plausible instead of only as a late theological elaboration by the Gospels' final editors.

28. Dunn, *Jesus*, 100.

29. Dunn, 101.

30. Cf. Dunn, 104.

31. Martin Hengel, *The "Hellenization" of Judaea in the First Century after Christ*, trans. John Bowden (Eugene, OR: Wipf and Stock, 2003), 9.

32. Hengel, *"Hellenization,"* 11.

33. Hengel, 17.

34. Hengel, 17.

Holistic Ecclesiology and Biblical Theology

Although the evangelical church has been present in Latin America for many decades, only recently has its ecclesiology started to develop. René Padilla and Tetsunao Yamamori recognized back in 2003 that "a remarkable deficit in Latin American evangelical theology is that found in the area of ecclesiology."[35] Padilla, in particular, has proposed an ecclesiology that can nurture holistic mission.[36] In order to articulate such an ecclesiology, Padilla uses the Gospels, mainly the Synoptic Gospels, in their final form. The driving question of his reading of the New Testament seems to be: How does the Gospels' ecclesiology support the theological concept of holistic mission?

Padilla argues for a holistic ecclesiology that has, at its center, the fulfillment of holistic mission.[37] Only a church that has a holistic ecclesiology is able to make a positive impact in its community and is capable of transforming society. This holistic ecclesiology has four intertwining characteristics. The first, and fundamental, characteristic is commitment to Jesus Christ as Lord of all. The heart of the New Testament is precisely the confession of Jesus as Lord (1 Cor 8:4–6). This confession is tied to the Greek version of the Old Testament, where Yahweh, the God of the Old Testament, was referred to as "Lord." This confession also was a protest against the first-century Roman imperial cult with its emphasis on the absolute authority of the Roman emperor. The church, then, that confesses that Jesus is Lord over all will have a mission that concerns all aspects of life: for example, economics, politics, culture, society, art, ecology, and community (1 Cor 1:2; cf. Acts 9:14, 21; 22:16). Christology, the acknowledgment that Jesus is Lord over all the earth, is the basis of ecclesiology.[38]

The second characteristic of a holistic ecclesiology is discipleship. Following Jesus means a process of transformation (Rom 10:12–15). The disciple is one who follows Jesus's example and obeys his teachings (Acts 2:42; Rom 6:17; Gal 1:8–9). Jesus taught and showed how to love God,

35. Padilla and Yamamori, eds., *Iglesia local*, 7.

36. Padilla, "Introducción," 13–45.

37. In what follows, I summarize the arguments found in Padilla, "Introducción," 13–45.

38. Ecclesiologies from other contexts, however, operate within a trinitarian framework that, in turn, allows a more ecumenical understanding. Cf. Kärkkäinen, "Ecclesiology."

love our neighbors, serve others, be in solidarity with the poor, and be committed to the truth (Mark 10:43–45; Luke 14:25–33; John 10:15). The "holistic disciple" should live as Jesus lived. However, discipleship is not a lonely business. The disciple is part of a Christian community where he or she finds God's grace. Therefore, the third characteristic of a holistic ecclesiology is community. The holistic church is actually a new humanity. Its testimony is incarnational – that is, it becomes real in the world just as God's Word became flesh and dwelt among us (John 1:14; 20:21). The church embodies God's word and is a witness of God's purpose for the whole of creation. The paradigm of the church's mission is Jesus's life, ministry, death, resurrection, and exaltation (Matt 10:18, 24–25; Acts 2:36; 1 Cor 15:25, 56–57; Eph 1:19–20).

This community of disciples is not, however, an end in itself. The Christian community plays a priestly role as intermediary between God and the world. This is the fourth characteristic of a holistic church. Through gifts and ministries, the Holy Spirit empowers the church to perform transformative acts in society (1 Cor 12:4; Eph 4:11–12). These transformations reflect God's purposes for human life and for his whole creation. Each member of the church should use his or her gifts to advance the transformation of this world. There should not be a sharp distinction between clergy and laymen and laywomen. Every Christian should be actively involved in the mission of the church. The clergy should be more like laypeople, and laypeople should be involved in the ministry of the church.

If our understanding of Christology is based on the confession that Jesus is Lord over all creation, our ecclesiology can then only be a holistic ecclesiology that inevitably leads to a holistic mission. That is, the whole church and all of its members are committed to the transformation of the whole world, following Jesus's example and living under his death, resurrection, and exaltation.

In evaluating Padilla's proposal we should start with his approach. It is a valuable contribution to look at the Gospels in their final form. This is the way that many "lay" Christians in Latin America would read the New Testament. He hardly makes a distinction between what Jesus taught and what the Gospel writers wrote. This, however, could play against his proposal. Reading the Gospels in their final form and extracting from them a holistic ecclesiology runs the risk of not paying enough attention to the theological distinctiveness of each Gospel and, indeed, of each book of the New Testament.

There is unity of thought across the New Testament. However, this unity should not be maximized beyond what can be seen from the New Testament itself. There are dimensions, perspectives, and contributions from each New Testament book on the topic of ecclesiology. This diversity does not necessarily oppose a holistic ecclesiology. It might be the case that paying attention to the distinct contribution of each Gospel from an ecclesiological perspective may enhance and enrich what Padilla calls "holistic ecclesiology."

From Exegesis to Ecclesiology

In what follows, I attempt to undertake constructive contextualized biblical reflection on the Gospel of John. My aim is to make a small contribution to Latin American ecclesiology by highlighting some distinctive features of Johannine ideas about community in John 13:34–35.[39] I have intentionally selected the Gospel of John because this seems a neglected text in classic Latin American liberation theology.[40] When it is used as a source of theology, the favorite passage seems to be the story of the Samaritan woman in John 4.[41] I will suggest three dimensions that should be considered in articulating the nature and mission of the church. I will preface each dimension with a brief description of my own observations and experience as a member of the Guatemalan church and society.

Although there is much debate about the extent and form of ecclesiological thought in the Gospel of John,[42] there are at least three indications in 13:34–35 that point to the idea of a new community of disciples. The first indication is the separation of Jesus from his disciples explained in verse 33. Jesus is leaving for a place where his

39. A Latin American "popular reading" of this passage is found in Ernesto Cardenal, *The Gospel in Solentiname* (Maryknoll, NY: Orbis, 2010), 543–549.

40. A notable exception is José Miranda, *Being and the Messiah* (Maryknoll, NY: Orbis, 1976).

41. For example, Néstor Míguez, "Reading John 4 in the Interface between Ordinary and Scholarly Interpretation," in *Through the Eyes of Another: Intercultural Reading of the Bible*, ed. Hans de Wit, Louis Jonker, Marleen Kool, and Daniel Schipani (Elkhart, IN: Institute of Mennonite Studies, 2004), 334–347.

42. For example, Francis J. Moloney, "John 18:15–27: A Johannine View of the Church," in *The Gospel of John: Text and Context*, Biblical Interpretation Series 72 (Leiden: Brill, 2005), 313–329.

disciples cannot come. This separation entails a new form of existence for the disciples as a group. The second indication is the reference to a "new commandment" in verse 34. The adjective "new" already points to a distinctive form of community among the disciples. The disciples will maintain a relationship with Jesus through obeying a new commandment. The third indication is the use of the ideas found in John 13:34–35 in latter Johannine works. In 1 John 3:23 (ESV) we read, "this is his commandment . . . love one another, just as he has commanded us." Similarly, in 2 John 5 (ESV) we find, "I ask you . . . – not as though I were writing you a new commandment, but the one we have had from the beginning – that we love one another." This would imply that the commandment found in John 13:34 was taken as foundational for Jesus's followers after his departure.[43]

How might the Johannine ideas of community found in 13:34–35 speak to the Latin American context? From a Latin American perspective, I suggest that churches should see themselves as (1) local communities with global awareness, (2) suffering communities that love the world, and (3) communities where diversity is reconciled.

Local Communities with Global Awareness

Latin American realities are deeply influenced by the global context. In Guatemala, for example, the US Embassy is often found expressing public opinions about the social and political situation of the country. The DR-CAFTA (Dominican Republic-Central America Free Trade Agreement) and the EU-CA (Economic Agreement between the European Union and Central America) put Guatemala in an economic relationship with the United States and the most powerful countries of Europe. This context might point to specific international applications of the love motif found in John 13:34–35. The following thoughts do not attempt to argue that the love command become a central place in all trade agreements. Instead, I suggest that the Johannine love command should be at the center of reciprocal activities between fellow Christians, including business relations.

---

43. A few scholars suggest that the Johannine letters were written before the Gospel of John. See Udo Schnelle, "Die Reihenfolge der johanneischen Schriften," *New Testament Studies* 57 (2011): 91–113. This view, however, is not dominant among scholars.

According to this Johannine text, the most important characteristic of a community of disciples is love. This idea is repeated three times in these two verses: "that you love one another" (v. 34); "you are to love one another" (v. 34); "have love for one another" (v. 35).[44] In the Gospel of John "love" is a divine characteristic. The first reference to "love" in this Gospel is found in 3:16: "For God so loved the world . . ." (cf. 17:23). God is portrayed several times as loving the Son (e.g. 3:35; 10:17), and Jesus is likewise portrayed as loving the Father (14:31). This divine "community" between Jesus and the Father is maintained by love. The Father loved the Son even before the foundation of the world (17:24, 26). The way the Father shows his love for the Son is by sharing all things with him. The Father has given all things into his hands (3:35; 13:3).[45]

This love between Christians should extend to all those followers of Jesus living in different countries (17:20–21). Laws that regulate economic agreements between Guatemala and the US and the EU are not based on the Johannine idea of love. Therefore, Christian business people from those regions that benefit from trade with Guatemala should ask: "What would be the best way to show love to my Guatemalan fellow Christians when doing business with them?" "Is it enough to follow the official international laws?"

The way Christians should show love among themselves is by imitating the love that God has for his Son: sharing all things and placing them in his hands (3:35; 13:3). The love command should be at the center of any kind of relation between Christians from different countries. Even those Christians in the so-called "first world" who profit from trade with fellow Christians from countries like Guatemala should reflect on the place of the love command in their business interactions.

---

44. ESV. This idea is repeated again in 15:12 and 15:17 (cf. 17:26). The love motif is prominent in the Gospel of John. For a classic study of this topic, see A. Feuillet, *Le mystère de l'amour divin dans la théologie johannique* (Paris: Gabalda, 1972). For a more recent treatment of this topic, see Sjef van Tilborg, *Imaginative Love in John*, Biblical Interpretation Series 2 (Leiden: Brill, 1993).

45. This Johannine idea about divine community shaping ecclesial community is an emphasis found in Eastern Orthodox tradition. A robust vision of divine community should be echoed in an ecclesiology of relational existence (Kärkkäinen, "Ecclesiology").

Suffering Communities That Love the World

Christianity is the majority religion in most Latin American countries. This is taken as a blessing by many internal and external observers. However, it carries a risk: society's values and worldview can negatively influence the mission of the church. Guatemala's elected president and vice president (2012) had to resign in 2015 due to allegations of corruption. The president was the guest of honor at the inauguration of the new church building of one of the largest neo-Pentecostal churches in Guatemala in 2013. He was given the pulpit to address thousands of parishioners, although he had never publicly indicated his adherence to any evangelical church. The elected vice president also donated a very expensive flag to be put in this new church building. Three years later it was discovered that money to finance the flag came from corruption in the government. The church was forced to give the flag back.

The Gospel of John indicates clearly that God loves the world (3:16; 17:23). God loves the world because he created it in the beginning (1:3, 10; 17:5, 26). Jesus shows his love for the Father by loving sacrificially what the Father loves, namely, the world. Jesus's love for the world has two dimensions. The first dimension is his giving his life in order to take away the sins of the world (10:17; 15:13; 13:1). Through his suffering on the cross, he showed his sacrificial love for the world. The second dimension is his testifying about the world that its works are evil (7:7). On the one hand, Jesus speaks the truth because he is the light. On the other hand, the world is attached to falsehood and is enslaved in darkness. This is why the world hates Jesus. Ironically, Jesus's love for the world was the cause of his earthly suffering. Because he spoke against falsehood and darkness in the world, he suffered during his earthly ministry. He faced opposition, accusations, threats of death, and persecution.

Christians living in countries like Guatemala with complex social problems where politics plays a major role might conclude that a "neutral" position is the best way to show love for the world. However, John 13:34–35 clearly indicates that love for the world implies taking a position in favor of the light and the truth and against darkness and falsehood.

If Christians are called to imitate Jesus, one might conclude that evidence that a church follows Jesus is its speaking the truth in the midst of a world full of lies. As long as the church loves the world, the church will suffer hate from the world. This means that an important component of the church's mission is testifying about the world that its works are evil. The disciples who live in a new covenant with Jesus (13:34) cannot live in covenant with the world.

The "new command" found in 13:34 is the Johannine equivalent of the "new covenant" elsewhere in the New Testament.[46] During his last meal, Jesus instituted the observance of the Lord's Supper (Matt 26:28; Mark 14:24; Luke 22:20; 1 Cor 11:25). This celebration would determine the way the disciples would live as a group.[47] The regular, perhaps weekly, observance of the Lord's Supper should shape their existence as a community. The Johannine passage we are considering (13:34–35) is also set in the context of Jesus's last supper (13:1–2). However, John omits any overt reference to the actual supper with bread and wine and instead focuses on a dramatic action, Jesus's washing of his disciples' feet (13:4–12). The Gospel of John lacks the actual institution of the "new covenant" and instead focuses on the "new command" that should characterize not the weekly but the daily life of his disciples. This new command should be fulfilled in the context of sacrificial service, just as Jesus washed his disciples' feet.

Communities Where Diversity Is Reconciled

Oppression and injustice have deeply marked the history of Latin America. Complex problems have divided Latin American societies and have even created alienation. Guatemala is regarded as one of the most diverse and multicultural countries in the world. Four groups coexist in this country: Maya, Xinca, Garifuna, and Ladinos.[48] Sixty percent of the population is Maya, but the central government is run by a huge majority of Ladinos. Although Mayan people contribute to the rich cultural

---

46. J. Ramsey Michaels, *The Gospel of John*, New International Commentary on the New Testament (Grand Rapids: Eerdmans, 2010), 758–759.

47. Michaels, *John*, 758.

48. People with strong ethnic ties with pre-Columbian inhabitants of Mesoamerica are called "Mayas." Indigenous people culturally different from "Mayas" are identified as "Xincas." People called "Garifunas" have strong ethnic links with West and Central African people brought to Latin America by Spanish people in the sixteenth century. "Ladinos" is a general term used to refer to all those contemporary inhabitants of Guatemala who can claim Spanish or Portuguese ancestors.

diversity of Guatemala, one of the major social problems of the country is racism.[49] In the midst of such intricate realities, the church should be the epicenter of reconciliation, transforming the world through the powerful testimony of God's love among them. The church should demonstrate a reconciled diversity.

The diversity of people attracted to Jesus in the Gospel of John is noteworthy. The Johannine Jesus indicates: "when I am lifted up from the earth, I will draw *all people* to myself" (12:32 ESV). Indeed, we find significant diversity among the people who approach Jesus in the Gospel of John: for example, disciples of John the Baptist (1:37), a true Israelite such as Nathanael (1:47), a ruler of the Jews (3:1), a woman from Samaria (4:7), a royal official (4:46), a former blind man (9:35), a family from the village of Bethany (11:1–3), Greek pilgrims in Jerusalem (12:20), the wealthy Joseph of Arimathea (19:38), and fishermen from Galilee (21:1–2). This is not surprising because the Word was actively involved in the creation of everything that exists (1:3, 10), and Jesus's mission as portrayed in the Gospel of John concerns the whole world (3:16; 12:44–50).

The church, then, should be taken as the privileged space where creation is reconciled to its creator and where diversity is redeemed. As Jesus departs from the world, he commands his disciples to love one another, just as he loved them (13:34).[50] During his earthly ministry, Jesus showed his love for his disciples by revealing the Father to them and teaching them the truth. Jesus loved them just as the Father loved him (15:9). Jesus also loved the world sacrificially, giving his life for the world (15:13). Jesus showed his love for the Father through obedience to his commandments (14:31). The love between the Father and the Son is sustained by Jesus's obedience to him (15:10). In loving one another, the disciples must reflect the same "divine community" between the Son and the Father. Since God loves his creation, the disciples show their love for the Father when they love what God loves, namely, his Son and his creation.

---

49. Heather E. Mitchel, "Guatemalan Indigenous Youth: Experiences of Ethnic Discrimination and Its Impact" (PsyD diss., Wheaton Graduate School, 2013).

50. It is worth noting that while the Synoptic Gospels emphasize love for enemies, the Gospel of John highlights love among disciples. Cf. Hugo Zorrilla and Daniel Chiquete, *Evangelio de Juan*, Comentario para Exegesis y Traducción (Miami: Sociedades Bíblicas Unidas, 2008), 443.

Leonardo Boff was correct to indicate that Jesus's resurrection ensures his presence among his followers. René Padilla also correctly highlighted the importance of the confession of Jesus as Lord among the community of disciples. However, from a Johannine perspective, the risen Jesus is present among those disciples who follow the new command to "love one another." Jesus will "manifest himself" to those who love him (14:21). Even the Father and the Son will come to abide and make their home with those who love Jesus (14:23). It is not only the confession of Jesus as Lord that ensures his presence among his followers. Jesus is present among those disciples who love one another.[51]

Love is actually what brings God closer to his world. Although the world loves darkness (3:19), God approaches his creation by sending his Son into the world (3:16). Those who love Jesus experience a very close encounter with their creator, since both the Son and the Father come to them and make their home with them (14:23; cf. 8:42).

This love has what we might call a missionary goal. If the community of Jesus's followers love one another, "all people will know" that they are his disciples (13:35 ESV). When the disciples love one another just as Jesus loved them, they become perfect in unity (17:23). The world will then know that Jesus was sent and loved by the Father (17:23). A community that fulfills the new command is a powerful testimony to the world of the love between the Father and the Son (14:31). Since loving God is the way creation can re-establish a proper relationship with its creator, and since loving Jesus means loving God, a community of disciples in which each loves the other as the Son loves the Father is in itself a testimony to the world of God's love.

This threefold perspective provided by John 13:34–35 has the potential to enrich our understanding of the historical confession of the church as contained in the Nicene-Constantinopolitan Creed (AD 381). For centuries, Christians around the world have confessed that the church is "one, holy, catholic, and apostolic."[52] Since the church is "one" and "universal," the idea of local communities with global awareness

---

51. This insight is also found in Cardenal, *The Gospel in Solentiname*, 443.

52. The received text of the Greek church and the Latin version of Dionysius Exiguus are found in Philip Schaff, *The Creeds of Christendom with a History and Critical Notes*, 3 vols. (New York: Harper & Brothers, 1877), 2:58. Actually, the characteristic construction of this confession in the Greek reception, "we believe in" (πιστεύω + εἰς), is found several times in the Gospel of John (e.g. 2:11; 3:16; 6:35; 11:48; 16:9).

is more than an ideal; it should be our commitment.[53] Local Christian communities are churches "insofar as they are in communion with other similar communities."[54] Christians from different contexts and geographies should constantly seek collaboration and communion not only for "ecclesiastically related" issues but also for larger social issues such as those described in this essay. This unity and universality also means that all the wonderful dimensions of God's diversity found in creation (John 1:3, 10; 17:5, 24) can and will be reconciled in Jesus through his disciples.

The confession of the church as "holy" does not make it impossible to have contact with the world which is in darkness. God loves the world and has sanctified Jesus's disciples (John 13:10; 17:11, 17) so that they can keep engaging the world with his Word. The only way the church can honor its title of "holy" is by continually shining its light in the darkness, by constantly bringing life to the world, and by loving a world that hates God. By keeping the tradition of the apostles, especially as contained in the New Testament texts, the church remains faithful to the truth, is sanctified in the truth, and engages a world dominated by lies in order to transform it.

Latin American churches with their distinctive liturgies, traditions, and confessions are part of the holy, catholic, and apostolic church. However, the church is not going to be recognized by the world as followers of Jesus primarily because of its dogmas, rules, or liturgy.[55] Love among one another is what makes churches part of the universal church.

Conclusion

Latin American ecclesiology still needs development. The two proposals evaluated here (Boff's and Padilla's) are helpful but they can be improved. There is a need for more exegetical work on the New Testament, paying attention to the individual theological contributions of each text.

---

53. For Jürgen Moltmann, *The Church in the Power of the Spirit: A Contribution to Messianic Ecclesiology*, trans. Margaret Kohl (London: SCM, 1977), 339–340, the Creed provides "statements of hope" that should become "statements of action." See Kärkkäinen, "Ecclesiology."

54. Kärkkäinen, "Ecclesiology."

55. Zorrilla and Chiquete, *Evangelio de Juan*, 443.

There is also need for an integrative work that can accommodate the rich diversity found in the New Testament texts and their significance to the contemporary church and society.

A reading of John 13:34–35 with attention to the Latin American context, particularly the Guatemalan context, has shown that the category of "love" should take a prominent place in any ecclesiological articulation. The meaning of this noun is framed and shaped by the larger Johannine thought in which love is the foundation of the unique relationship between the Father and the Son. This "divine community" is actually extended to all those who love the Son. Jesus and the Father are present with those who love each other. Furthermore, Jesus's followers should follow his example by loving what the Father loves, namely, the world.

A constructive contextualized reading of John 13:34–35 has the potential to nurture Latin American ecclesiology by highlighting the nature of the church as a local community with global awareness, by emphasizing the being of the church as a suffering community that loves the world, and by underscoring its mission of reconciling the creation with its creator and redeeming diversity.

Further Reading

Azevedo, Marcelo de C. *Basic Ecclesial Communities in Brazil*. Washington DC: Georgetown University, 1987.

Boff, Leonardo. *Church, Charism and Power: Liberation Theology and the Institutional Church*. Translated by John W. Diercksmeier. New York: Crossroad, 1985.

Hewitt, W. E. *Basic Christian Communities and Social Change in Brazil*. Lincoln: University of Nebraska, 1991.

Kärkkäinen, Veli-Matti. *Introduction to Ecclesiology: Ecumenical, Historical and Global Perspectives*. Downers Grove: InterVarsity, 2002.

Núñez C., Emilio A., and William D. Taylor. *Crisis and Hope in Latin America: An Evangelical Perspective*. Pasadena: William Carey Library, 1996.

Padilla, C. René. *Mission Between the Times: Essays on the Kingdom*. Revised and updated. Carlisle: Langham Monographs, 2010.

Sobrino, Jon, and Ignacio Ellacuría, eds. *Mysterium liberationis: Fundamental Concepts of Liberation Theology*. Maryknoll, NY: Orbis, 1993.

CHAPTER 6

The Community as Union with Christ in the Midst of Conflict: An Ecclesiology of the Pauline Letters from a Chinese Perspective

Xiaxia E. Xue

ABSTRACT

This essay explores from a Chinese perspective the essence of the church as described in the Pauline letters. After a brief survey of the historical forms of Chinese ecclesiology, the essay argues that the essence of the church is the community in union with Christ in the midst of conflict. It examines the Pauline churches in Galatia and Corinth, and also the churches in Hong Kong. The essay considers both the earthly and transcendental dimensions of the church. On the one hand, the church is fully human because Christian communities share the human characteristics of tension and fragility. On the other hand, the church is transcendent because its true identity is the body of Christ and it is created by Christ. The church stands as a dynamic community in the process of growing into its fullness. In its continuous struggle and unceasing efforts to achieve unity, the church grows toward greater maturity.

The church is the assembly of the faithful whose marks the Nicene Creed proclaims as "one, holy, catholic, and apostolic." It is, however, not a pure instrument representing God's presence since throughout history it becomes manifest in the imperfect nature of its members. Conflict is natural to Christian churches. Starting from the early church in the first century and throughout every following age, people have experienced divisions in the church.[1] One instance is the church in Corinth. It was reported that there were several parties in this church. Some claimed to belong to Paul, some to Apollos, some to Cephas, and some even to Christ. Paul cried out to the Corinthian church, "Is Christ divided? Was Paul crucified for you?" (1 Cor 1:13 ESV).

Tension and conflict, even division, were characteristic of the early church, for the church consists of people who think differently due to each one's experiences and identity. Does such intrachurch struggle and fragmentation contradict the great gospel of reconciliation? Of course not. These conflicts and how the early followers dealt with them demonstrate that the church community is not an "otherworldly entity" but a real body of flesh-and-blood humans in the process of growing into maturity.[2] The tensions created by the differences of divergent Christian groups challenge the church to become more mature.[3] L. Vischer states, "From the very beginning the community had to struggle for its unity . . . Unity shatters when this struggle ceases. It is destroyed primarily by the hardening of positions, by exclusivity and self-contented isolation."[4] In other words, dealing with the struggle helps to push forward the growth and maturity of the churches.

These conflicts are also rooted in modern churches, as we see in churches in Hong Kong. In contemporary Hong Kong churches, Christians are divided according to their attitudes toward the Chinese central government. Strongly held attitudes trigger fragmentation within the churches. Some wish to continue to relate to and support the churches in Mainland China and some do not want to. From this conflict arise divisions among them.

This essay aims to explore through Pauline texts how the first Christians dealt with their fragmenting struggles and then make application to modern Asian churches in Hong Kong to clarify the essence and nature of the church. However, one may question how texts from two thousand years ago can address modern church issues. With great insight, Vischer has provided a good reason to use these texts:

---

1. Lukas Vischer et al., *Unity of the Church in the New Testament and Today* (Grand Rapids: Eerdmans, 2010), 1–2.

2. Vischer, *Unity of the Church*, 5.

3. Luke Timothy Johnson, *The Creed: What Christians Believe and Why It Matters* (New York: Doubleday, 2003), 275.

4. Vischer, *Unity of the Church*, 14.

Reasons that compelled the first generations to struggle for community are still valid today. What was true for the authors of the New Testament is still true for the modern ecumenical movement – that with his reconciling work in Christ God has laid the foundation for a community in love, and that obedience to God involves giving visible expression to this unity. The call to unity is the same, and it is therefore not surprising that the great texts of the New Testament in which the drive to unity has been formulated are also relevant today.[5]

Therefore, this essay will examine the origins of the church and the Nicene Creed to describe and explain both the reality and the ideal nature of the church. Then it will focus on the conflict in Pauline churches and in today's churches in Hong Kong. Third, the way Paul deals with conflicts within the churches will be examined, from which the essence of the church will be derived. Finally, the essay will apply Paul's principles in dealing with such conflicts to the current conflicts in the churches in Hong Kong. But first I will offer a brief survey of Chinese ecclesiologies as examples of dynamic Christian communities and their contexts.

A Brief Survey of Chinese Ecclesiologies

There are many different types of Chinese churches. These include the Three-Self (Self-governance, Self-support, Self-propagation) Patriotic Church, house churches, local assemblies, registered churches, and the True Jesus Church. The Three-Self Patriotic Church is an institutional, state-approved church which was constituted after the communists established the new Red China in 1949. In order to adapt to the new political environment, Three-Self Church leaders decided to show their loyalty to the state by rejecting the influence of foreigners in the areas of leadership, finance, and mission.[6] According to K. H. Ting, the Three Self-Church needed to be independent from foreign countries and to carry out the Three-Self policy because the revival of China required

5. Vischer, 15.
6. 丁光訓著，《論三自與教會建設》(上海: 中國基督教兩會出版，2000年)，5 (English translation: K. H. Ting, *On Three-Self Policy and the Construction of the Chinese Churches* [Shanghai: National Committee of Three-Self Patriotic Movement and National Christian Council of China, 2000], 5).

Christians to be in line with the state. Christians henceforth would be accepted as patriotic citizens, thereby enabling more effective evangelism.[7] Also, Y. T. Wu, the first Three-Self Church leader after the establishment of the People's Republic of China, maintained that the most significant expressions of the church were in social action and moral doctrine. Therefore, it was important for him to respond to social and political issues,[8] and Wu participated actively in political movements.[9] For him, Christian ethics which responded to particular social and political issues were important.[10]

If the Three-Self Church's close connection with the Chinese social and political environment is at one end of the spectrum, at the other end are the house churches and their relationship with their political and cultural environment. Wang Mingdao represents those conservatives who refused to compromise with the communist government.[11] In Wang's view, the church is independent of any worldly structure, since "no particular form of church government was essential for the existence of the church."[12] For such conservatives, the function of the church is twofold: "One was to be separate from the world, and not be conformed to the world. Everything must be done according to the will of God. The other side was to bear witness to the world. It was because the church did not conform to the world that it could be a witness of God."[13] In sum, most conservatives remain separate from social and political issues and believe the church should exist independent from any worldly structure. They insist on walking the way of non-conformity to the world.

The third type of church is the "local assembly" established by Watchman Nee, whose ecclesiology was influenced by the Brethren.[14]

7. 丁光訓, 《論三自與教會建設》, 55–65 (English translation: Ting, *On Three-Self Policy*, 55–65); Chee Nan Pin, *The Search for the Identity of the Chinese Christian Church: Ecclesiological Response of the Chinese Church in 1949–1958 to the Political Changes* (Hong Kong: WEC International of HK, 2016), 69.

8. Chee, *Search for the Identity*, 111.

9. Philip L. Wickeri, *Reconstructing Christianity in China: K. H. Ting and the Chinese Church* (Maryknoll, NY: Orbis, 2007), 97.

10. Chee, *Search for the Identity*, 111.

11. Thomas Alan Harvey, *Acquainted with Grief: Wang Mingdao's Stand for the Persecuted Church in China* (Grand Rapids: Brazos, 2002), 93–101; Chee, *Search for the Identity*, 124.

12. Chee, *Search for the Identity*, 125.

13. Chee, 126.

14. Chee, 128.

Dissatisfied with the fragmentation of the churches caused by denominational differences, Nee called for the unity of different denominations.[15] He introduced the local assembly model of church – one geographical locality, one church.[16] Nee's understanding of God's kingdom was church-centered, and he did not consider it necessary for Christians to exert moral effort to change society[17] since the church revealed and manifested God's kingdom.[18]

Besides these three types of Chinese churches, other churches are affiliated with the state, with and without being affiliated with the Three-Self official churches. In sum, the forms of the church in China are varied. Each type reflects the church's understanding of its nature and its relationship with God, God's kingdom, and its socio-political and cultural context.

The Origin of the Church and the Nicene Creed's Statement about the Church

The Origin of the Church

The word *ekklesia* focuses on two points, evoking associations in two ways. First "The assembly of the nation Israel, the assembly of God, is behind the word."[19] Second, it evokes associations with popular assemblies in ancient cities, so a local church could be referred to as an *ekklesia*.[20] Regarding the origin of the church, scholars argue one of two positions. The first is to view the church as being "instituted immediately and directly by the true and historical Christ himself."[21] The second is to regard the church as a post-Easter creation.[22] The second declaration

15. Chee, 128.
16. Chee, 128.
17. Chee, 132.
18. 倪柝聲, 《權柄與順服》, 第二版, (台北: 台灣福音書房, 1979), 52–53 (English translation: Watchman Nee, *Authority and obedience*, 2nd ed. [Taipei: Taiwan Gospel Book Room, 1979], 52–53).
19. Vischer, *Unity of the Church*, 55.
20. Vischer, 55.
21. For the Latin text please see Heinrich Denzinger and Adolf Schönmetzer, *Enchiridion Symbolorum*, 36th ed. (Freiburg: Herder, 1976), no. 3540. Also see Vischer, *Unity of the Church*, 34.
22. Vischer, *Unity of the Church*, 34.

would lead to the ecclesiological discontinuity between the historical Jesus and the risen Jesus. I agree with Vischer's view that "one can speak only of starting points or roots in Jesus that then after Easter led to the formation of the church."[23] In other words, there is no historical root for the church without Jesus, and without the post-Easter proclamation of Jesus's resurrection, there is no formation of the church. The unity of the church hinges on Jesus whose coming, death, and resurrection are the core of the proclamation of the church community.

The disagreements within the church arise mainly out of the varied identities of church members and the conflicting viewpoints among them. With Jesus, we find there are two groups: the twelve disciples and the other disciples who followed Jesus. The personal identities of the first group varied sharply; for example, Matthew the tax collector and Simon the Zealot would have represented opposing parties in Israel.[24] The second group is larger than the first and includes unclean people, women, and Samaritans, suggesting the openness of the group.[25] The strains within the church in Jerusalem are reported in Acts 6:1 by Luke who writes of the tensions between the Greek-speaking Jewish followers of Jesus and the Aramaic-speaking disciples.[26] It can be inferred that there were various disputes among group members from the very beginning of primitive Christianity.[27] Surely, members emphasized different points about Jesus and his mission.

The Nicene Creed: "One Holy Catholic and Apostolic Church"

Although from the beginning of the primitive church conflicts existed among church members, this does not mean that they are the essence of the church. We need to turn to a very early statement of faith to understand the concept of ecclesiology. As the oldest of the three ancient creeds, the Nicene Creed stands closest to the original sources of faith, being issued by over three hundred bishops gathered at Nicea on

23. Vischer, 36.
24. Vischer, 38.
25. Vischer, 39.
26. Cf. Johnson, *The Creed*, 44.
27. Johnson, 45.

19 June 325.[28] Moreover, the Creed was an innovation for the church which clearly brought the churches into a position of cooperation with a universal creed which took precedence over local versions.[29] The Creed places the statement of the church under the third article:

> We believe in the Holy Spirit,
> the Lord, the giver of life,
> who proceeds from the Father.
> With the Father and the Son he is worshipped and glorified.
> He has spoken through the prophets.
> *We believe in one holy catholic and apostolic church.*
> We acknowledge one baptism for the forgiveness of sins.
> We look for the resurrection of the dead,
> and the life of the world to come. Amen.[30]

The relevant part for the church is the statement, "We believe in one holy catholic and apostolic church." However, what do these four categories (one, holy, catholic, apostolic) say about the essence of the church? Does it mean that the church has these characteristics? The answer is, "No." In other words, the four characteristics "are the directions into which the church is growing."[31] First, the church is "one." This declaration points to the unity (not the uniformity) of the church through the work of the Holy Spirit. The church as "God's chosen people" who call on the name of the Lord (Rom 10:13) is the body of Christ. This unity requires diversity within the community (Eph 4:3–12; 1 Cor 12:4–11). The second mark is "holy." It indicates that the church as a corporate entity is called to be different from the world. The otherness of the church makes it challenge and even transform the world through the Holy Spirit's leading. The third mark is "catholic." Catholicity refers to the church's universality and its embrace of ethnic and cultural differences (Gal 3:28). The fourth mark of the church is "apostolic." This characteristic refers to the standard by which the church is measured.

---

28. Hans-Georg Link, "Fullness of Faith: The Process of an Ecumenical Explication of the Apostolic Faith," in *One God, One Lord, One Spirit: On the Explication of the Apostolic Faith Today*, ed. Hans-Georg Link, Faith and Order Paper No. 139 (Geneva: WCC, 1988), 5. Also see Johnson, *The Creed*, 34.

29. Johnson, *The Creed*, 33.

30. Link, *One God, One Lord, One Spirit*, 1. Emphasis mine.

31. David Willis, *Clues to the Nicene Creed: A Brief Outline of the Faith* (Grand Rapids: Eerdmans, 2005), 142.

Johnson states, "The church in every age must be measured by the standard of the apostolic age as witnessed not by the later tradition but by direct appeal to the writings of the New Testament."[32] These four marks point to the ideal church which has not been and will not be realized yet, for tension and conflict remain natural to human communities, including the church.[33]

The church in its essence is a community that is united with Christ in the midst of tension. On the one hand, it is the body of Christ, the assembly of the faithful in the Spirit, with the four traits as marks of the ideal church. On the other hand, the church through history has been composed of real people with human frailties and natural passions.[34] It has never been a pure instrument perfectly representing God's presence on earth[35] since tension is natural in Christian communities.

A Brief Summary

Tension within the church is not an accidental or alien factor. It has its place in the historical churches. It already existed in the early church from its beginning since these Christian communities consisted of people with different experiences who came from various ethnic groups (e.g. the Greek-speaking Jewish Christians, the Aramaic-speaking disciples, and the Gentiles among the Greco-Roman citizens, etc.). Nevertheless, the Nicene Creed describes the four classic marks of church which provide an ideal goal for the church to realize. Therefore, tension and conflict share a place with the four classic marks of church. The former have existed since the beginning of the earliest church and the latter will never be fully realized.

32. Johnson, *The Creed*, 274.
33. Johnson, 275.
34. Johnson, 254–262.
35. Johnson, 254–262.

The Tensions in Pauline Churches and in Today's Hong Kong Churches

Many factors cause tensions in the Christian communities. Tension started in Jerusalem between the Greek-speaking Jewish followers of Jesus and the Aramaic-speaking disciples because of an argument over the daily distribution of food (Acts 6:1–2).[36] Moreover, different attitudes toward the Torah caused further divisions between the followers of Jesus.[37] In addition, local religious or ethnic factors would bring about conflict (e.g. the table-fellowship disputation between the Jewish and non-Jewish Christians in the Antioch event, Gal 2:11–14). Fourth, socio-cultural factors led to tensions, such as the partisan problems in the Corinthian church. The last, but not least, aspect is socio-political issues. The conflict between Hong Kongers and Mainlanders in China stems from a political issue. In the following pages, the tensions in Galatian churches, Corinthian churches, and modern Hong Kong churches will be examined.

The Conflict in the Galatian Church[38]

The Gentile mission soon led to the dispute over whether the Gentiles should be circumcised and be obedient to the law. This contention threatened the unity of the church.[39] The conflict in the Galatian church was between the Judaizers and Gentile Christians. Paul describes those Jewish Christians as "troublemakers" or "agitators" (Gal 1:7, 10; 4:17) and views their gospel as another, different gospel (1:6). Regarding the Antioch crisis, when the Torah-faithful visitors came from Jerusalem to Antioch, Peter, Barnabas and some other Jews separated from the table-fellowship with Gentile Christians, for they feared the circumcision faction (2:12). What Peter did gave the Gentile Christians the impres-

---

36. Vischer, *Unity of the Church*, 44.

37. Vischer, 45.

38. Regarding Paul's general concept of church in Romans and Galatians, please see Stanley Porter, "The Church in Romans and Galatians," in *The New Testament Church: The Challenge of Developing Ecclesiologies*, ed. John Harrison and James Dvorak (Eugene, OR: Pickwick, 2012), 85–102. However, this essay explores Paul's view of church from the perspective of conflict.

39. Vischer, *Unity of the Church*, 58.

sion that they must participate in the Jewish rite of circumcision and other rituals, otherwise they could not continue to eat with the Jewish Christians.[40] Paul reproaches Peter sharply for being a hypocrite since he was not acting consistently with the true gospel (2:14). At Antioch he resisted the troublemakers from Jerusalem, which was a way of expressing his persuasion of the Galatians to stand firm against the agitators in Galatia.[41] For those agitators, Jewish rituals were valued more highly than the new community of Jewish and Gentile Christians. In Galatians Paul argues sharply against this tendency.

The Conflict in the Corinthian Church[42]

Scholars have suggested that there were different parties in the Corinthian church that followed different leaders (1 Cor 1:12).[43] The factions were reported to Paul through Chloe's household (1 Cor 1:11). The following will explore the underpinnings of the conflict.

First, the opening four chapters of this letter illustrate the factions, quarrels, and divisions among the Corinthian congregation. This tension extends through the entire letter, as Mitchell suggests.[44] In 1:10–12, the opening section of the body of the letter, Paul indicates that there are quarrels (ἔριδες, v. 11) and parties who dispute with each other. They claim to belong to Paul, or to Apollos, or to Cephas, or to Christ (v. 12). He reproaches them for being of the flesh because they behave according to their human inclinations, with jealousy and quarreling (3:3). The Corinthians' divisions depict the rivalry among them. As DeSilva says, "In many respects these divisions reflect the age-old problem of 'looking out for number one' rather than looking out for

---

40. Vischer, 67.

41. Frank J. Matera, *Galatians* (Collegeville, MN: Liturgical Press, 1992), 88.

42. For a general idea of the Corinthian church, please see Eckhard J. Schnabel, "The Community of the Followers of Jesus in 1 Corinthians," in *The New Testament Church: The Challenge of Developing Ecclesiologies*, ed. John Harrison and James Dvorak (Eugene, OR: Pickwick, 2012), 103–129.

43. Craig S. Keener, *1–2 Corinthians* (Cambridge: Cambridge University, 2005), 8.

44. See Margaret M. Mitchell, *Paul and the Rhetoric of Reconciliation: An Exegetical Investigation of the Language and Composition of 1 Corinthians* (Louisville: Westminster John Knox, 1992), 81–83. Also, John M. G. Barclay, *Pauline Churches and Diaspora Jews* (Tübingen: Mohr Siebeck, 2011), 34–35.

the interests of fellow believers."[45] Paul criticizes the Corinthians for being puffed up for following one leader rather than another (4:6–7, 18–19). Their claim of superiority is based on the teacher they consider most authoritative.[46] Moreover, this rivalry or competitiveness exists in the way they measure spiritual gifts and charismatic endowment (chs. 12–14). Even at the celebration of the Lord's Supper they compete for the hierarchy of social status.[47]

Second, the conflict in the Corinthian church results in part from their close interaction with Corinthian society. The issue is that they are so attached to the culture that they are very much influenced by it. In 1 Corinthians 1:18 – 2:5 we read that they are deeply attracted to the wisdom of the world, which is contrary to the gospel.[48] Corinthian society is very competitive and so are some believers in the church. In chapters 12–14, Paul indicates that these believers regard themselves as spiritually superior to other members. As people of the Spirit, they see themselves as above any responsibility toward weaker members. For them, the church has no claim on their lives outside the worship gatherings.[49] Some may even have participated in temple dinners (10:14–22) for they would meet with socially higher-positioned people there. Barclay suggests that "from their continued participation in temple-dinners . . . those who are socially well-placed set much more store on the opinions of their non-Christian friends than on the feelings of their 'weaker' Christian brothers."[50]

Third, the divisions within the church are also expressed in the hierarchal gaps between the rich and the poor. Paul, discussing the Lord's Supper in 1 Corinthians 11:17–34, teaches the Corinthians not to abuse the church's common meal; in other words, the shared fellowship of the Lord's Supper has been superseded by a divided meal.[51] The rich

---

45. David A. DeSilva, *An Introduction to the New Testament: Contexts, Methods and Ministry Formation* (Downers Grove: IVP Academic, 2004), 566.

46. Barclay, *Pauline Churches and Diaspora Jews*, 41.

47. DeSilva, *An Introduction*, 566. DeSilva indicates, "It [the mindset of competition] led to the replication of the hierarchy of social status at the celebration of the Lord's Supper as the rich provided fine fare for themselves and their guests of equal rank in addition to the bread and wine that was distributed to the 'masses' (1 Cor 11:17–31)."

48. Barclay, *Pauline Churches and Diaspora Jews*, 190.

49. Barclay, 191.

50. Barclay, 191.

51. Gordon D. Fee, *The First Epistle to the Corinthians* (Grand Rapids: Eerdmans, 1987), 535.

members came early and went ahead with their own private meals. The poor or the slaves who had nothing came late with nothing to eat. Paul blames the wealthy: "Do you not have homes to eat and drink in? Or do you show contempt for the church of God and humiliate those who have nothing?" (11:22 NRSV). Barclay comments, "The behavior of the wealthier members at the Lord's Supper and the legal disputes between members are eloquent testimony to the lack of close affective ties within the church."[52]

In summary, the tensions and fragmentation in the Corinthian church were caused by several factors, such as the low (the poor) and high status (the elites) of the members, and the personal desire to seek superiority in society as well as in the church through spiritual experiences. In a nutshell, the conflict among the Corinthian congregants resulted from their removing Christ from the center and reducing him to the periphery so that they were principally influenced by their cultural value systems. Those who were to overcome the world were overcome by the world.

The Conflict in Today's Hong Kong Churches

In recent years, the tension between Hong Kong and Mainland China has increased sharply, which in turn has influenced the relations of the churches on the two sides. The conflict, on the one hand, has its roots in divergent political opinions and, on the other hand, is caused by their different cultural value systems.

First, the conflict inside the Hong Kong churches results from the socio-political context of Hong Kong society. When speaking of the Christian churches in Hong Kong today, this Hong Kong–Mainland conflict has to be kept in sight. Since the handover of Hong Kong's sovereignty to China in 1997, the tensions between people from Hong Kong and Mainland China have increased, especially in the late 2000s and early 2010s.[53] Most of all, the Hong Kong–Mainland conflict can be attributed to differences in cultural value systems, those of the former

---

52. Barclay, *Pauline Churches and Diaspora Jews*, 191.
53. See Custer Charles, "The Conflict of Hong Kong vs. China: What's All the Fighting About?," updated 17 October 2016, https://www.thoughtco.com/china-vs-hong-kong-687344, accessed 22 March 2017.

being more international while those of the latter are more traditional Chinese. Also, Hong Kong people and Mainlanders have different spoken languages. Most Hong Kongers cannot understand Mandarin, which makes communication complex. The tension can be illustrated in the derogatory names they give each other; for example, the Mainlanders call Hong Kongers "old dogs" and the latter call the former "locusts."[54] Moreover, the conflict is due to the allocation of resources in different sectors. For example, the number of "anchor babies" of Mainland mothers in Hong Kong has been increasing, which results in increased competition for welfare in the city.[55]

The tension between Hong Kongers and Mainlanders is reflected in the churches. For one thing, the Hong Kong churches' ministries on the Mainland have diminished in recent years, for the Hong Kong sponsors have reduced or even canceled their donations to their ministries on the Mainland. For another thing, mutual distrust leads to the doubts that Mainlanders have about the purpose of the Hong Kong churches' aid. This distrust creates obstacles for gospel ministry toward the Mainlanders. In addition, the cultural differences make it difficult for the Mainlanders to integrate into local Hong Kong churches, which creates further misunderstanding or distrust between both sides.

Second, churches are also torn apart due to the divergent political opinions between different generations, especially after the Umbrella Movement. The Umbrella Movement started on 28 September 2014 and is "usually considered the day that the theological landscape in Hong

---

54. The label "old dogs" comes from a well-known outspoken professor at Peking University, who indicated that some Hong Kongers in the former colony were "British running dogs." This insulting label caused some Hong Kongers to take to the streets to protest. Then a Hong Kong newspaper called some Mainlanders "locusts" swarming into Hong Kong to grab the resources. See "Dogs and Locusts" in *The Economist* (4 February 2012). The article can be accessed online at http://www.economist.com/node/21546051, accessed 5 June 2017.

55. <800人捐款五日籌十萬高登下週登報促截'雙非'>, 載於蘋果日報 ("Hong Kong–Mainland Contradictions," *Apple Daily*, 27 January 2012, http://hk.apple.nextmedia.com/news/art/20120127/16018621, accessed 22 March 2017). "Anchor babies" refers to the babies born in Hong Kong by Mainland mothers. Hong Kong opened its door to Mainland Chinese in 2003. Then some Chinese pregnant women went to Hong Kong to give birth so that their babies could obtain Hong Kong citizenship. By doing this, they could skirt the Mainland's one-child policy and gain access to Hong Kong's social welfare benefits.

Kong changed."[56] It lasted for seventy-nine days and deeply affected Hong Kong's economy, the people's livelihood, and the churches. Some Hong Kongers affirmed the movement as a kind of liberation theology in Hong Kong; others opposed it because for them it had torn society apart.[57] The conflicts and disagreements among citizens also exist in the family, among friends, and within churches. The Archbishop of Hong Kong, Paul Kwong, indicated that these political struggles have made many people lose their mutual trust and respect.[58]

A Brief Summary

Serious conflict resided in the Pauline assemblies (e.g. in Galatia and in Corinth), and continues to be present in Christian communities in modern society. Where there are people, tension occurs. God's assembly consists of human beings, so the tension is natural to Christian institutions. The conflict created by differences among people (e.g. different ethnic groups, various political viewpoints, differences in social status and goals, or incompatible cultural value systems) results in divisions within the church. However, this does not mean that we do not need to deal with the tension, for the essence of the church is based on Christians' union with Jesus Christ. The reality of the church still points to the unity of all God's assemblies with Christ through the work of the Holy Spirit. We may not have realized our ideal yet, but we are in the process toward that final eschatological reality. We are called to move this process forward.

---

56. Justin K. H. Tse, "Introduction: The Umbrella Movement and Liberation Theology," in J. K. H. Tse and J. Y. Tan, eds., *Theological Reflections on the Hong Kong Umbrella Movement* (New York: Palgrave Macmillan, 2016), 1.

57. Yan Kung, "The Umbrella Movement and Kairos: The Church's Theological Encounter with a Political Movement," in Tse and Tan, *Hong Kong Umbrella Movement*, 107.

58. Cardinal John Tong, "Church Leaders Call for Reconciliation in Society," http://rthk9.rthk.hk/rthk/news/englishnews/20141222/news_20141222_56_1063428.htm, accessed 23 March 2017.

The Essence of Church: The Community as Union with Christ in the Midst of Conflict

In the midst of tension, how did Paul respond to the situation? The way Paul reacted to the tension of the church helps us explore his opinion of ecclesiology, particularly the essence of the church. Paul's handling of the disputes in the Galatian and Corinthian churches will be examined using the four marks found in the Nicene Creed.

Paul's Viewpoint of Ecclesiology Based on Galatians

The Mark of Catholicity: Dealing with the Ethnic Conflicts between Jewish and Gentile Christians One of the characteristics of an ideal church is catholicity, a trait expressed in the church's embrace of differences. The conflict in many churches is caused by church members' exclusivity toward others. Paul urges God's assemblies to embrace the diversity of the community.

The conflict between the Jewish and Gentile Christians is firstly represented in the Antioch table-fellowship event in Galatians 2. In Antioch, obedience to Jewish ritual was vigorously discussed because some Jews demanded exact obedience to the Jewish rites of circumcision and table-fellowship so as to differentiate themselves from the Gentiles. This led to tensions between the Jewish and non-Jewish Jesus-followers.[59] In the Antioch crisis, Paul confronted Peter because he was in fear of the circumcision faction (2:12). Moreover, these tensions in the Galatian church had been expressed through hostility shown among the believers, as Paul implied in 5:15: "If, however, you bite and devour one another, take care that you are not consumed by one another" (NRSV). Paul also used an allegorical story of Hagar and Sarah in 4:21–29 to explain the conflict relationship in the church: "But just as at that time the child who was born according to the flesh persecuted the child who was born according to the Spirit, so it is now also" (4:29 NRSV).

To address the ethnic conflict issue, Paul appeals to both Christ and Abraham to redefine who God's heirs are. First, Paul deals with the crucial factors (the Gentiles' circumcision and law observance) that caused the ethnic conflicts. He sets Abraham as a universal ancestor (3:29), and

---

59. Vischer, *Unity of the Church*, 46.

then dissociates the ancestor from the law of Moses and connects him with faith (3:10–14, 23–25). Second, Paul identifies the descendants of Abraham by their faith in God. Those who believe are the descendants of Abraham (3:7; οἱ ἐκ πίστεως, οὗτοι υἱοί εἰσιν Ἀβραάμ).[60] By employing Genesis 15:6, he bases descent from Abraham on faith, not circumcision. The third and most important factor for the redefinition of God's people is the role of Christ. Paul intentionally links the singular form of the "seed" (σπέρμα) with a single descendant, Jesus Christ (3:16). In 3:26–29 he includes both Jew and Gentile in Christ: "If you belong to Christ, then you are Abraham's offspring, heirs according to the promise" (3:29 NAS 1977). Therefore, Paul argues that the ethnic tension between the Jewish and Gentile Christians should be overcome by their faith in Jesus Christ, for all the believers are united with Christ to become the body of the one church.

The Mark of Apostolicity: Crucified Love on the Cross in Galatians The mark of apostolicity refers to the measure of the real church which is founded upon the apostles and their writings. In the midst of the conflicts, Paul's way of reunification is based on Christ's sacrificial love on the cross, and he himself sets an example as a paradigm of conformity to Christ. In Galatians 5:11 Paul says that he was persecuted for the sake of the cross because he does not preach circumcision. Then he reproaches the Judaizers for compelling circumcision in order to avoid persecution (6:12). All the believers in Galatia are called to imitate the crucified Christ as Paul did: "Brothers, I entreat you, become as I am . . ." (4:12 ESV). As Paul says in Galatians 2:20 (NRSV), "It is no longer I who live, but it is Christ who lives in me. And the life I now live in the flesh I live by faith in the Son of God, who loved me and gave himself for me." If we live in conformity to Christ, we have no reason to fight against each other due to our different opinions or ethnic identities.

---

60. G. Walter Hansen, *Abraham in Galatians: Epistolary and Rhetorical Contexts*, Journal for the Study of the NT Supplement Series 29 (Sheffield: JSOT, 1989), 109–116; Karin B. Neutel, "'Neither Jew Nor Greek': Abraham as a Universal Ancestor," in *Abraham, the Nations, and the Hagarites: Jewish, Christian, and Islamic Perspectives on Kinship with Abraham*, ed. Martin Goodman et al. (Leiden: Brill, 2010), 292–293.

Paul in his letters already expressed that Christ's crucified love binds the diverse members into one unified, but not uniform, community.

Paul's Viewpoint of Ecclesiology Based on Corinthians

The Mark of Holiness: Dealing with Cultural and Secular Conflict Instead of being assimilated into contemporary cultures, the church's holiness requires it to be different from its surrounding social milieu and also to challenge and transform culture.

I have discussed the cultural and secular conflict above. First, the Corinthians tore the church apart by splintering into partisan groups following Paul, or Apollos, or Peter. However, they saw no wrong in the divisions, because division was quite common in the hierarchical society of the ancient Mediterranean world.[61] But Paul considers division to be very serious, regarding it as a division of Christ. He asks in 1 Corinthians 1:13, "Has Christ been divided? Was Paul crucified for you? Or were you baptized in the name of Paul?" (NRSV). For Paul, it is Christ himself, not these apostolic leaders, who created the church community. And it is Christ in whom they should boast, not the apostles (1:31). It is Christ alone who is the source of our life and it is he who became for us wisdom from God, and righteousness and sanctification and redemption. Thus the honor belongs to Christ alone (1:29–31).

Second, the competitive secular culture had an effect on the church. The members competed for alliance with these distinguished apostles, and they even participated in the city's temple feasts to make a connection with higher-status groups in society.[62] Paul instructs them that the full power of God is made perfect in weakness (2 Cor 12:9). Paul himself did not teach with words of wisdom, but came in weakness and in fear and in much trembling (1 Cor 2:3–4). In addition, he even regarded himself as the rubbish of the world, the dregs of all things (1 Cor 4:13).

Third, the divided Lord's Supper further widened the gap or divisions among church members. Paul asks for true fellowship among all members without any social disruption. Destroying the church's fellowship is an affront to Christ; as he states, "when you . . . sin against

---

61. David DeSilva, *Honor, Patronage, Kinship and Purity: Unlocking New Testament Culture* (Downers Grove: InterVarsity, 2000), 95–104.

62. Vischer, *Unity of the Church*, 86.

members of your family, and wound their conscience when it is weak, you sin against Christ" (8:12 NRSV). It is Christ who creates the community, and all the behaviors that damage the fellowship of the community are sin against Christ.[63]

In summary, the problem of the Corinthians was that they were too closely attached to the society so that cultural values infiltrated their lives. Paul asks the Corinthian church to be holy and to live lives different from the social milieu by living out their union with Christ.

The Mark of Unity: Union with Christ as One Body with Many Members That the church is one declares its unity, and this unity requires the diversity of the community (1 Cor 12:4–11). When managing the problem of divisions, Paul keeps returning to our union with Christ. The conflict in the Corinthian church resulted from two sets of disordered relationships. Vertically, the members' relationship with Christ had been viewed through their relations with the apostolic leaders. Horizontally, the relationship among members was disordered for they saw themselves via the secular value system. They favored one over another based on each other's religious authority or social position (1 Cor 4:6).

Paul provides some foundational principles to deal with these tensions. First, for Paul, church takes place not only in the physical arena, but also in the spiritual arena. All members are united with Christ through one Spirit: "For in the one Spirit we were all baptized into one body – Jews or Greeks, slaves or free – and we were all made to drink of one Spirit" (12:13 NRSV). In other words, the Spirit or Christ is the foundation of the unity of church communities. Christ is the center for the creation of a church community. We are called by God into fellowship with Jesus Christ (1:9) and not with any superior human being. All the members who share in this union with Christ are in fellowship with one another.

Second, the horizontal fellowship with one another is like the relationship that our body parts have with each other.[64] Our body cannot live without the parts. Because each member is reliant on the others, when one suffers, all suffer together, and the weaker part is indispensable for the other members of the body. Moreover, the inferior member should be given greater respect and honor. According to Paul,

63. Vischer, 86.
64. Vischer, 88.

the members of the body that seem to be weaker are indispensable, and those members of the body that we think less honorable we clothe with greater honor, and our less respectable members are treated with greater respect; whereas our more respectable members do not need this. But God has so arranged the body, giving the greater honor to the inferior member, that there may be no dissension within the body, but the members may have the same care for one another. If one member suffers, all suffer together with it; if one member is honored, all rejoice together with it. (12:22–26)

A Brief Summary

Paul's way of dealing with these tensions in the churches in Galatia and Corinth helps us to understand the essence of God's assemblies. Since the beginning of the church, the struggle for unity has not ceased. In his letters, Paul demonstrates an ideal community of Christ – that is, in the midst of conflict the crucified love of Christ has been given so that all Jesus's followers can be renewed and reunited with the Son of God as one body. Christ's community should be one holy, catholic, apostolic church. Each part of the body is indispensable for every other part and they all build each other up. The communities' fellowship with Christ empowered them to live differently from their social surroundings. The unity of the church is measured by the apostles and their writings. In short, church is a community united with Christ in the midst of conflict. Its true identity is sanctified but it lives in earthly bodies (1 Cor 15:40).

How Paul's View of Ecclesiology Relates to Today's Churches in Hong Kong

Are the struggles for unity of the first generations of Christians in church communities still valid today? Is what was true in the apostolic period still applicable to today's churches in Hong Kong? At the start of this essay we quoted the good answer provided by Vischer: "The call to unity is the same, and it is therefore not surprising that the great texts of the New Testament in which the drive to unity has been formulated are also relevant today."[65]

It is necessary to admit that tension and conflict are as natural to Hong Kong churches as to any other communities consisting of human beings. Since the Umbrella Movement of September 2014, the deteriorating relationships within different groups, communities, and churches have become a thorny social issue. Even parents were set against their children and children against their parents. Friends disputed with each other due to their different attitudes toward the central government and Mainland China. These issues remain a serious concern in some Hong Kong churches. Having accepted that the issue of tension is rooted in the churches, we must now explore how Paul's view of ecclesiology might help produce the desired unity.

If Paul could write a letter to the Hong Kong churches, what would he say?

First, Paul might remind us of the crucified love on the cross as the foundation for our mutual love in a community. No matter what kind of tensions exist between Hong Kongers and Mainlanders, as Christians we embrace the same sacrificial love of Christ. Christ so loved us that he gave his life for us, so how can we level charges against those whom God has chosen? How can we separate from each other over different political viewpoints or cultural value systems? We discover Christ in fellowship with our brothers and sisters, particularly in the midst of conflict.

Second, as we are all united with Christ as one body, each member has an indispensable position in the body. Neither Hong Kong churches nor Mainland Chinese churches can live without the other. On the one hand, Hong Kong churches are more developed and have more resources. In many respects, Mainland people can benefit from the advanced resources in Hong Kong, such as the developed administration in churches, valuable theological resources, and well-disciplined theological educators. On the other hand, following the reunification of Hong Kong with Mainland China, Hong Kong churches need skill and wisdom to deal with the Chinese Central government. In this the Mainland churches can share various kinds of lived experiences learned over many long years in which their faith has grown strong. In this sense, both Mainland Chinese Christians and Hong Kong Christians

65. Vischer, 15.

are called to embrace and love each other, since we are all members of this one body, Jesus Christ.

In sum, Paul's view of handling the tensions in the church is still applicable to modern churches in Hong Kong. The types of conflicts may vary, but the foundations for dealing with the struggle for unity remain the same.

Conclusion

A church in its essence is a community that is united with Christ in the midst of conflict. It demonstrates two perspectives: one earthly and the other transcendental. It is earthly because Christ's communities share the fully human characteristics of tension and fragility. It is transcendental because the true identity of church is the body of Christ and it is created by Christ. The church stands as a dynamic community in the process of growing into its fullness. The continuous struggle and unceasing efforts to achieve unity will make the church grow into greater maturity.

Further Reading

Cao, Nanlai. *Constructing China's Jerusalem: Christians, Power, and Place in Contemporary Wenzhou*. Stanford, CA: Stanford University, 2011.

Chee, Nan Pin. *The Search for the Identity of the Chinese Christian Church: Ecclesiological Responses of the Chinese Church in 1949–1958 to the Political Changes*. Hong Kong: WEC International of HK Ltd., 2016.

Clapp, Rodney. *A Peculiar People: The Church as Culture in a Post-Christian Society*. Downers Grove: InterVarsity, 1996.

Harvey, Thomas Alan. *Acquainted With Grief: Wang Mindgao's Stand for the Persecuted Church in China*. Grand Rapids: Brazos, 2002.

Pavey, Stephen C. *Theologies of Power and Crisis: Envisioning/Embodying Christianity in Hong Kong*. Eugene, OR: Pickwick, 2011.

Wickeri, Philip L. *Reconstructing Christianity in China: K. H. Ting and the Chinese Church*. Maryknoll, NY: Orbis, 2007.

丁光訓。《論三自與教會建設》。上海：中國基督教兩會，2000。(English Translation: Ting, K. H. *On Three-Self Policy and the Construction of the Chinese*

Churches. Shanghai: National Committee of Three-Self Patriotic Movement and National Christian Council of China, 2000.)

林榮洪。《王明道與中國教會》。香港：中國神學研究院，1982，1987。(English translation: Lam, Wing-hung. *Wang Ming-Tao and the Chinese Church*. Hong Kong: China Graduate School of Theology, 1982, 1987.)

彭淑卿。《倪柝聲的末世論教會觀》。台灣：中原大學宗教研究所及台灣基督教文藝出版社聯合出版，2011。(English translation: Peng, Shu-Ching. *Watchman Nee's Eschatological Ecclesiology*. Taiwan: Graduate School of Religion of Chung Yuan Christian University and Taiwan Christian Literature, 2011.)

CHAPTER 7

The Church as an Assembly on Mt Zion:
An Ecclesiology from Hebrews for African Christianity

PETER NYENDE

ABSTRACT

In this paper I classify ecclesiological studies, against which I briefly survey African ecclesiological scholarship. From this survey I show that, relative to ecclesiological studies elsewhere, there is a paucity of literature on ecclesiology within African scholarship. I argue that this paucity puts African Christianity at a disadvantage in the quest of African Christians to be simultaneously African and biblical, thereby embodying an African biblical Christianity. In an effort, therefore, to contribute to African ecclesiological scholarship, I offer a conceptual ecclesiology drawn from Hebrews in which the church is understood as a community approaching God, in Christ, in his heavenly dwelling (the heavenly Mt Zion) to offer him, through the same Christ, prayers and immaterial sacrifices, and to live in obedience to him en route to partaking in the coming fullness of his presence and kingdom. This fullness will result in the realization of God's purposes for creating the world.

I wish to propose from Hebrews a biblical theological ecclesiology that is at home in African Christianity. But since the subject of ecclesiology is vast I will begin my paper by classifying academic discourse on ecclesiology, and within that classification give an overview of ecclesiological studies in Africa. This overview will support the view that, although all types of ecclesiological study are found in Africa, more ecclesiological studies from Africa are needed, especially in the area of conceptual ecclesiologies, if the quest for an authentic but biblical African Christianity is to be achieved.

Global and African Ecclesiological Studies

Ecclesiological studies can be classified into three distinct areas of study, namely, identity ecclesiologies, concrete ecclesiologies, and conceptual ecclesiologies. In identity ecclesiologies the content of ecclesiology is focused on, and/or is from the perspective or in the interests of, a given denomination.[1] Ecumenical ecclesiologies are also included in identity ecclesiological studies although their intent is to transcend denominational boundaries.[2] African identity ecclesiological studies are found in historical studies literature on African Initiated Churches (AICs),[3] which are churches in Africa that were founded by Africans, in historical studies literature on various African churches which were started by missionaries,[4] and, in exceptional cases, in studies of the church in a given African country.[5] These African identity ecclesiologies

1. See, for example, Walter Kasper, *The Catholic Church: Nature, Reality, and Mission* (New York: Bloomsbury Academic, 2015); and Paul Avis, *The Anglican Understanding of Church* (London: SPCK, 2013).

2. See, for example, Gillian R. Evans, *The Church and the Churches: Towards an Ecumenical Ecclesiology* (Cambridge: Cambridge University, 1994); and Gesa Elsbeth Thiessen, *Ecumenical Ecclesiology: Unity, Diversity, and Otherness in a Fragmented World* (London: T&T Clark, 2009).

3. See, for example, F. B. Welbourne and B. A. Ogot, *A Place to Feel at Home* (London: Oxford University, 1966); David B. Barrett, *Schism and Renewal in Africa: An Analysis of Six Thousand Contemporary Religious Movements* (Nairobi: Oxford University, 1968); Bengt Sundkler and Christopher Steed, *A History of the Church in Africa* (Cambridge: Cambridge University, 2000); H. J. Becken, "A Healing Church in Zululand: 'The New Church Step to Jesus Christ Zion in South Africa,'" *Journal of Religion in Africa* 4 (1972): 213–222; M. C. Kitshoff, ed., *African Independent Churches Today: Kaleidoscope of Afro-Christianity*, African Studies 44 (Lewiston, NY: Edwin Mellen, 1996); and Allan H. Anderson, *African Reformation: African Initiated Christianity in the 20th Century* (Asmara: Africa World, 2001).

4. See, for example, Walter L. Yates, "The History of the African Methodist Episcopal Church in West Africa: Liberia, Gold Coast (Ghana) and Nigeria, 1900–1939" (PhD diss., University of Hartford, 1967); Adrian Hasting, *A History of African Christianity 1950–1975*, African Studies 26 (Cambridge: Cambridge University, 1979); and Ogbu Kalu, *African Pentecostalism: An Introduction* (Oxford: Oxford University, 2008).

5. See Kenneth R. Ross, "Current Ecclesiological Trends in Northern Malawi," *Journal of Religion in Africa* 19 (1999): 465–485; Christine Chaillot, *The Ethiopian Orthodox Tewahedo Church Tradition: A Brief Introduction to Its Life and Spirituality* (Paris: Inter-Orthodox

usually discuss the genesis and spread of African churches, together with their peculiarities.

Also to be found within identity ecclesiological research are studies along the lines of race and ethnicity and, to a lesser extent, gender.[6] They are highly contextual in nature and are usually fueled, for various reasons, by the need for ecclesial emancipation from Eurocentric or Western ecclesiologies. Black ecclesiologies in Africa belong to such studies where, for example, Vellem articulates a black ecclesiology based on the narrative of the uprising of liberation spirituality.[7]

Concrete ecclesiological studies are ecclesiological studies which focus on the practical and empirical matters of a church or churches. These practical studies include how to be church or a certain kind of church,[8] church order and church polity,[9] church ministry,[10] how to grow a church,[11] what successful or healthy churches look like,[12] church

---

Dialogue, 2002); and Frank-Ole Thoresen, *A Reconciled Community of Suffering Disciples: Aspects of a Contextual Somali Ecclesiology* (Frankfurt: Peter Lang, 2014).

6. See, for example, Letty M. Russell, *Church in the Round: Feminist Interpretation of the Church* (Louisville: Westminster John Knox, 1993); De Woong Park, "Towards an Asian Ecclesiology Based on Asian Liberation Theology and Minjung Theology," PhD dissertation (Drew University, 2008); and C. René Padilla, "A New Ecclesiology in Latin America," *International Bulletin of Missionary Research* 11 (1987): 156–164.

7. Vuyani S. Vellem, "Black Ecclesiology: Uprising Faith Praxis for the Blackness of Humanity," *The Ecumenical Review* 67 (2015): 651–663. See also Goba Bongonjalo, "Towards a Black Ecclesiology," *Missionalia* 9 (1981): 47–59.

8. See, for example, Michael Moynagh, *Being Church, Doing Life: Creating Gospel Community Where Life Happens* (Oxford: Monarch, 2014); and C. René Padilla et al., eds., *The Local Church, Agent of Transformation: An Ecclesiology for Integral Mission* (Buenos Aires: Ediciones Kairós, 2004).

9. See, for example, Mark Dever, ed., *Polity: Biblical Arguments on How to Conduct Church Life* (Washington DC: Center for Church Reform, 2001); and Steven B. Cowan, *Who Runs the Church? 4 Views on Church Government* (Grand Rapids: Zondervan, 2004).

10. See, for example, Robin Greenwood, *Transforming Church: Liberating Structures for Ministry* (London: SPCK, 2002); and Brian D. MacLaren, *The Church on the Other Side: Doing Ministry in the Postmodern Matrix* (Grand Rapids: Zondervan, 2000).

11. See, for example, Bob Jackson, *Hope for the Church: Contemporary Strategies for Growth* (London: Church Publishing House, 2002); and George Barna, *Grow Your Church from the Outside In: Understanding the Unchurched and How to Reach Them* (Ventura, CA: Regal, 2002).

12. See, for example, Mark Dever, *Nine Marks of a Healthy Church*, 2nd ed. (Wheaton: Crossway, 2012); and Eddie Gibbs and Ryan K. Bolger, *Emerging Churches: Creating Christian Community in Postmodern Cultures* (Leicester: IVP, 2006).

life and membership,[13] and church architecture[14] (from which "ecclesiology" as a technical term was first used).[15] There is a small amount of African literature on concrete ecclesiologies dealing with how to be an indigenous church,[16] being a local church,[17] types of congregations in Africa,[18] church ministry to youth in Africa,[19] and church architecture in Africa.[20]

Conceptual ecclesiologies address the topic of who or what the church is, or simply the nature of the church.[21] For this reason, they are considered ecclesiologies of the first order, are prescriptive in nature, and provide guideposts for concrete forms of being church, of church practice, and doing mission. Studies on the creedal pronouncement of belief in the "one, holy, catholic, and apostolic church" are in this group of ecclesiological studies and, as such, have inspired a variety of forms of being church. African literature on conceptual ecclesiologies is dominated by understandings of the church based on socio-cultural dynamics

13. See, for example, James P. Wind and James W. Lewis, eds., *American Congregations*, Vol. 2 (Chicago: University of Chicago, 1994); and Scott Thumma and Dave Travis, *Beyond Megachurch Myths: What We Can Learn from America's Largest Churches* (San Francisco: Jossey-Bass, 2007).

14. See, for example, Mark A. Torgerson, *An Architecture of Immanence: Architecture for Worship and Ministry Today* (Grand Rapids: Eerdmans, 2007); and Jeanne Halgren Kilde, *Sacred Power, Sacred Space: An Introduction to Christian Architecture and Worship* (Oxford: Oxford University, 2003).

15. Gerard Mannion, "What Is Comparative Ecclesiology and Why Is It Important? Roger Haight's Pioneering Methodological Insights," in *Comparative Ecclesiology: Critical Investigation*, ed. Gerard Mannion (London: T&T Clark, 2008), 13–40 (14).

16. E. Bolaji Idowu, *Towards an Indigenous Church* (London: Oxford University, 1965).

17. See A. Radoli, ed., *How Local Is the Local Church?* (Eldoret, Kenya: AMECEA Gaba, 1993); and John Gichinga, *The Local Church* (Kampala: IFES, 1995).

18. H. Jurgens Hendriks, *Studying Congregations in Africa* (Wellington, South Africa: Lux Verbi BM, 2004).

19. Jesse Jackson Mirega, *The Youth and the Church in the 21st Century: A Handbook for Youth Ministry and Pastors* (South Bend, IN: Sahel, 2010).

20. Richard Tambwe Mutibula, *Towards an African Ecclesiology in Stones: A Theological Cry of An African Newborn Child* (Saarbrücken: VDM Verlag Dr. Müller, 2011).

21. See, for example, Avery Dulles, *Models of the Church* (Garden City, NY: Doubleday, 1987); Everett Ferguson, *The Church of Christ: A Biblical Ecclesiology for Today* (Grand Rapids: Eerdmans, 1996); Miroslav Volf, *After Our Likeness: The Church as the Image of the Trinity*, Sacra Doctrina (Grand Rapids: Eerdmans, 1997); and Scott MacDougall, *More Than Communion: Imagining as Eschatological Ecclesiology* (London: Bloomsbury T&T Clark, 2015).

of family, such as family itself, clan, ethnic group, and ancestorhood.[22] Stephanie Lowery's essay in this volume concerned with ecclesiology in Africa from the perspective of its developments also points out the predominance of "church as family" in virtually all church groupings in Africa.[23] This dominance she pins on the metaphor's cultural resonance in Africa and the plentiful biblical support for it. But we also have conceptual ecclesiologies based on some aspect of mission,[24] on understandings of sacrament,[25] and on biblical imagery of pilgrims.[26]

The Need for African Ecclesiological Studies

The ecclesiological studies highlighted above from other parts of the world are but a representation of a vast literature on ecclesiology, while those from African ecclesiological studies are virtually all that there is. This state of affairs puts Christianity in Africa at a disadvantage in view of African Christians' ongoing need for both indigenousness and faithfulness to Scripture.

22. See Paul J. Sankey, "The Church As Clan: Critical Reflections on African Ecclesiology," *International Review of Mission* 83, no. 330 (1994): 437–449; John Mary Waliggo, "The African Clan as the True Model of the African Church," in *The Church in African Christianity: Innovative Essays in Ecclesiology*, ed. J. N. K. Mugambi and L. Magesa (Nairobi: Acton, 1998), 111–128; A. E. Orobator, *The Church As Family: African Ecclesiology in Its Social Context* (Nairobi: Hekima College, 2000); Oliver Alozie Onwubiko, *The Church in Mission in the Light of Ecclesia in Africa* (Nairobi: Paulines, 2001); Gerald K. Tanye, *The Church As Family and Ethnocentrism in Sub-Saharan Africa* (London: Transaction, 2010); and Charles Nyamiti, *Studies in African Christian Theology*, Vol. 4: *Christ's Ancestral Mediation through the Church Understood as God's Family: An Essay on African Ecclesiology* (Nairobi: Catholic University of Eastern Africa, 2010).

23. See also her *Identity and Ecclesiology: Their Relationship among Select African Theologians* (Eugene, OR: Pickwick, 2017).

24. See Solomon Andriatsimialomananarivo, "The Missiological Dimensions of African Ecclesiology" (PhD diss., University of South Africa, 2001); and Stan Chu Ilo, Joseph Ogbonnaya, and Alex Ojacor, eds., *The Church As Salt and Light: Path to an African Ecclesiology of Abundant Life*, African Christian Studies (Eugene, OR: Wipf and Stock, 2011).

25. Kambere Kasai Florent, "The Church as a Sacrament of Reconciliation and Healing in the Africa Context," *African Christian Studies* 30 (2014): 26–47.

26. See P. J. Arowele, "The Pilgrim People of God: An African's Reflection on the Motif of Sojourn in the Epistle to the Hebrews," *African Journal of Theology* 4, no. 2 (1990): 438–455; and David Zac Niringiye, *The Church: God's Pilgrim People* (Carlisle: Langham Global Library, 2016), although Niringiye does not focus on any African context.

The latest statistics project that by 2025, Africa will have the highest population of Christians on any continent, standing at more than 700 million.[27] Alongside this increase Africa has manifold forms of Christianity due to an unrivaled proliferation of churches and denominations.[28] But this numerical strength must be matched by the Christian faith taking root in African culture and thereby being authentically African. For this rooting to happen, African Christians must be helped to think about their faith in African terms; worship and liturgy must be African in thinking, conduct, and instrumentation; Bible interpretation must be through the lens of, and for, African contexts; and theologies must give priority to, and engage with, African needs and realities.[29] The extent, therefore, to which these requirements are met is the extent to which Christianity in Africa takes on authentic African forms. And given that African ecclesiologies are written for, or based on, African churches, more of them would contribute to shaping authentic African forms of Christianity.

Moreover, authentic African forms of Christianity must be matched by fidelity to the Bible for African Christianity to be biblical Christianity, that is, African biblical Christianity. The quest for authentic African Christianity must then be guided by biblical insight or else it will be left at the mercy of what is African, or what is locally expedient and pragmatic for the survival, sustenance, or growth of churches in African cities, towns, and countryside. Otherwise it will even be at the mercy of ecclesiastical entrepreneurs who are out simply to make money through churches. For this reason, ecclesiological studies, particularly the conceptual kind which are informed directly by the Bible, are critical since they help engender faithful forms of African Christianity. Such studies can help Christian communities in Africa to understand the nature of the church they are a part of and who they are in Christ, and, thereby, be guideposts for faithful forms of biblical Christianity that is also African.

27. Todd M. Johnson, Gina A. Zurlo, Albert W. Hickman, and Peter F. Crossing, "Christianity 2016: Latin America and Projecting Religions 2015," *International Bulletin of Missionary Research* 40 (2016): 1.

28. Paul Kollman, "Classifying African Christianities: Past, Present, and Future: Part One," *Journal of Religion in Africa* 40 (2010): 4.

29. The rooting of Christianity in Africa is what is called inculturation (or contextualization), and it has been a defining goal of African Theology; see K. Davis, "Third World Theological Priorities," *Scottish Journal of Theology* 40 (1987): 85–105.

I wish, therefore, to articulate an ecclesiology for African Christianity which not only comes from the book of Hebrews but, at the same time, resonates with Africa's spiritual enchanted world. But since Hebrews's ecclesiology can only be grasped against the background of the Old Testament's literature on God's dwelling from the garden of Eden to Mt Zion, my ecclesiology is invariably a biblical theological ecclesiology.

God's Dwelling from the Garden of Eden to Mt Zion: A Biblical Theology

The key to appreciating Hebrews's ecclesiology lies in the second of the Genesis creation accounts. The stories of creation are not a discourse with a lot of literary detail and precision telling us everything we need to know about how God created the world. Rather, they are brief stories imbued with imagery and symbolism whose meanings are foundational for understanding the purposes of God for creation, what jeopardized those purposes, and God's plan for restoring those purposes.

In Genesis's second account of creation (Gen 2:4–24), the garden of Eden is depicted as God's own dwelling where human beings are placed to care for and tend it (Gen 2:15). This depiction is first seen in God's full accessibility to human beings within the garden, symbolized in God being with the humans and talking with them face to face. Second, it appears in the words used to explain the duties of the human beings in the garden, that is, "work" (*avad*) and "taking care of" (*shamar*), words used to describe Levitical duties of guarding and ministering in the sanctuary (see Num 1:53; 3:7–8; 4:23–26; and 18:4). The use of *avad* and *shamar* to designate the duties of human beings in the garden, therefore, implies that the garden was God's dwelling place. Third, the depiction is seen when human beings sin against God, since the movement of God when he finds out the humans' sin is a movement (*hithallek*) specific to one's residence (Gen 3:8; cf. Lev 26:11–13; Deut 23:14).[30] It was as God was taking a walk in his garden that he confronted the human beings' disobedience to his express command. Fourth, the depiction is seen in the

---

30. The verb used for movement (*mithalek*) in Gen 3:8 is, as pointed out by Hamilton, "a type of Hithpael that suggests iterative and habitual aspects." Victor Hamilton, *The Book of Genesis Chapters 1–17*, New International Commentary on the Old Testament (Grand Rapids: Eerdmans, 1990), 192.

consequence of sin, when human beings are expelled from the garden as God's abode. The cherubim, who are associated with God's presence and throne, guard the garden from human beings so that they cannot re-enter it, lest they enjoy what it has to offer (Gen 3:22–24). Finally it is seen in the reference to the garden of Eden in biblical literature as God's garden (Gen 13:10; Isa 51:3; Ezek 28:13 and 31:9), thereby underscoring the view that the garden is indeed God's dwelling.

The depiction of the garden of Eden as God's dwelling where he is fully accessible to humans and where humans live to serve reveals a fundamental purpose of God's creation of the world: God intended the world to be the place of his dwelling with human beings. God's residence and kingship are inseparable, as later biblical literature makes clear with the ark, the mercy seat, and the cherubim (Exod 25:19–22) in the temple's inner room (*hekal*) making up God's throne or footstool (see Pss 11:4; 99:1, 5, 9; 132:7; Isa 6:1–3; 37:16; 60:13; Ezek 10:1–4; 43:6–7; cf. Num 10:35–36; 1 Sam 4:3–4; 1 Kgs 22:19; Mic 4:7). Therefore it is implicit that, by virtue of God's dwelling with humans, he intended to rule the world from his dwelling. In other words, God intended the world to be his place of residence with humans and a part of his kingdom.

However, these purposes were jeopardized by Adam and Eve sinning, which led to their expulsion from God's dwelling (Gen 3:22–24). In calling Abraham and promising him offspring, land, kings, and blessing to all nations (Gen 12:1–3, 7; 13:15; 15:18–20; 17:6, 16 [cf. 35:11]), YHWH sets out to restore his residency and kingdom purposes for creation (i.e. Edenic restoration). YHWH clarified this restoration plan by the person of Abraham when he spoke through Moses about Israel's identity as his people and himself as their God, including their vocation as a holy nation and a royal priesthood for the sake of other nations if they were obedient to him (Exod 19:1–6; cf. Deut 4:5–8; Jer 4:2). He commanded Moses to have the people of Israel build him a sanctuary according to his design (Exod 25:9–40) so that he could dwell with them (Exod 25:8). But it was through another prophet, Nathan, that YHWH clarified his restorative plan, according to his kingship promise made to Abraham. He chose David and his line for kingship which he would use to exercise his rule (2 Sam 7:4–17; 1 Chr 17:3–15). So the restoration plan of God's residency and kingdom by means of Abraham entailed God's dwelling with Israel in the land under Davidic kings and then using them to restore both his kingdom and his dwelling with human beings (the nations) in the world.[31]

In the tabernacle and later the temple we have the beginning of YHWH restoring his dwelling among humans and his kingdom in the world. This conclusion is supported by numerous correspondences between the tabernacle and the temple and YHWH's garden dwelling.[32] Furthermore, this correspondence is seen when human beings are referred to as trees in the temple (Pss 52:8; 92:12–13), and in the reference to a river in Jerusalem where the temple is located (Ps 46:4–5; cf. Ezek 47:1–12), both of which correspond to the setting in the garden of Eden. This parallelism is also witnessed in the Chronicler's consistent use of God's compound name (*YHWH Elohim*) in connection with the temple (see 1 Chr 17:16–17; 28:20; 29:1; 2 Chr 1:9; 6:41–42; 26:18), which corresponds to the use of the same name to refer to God in the garden story.[33]

It is important to note here that the temple as God's dwelling was referred to as Mt Zion. This reference was due to the association of mountains with divine dwellings in ancient Near Eastern cosmology. Numerous studies[34] show that, because they reached to the clouds, mountains were believed in the ancient Near East to be places where

31. See details of this, albeit with different shades and emphases, in T. Desmond Alexander, *From Eden to the New Jerusalem: An Introduction to Biblical Theology* (Grand Rapids: Kregel Academic, 2009); and C. Marvin Pate et al., *The Story of Israel: A Biblical Theology* (Downers Grove: InterVarsity, 2004), amongst others.

32. For details of correspondences, see, for example, Victor Avigdor Hurowitz, "YHWH's Exalted House: Aspects of the Design and Symbolism of Solomon's Temple," in *Temple and Worship in Biblical Israel*, ed. John Day (London: T&T Clark, 2007), 63–110 (80–81); Elizabeth Bloch Smith, "'Who Is the King of Glory?' Solomon's Temple and Its Symbolism," in *Scripture and Other Artifacts: Essays in Honor of Philip J. King*, ed. Michael D. Coogan and Philip J. King (Louisville: Westminster John Knox, 1994); Gregory K. Beale, *The Temple and the Church's Mission: A Biblical Theology of the Dwelling Place of God* (Downers Grove: InterVarsity, 2004), 66–80; D. Sawyer and P. Morris, eds., *A Walk in the Garden: Biblical, Iconographical and Literary Images of Eden*, Journal for the Study of the OT Supplementary Series 136 (Sheffield: JSOT, 1992); and Margaret Barker, *The Gate of Heaven: The History and Symbolism of the Temple in Jerusalem* (Sheffield: Phoenix, 2008).

33. I am indebted on this point to Stordalen's comprehensive study. For a fuller discussion, see T. Stordalen, *Echoes of Eden: Genesis 2–3 and Symbolism of the Eden Garden in Biblical Hebrew Literature* (Leuven: Peeters, 2000), 457–458.

34. See, for example, Mircea Eliade, *Patterns in Comparative Religion* (Cleveland: Meridian, 1958), 367–387; Richard J. Clifford, *The Cosmic Mountain in Canaan and the Old Testament* (Cambridge, MA: Harvard University, 1972); and Robert L. Cohn, "The Mountains and Mount Zion," *Judaism* 26 (1977): 97–115.

the nether-world, earth, and heaven met (the fulcrum of the world, the *axis mundi*), and were therefore believed to be the dwelling place of divinities. As such, mountains were viewed as the hot spots of encounters and communications between humans and divinities. And so the temple, and by extension Jerusalem as YHWH's abode, was referred to as a mountain, namely, Mt Zion (Pss 2:6; 3:3–4; 24:3; 99:9; Isa 4:5; 8:18; 11:9; 56:6–7; Mic 4:7; Joel 2:1; 2:32), although it was not a mountain. Indeed, the movement of God to the temple as his permanent dwelling was seen to be the movement of God from Mt Sinai, where his presence was felt by the people of Israel definitively (Exod 24:17), to Mt Zion (Ps 68:15–18).

We have already mentioned that the purpose of God having residence in Israel was to restore his dwelling among humans and his kingdom in the world. This was first to start taking effect with Israel, who approached YHWH in his dwelling through all manner of prayers, such as thanksgiving, praise, and petition, as the prayer of Solomon (1 Kgs 8:30–45) and the psalmists' petitions and thanksgiving indicate, and through sacrifices and feasts (Lev 1 – 7:19; 16; 23) which YHWH had prescribed. YHWH would in consequence respond to their approaches (Ps 73:15–20; Isa 37:14–34) besides revealing his presence one way or another on account of them being in his house. This explains the psalmists' longings for visits to and residence in the temple (Pss 42:1–2; 27:4–5; 84:1–4; 122:1–2), and even their eschatological-like hopes of living there forever (Pss 23:6; 26:8; 27:4). The people of Israel would then go back to their homes and daily lives to live in obedience to God (Pss 15:5; 24:3–4; 36:7–9; cf. 65:4), consequently experiencing his blessings of life in the land (Exod 19:5; Lev 26:3–13, 14–39; Deut 7:12–16; Ps 24:5) and becoming a light to the nations (Exod 19:1–6; Deut 4:5–8). Other nations would in turn flock to Zion to be in God's presence and be exposed to his law and ways (Pss 47; 48:1–2; 50:1–2; 67:1–2; 68:28–34; 84:5–7; 87; 96:3–4; 99:1–3; Isa 2:2–4; Mic 4:2) and, as a logical implication, go back to their nations and kingdoms to live in obedience to YHWH, as seems to have been the case with the queen of Sheba (1 Kgs 10:1–13). Mt Zion as God's dwelling would become a magnet to Israel and to all nations, who would then, respectively, be and come under God's kingdom. Unfortunately, due to Israel's disobedience to God's commandments, this plan did not come to pass.

The pre-exilic prophets then proclaimed God's judgment on Israel on account of their sins, which ranged from rebellion (e.g. Hos 1:2; 4:1–2, 6–10), injustice, lies, and deceit (e.g. Mic 2:1–2, 8–10; 3:1–3, 9, 11), to violence and murder (see Jer 5:26–28; 9:4–6). In regard to false worship in the temple, their drawing near to God in the temple was not accompanied by obedience to God in their daily living, and this was tantamount to rejecting him (e.g. Amos 2:8; Isa 1:12–17), and to idolatry (see Ezek 8:1–18; 16:1–52). Judgment upon Israel included the destruction of Jerusalem and the temple, the decimation of Israel's population but for a remnant (e.g. Isa 1:7–9; 3:1–8; Ezek 2:10; 4:9–17), and exile (e.g. Hos 9:3–6; 10:3–6; Jer 1:14–15; 5:8–19).

In the same breath the prophets also proclaimed God's restoration of Israel, which showed his intent to still use Israel, Davidic kings, and Mt Zion to restore his dwelling and kingdom. However, the future restoration which the prophets prophesied was in some of their oracles indicative of a transformative restoration and not simply a restoration of what had gone before, since some descriptions of the restored state of Israel, Davidic kingship, covenant, land, Jerusalem, and temple could not be reconciled with their current or past states. This transformative restoration is explicit in covenant restoration, since Jeremiah's description of a new covenant meant a radical transformation of the existing one (Jer 31:31–34).

In regard to the prophecy of temple restoration, the restored temple would not just be a rebuilt temple but would be transformed into the highest mountain (Isa 2:2–4; Mic 4:1–3), which was in all probability symbolic of Mt Zion's superiority over other houses of divinities because YHWH, its resident, is superior to all other gods. The restored temple would have life-giving waters flowing from it (Ezek 47:1–12; Zech 14:8), perhaps symbolic of God's dwelling supporting life, as was the case with the rivers in the garden of Eden. It would also be the eschatological site of a great feast for all peoples and the destruction of death and all things that hurt (Isa 25:6–8). However, it was not until the advent of Christ that the nature of this transformative restoration was clarified. This clarity is the case in point when the author of Hebrews admonishes his audience to be aware that in Christ they have come to a heavenly temple and city which are ontologically superior to God's dwelling in the past. Indeed the clarity which Hebrews provides on the nature of the restored Mt Zion to which the church has come is central to its ecclesiology. It is this connection of Hebrews' ecclesiology with God's past dwelling which makes the discussion of a biblical theology of God's dwelling necessary, without which Hebrews' ecclesiology would not be comprehensible.

Ecclesiology in Hebrews

We can view Hebrews as a sustained rhetorical discourse[35] on Jesus as mediator par excellence. Jesus's mediatorial functions are articulated in comparison with Old Testament prophets and Moses in particular (Heb 1:1–2; 3:1–6), angels (1:4 – 2:18), and, for the most part, Aaronic high priests (1:3; 2:14–18; 4:14 – 5:10; 6:16 – 8:7; 9:1 – 10:18). Given that Jesus's mediatorial functions are largely spelled out in comparison with those of Aaronic high priests, God's dwelling forms a significant part of the content of Hebrews since priests and Aaronic high priests served in the tabernacle and then in the temple. In consequence, the author of Hebrews (referred to from here on simply as Hebrews, given the book's unknown authorship) envisions his audience (community of faith from here on) as a worshipping community both in their approach to God in his dwelling and in obedient living. This vision of the church is most prominent in Hebrews' unique revelation to the community of faith that they are approaching God on the heavenly Mt Zion and Jerusalem (12:22) and, therefore, are also receiving God's unshakable kingdom (12:28).

The subject of God's dwelling (*skēnē*) is articulated in Hebrews in relationship to Jesus's high priestly role for the community of faith. For the purposes of discussing Hebrews' ecclesiology, we shall pay attention to God's dwelling in relationship to the community of faith. With regard to Jesus, it suffices for the purposes of this paper only to note that in contrast to Aaronic high priests, Jesus is said to be a minister in the true tent pitched by the Lord (Heb 8:1–2; 9:11, 24).

In the above study on God's dwelling which was a necessary backdrop to Hebrews' ecclesiology, we pointed out that the people of Israel approached God in his dwelling through prayers and the feasts and sacrifices which YHWH had prescribed. YHWH would then respond to their approaches and reveal himself to them. This is one half of what constituted worship. Accordingly, in four instances (Heb 4:16; 10:19; 12:18–29; 13:15–16) Hebrews' audience is called upon to worship God in his house in ways similar to the people of Israel's worship in the temple.

In the first call, the recipients of Hebrews are encouraged, in view of Christ's high-priestly sympathetic intercessions (4:14–15), to approach

---

35. Indeed, the speaker in Hebrews characterizes it as "a word of exhortation" (*logos tēs paraklēseōs*, Heb 13:22), which is usually understood as an oral discourse, that is, a sermon (cf. Acts 13:15).

the throne of grace with confidence to receive mercy and grace to help them in their moments of need (4:16). This has to do with prayers in the house of God, because the mention of God's throne of grace corresponds to God's mercy seat in the temple. In addition, the verb used for "approach" (*proserchōmetha*), also found elsewhere in Hebrews (7:25; 10:1, 22; 11:6; 12:18, 22), corresponds directly to its use in the Septuagint to denote prayers in the temple where God's mercy seat resides.[36]

The second call to Hebrews' community of faith to worship God in his house comes in the exhortation to have confidence to enter God's house ("holy places," *tōn agiōn* – 10:19) and to draw near to him (10:22) because of the blood of Jesus (10:19). The entering into God's house and drawing near to him presumes that they will engage in worship of the kind that occurred in the temple – prayers and sacrifices – for that is what was prescribed and done there. This presumption is, again, supported by the word for drawing near (*proserchōmetha*) to God being similar to that used for worship in the temple.

Given the preeminence of the third call to the community of faith to worship God in understanding Hebrews' ecclesiology, we shall look at it last. The fourth call to worship comes in the pastoral admonition to the community of faith to offer to God a continuous sacrifice of praise through Jesus, a sacrifice of good deeds and sharing what they own (13:15–16). Here sacrifices in the prescribed way are commended to the community of faith since they too worship in God's house. However, in this case the sacrifices commended are not material, as was the case on Mt Sinai, the tabernacle, and Mt Zion, but immaterial. The immaterial sacrifices are in keeping with the kind of house that it is. Before we turn to this house below, it is important to note here that Hebrews makes it clear to the community of faith that their approach to God in his house is enabled by Christ: by his sympathetic priesthood (4:14–15), by his blood (10:19), and through him now in God's very presence (13:15).

The third call to Hebrews' audience to worship God in his house (12:18–29) is essential for understanding Hebrews' ecclesiology given its content: (1) it clarifies the location and nature of God's dwelling; (2) it points to the nature of God's dwelling in relationship to God's past dwelling among the people of Israel, and in so doing helps us to relate

---

36. For more on this word and its cultic context, see J. M. Scholer, *Proleptic Priests: Priesthood in the Epistle to the Hebrews*, Journal for the Study of the NT Supplement Series 49 (Sheffield: JSOT, 1991), 91–95.

God's dwelling to the prophets' prophecies of temple restoration; (3) it ties God's dwelling to God's kingdom; and (4) it mentions both halves of worship (prayers and sacrifices on the one hand, and obedience on the other) as integral to being in God's dwelling.

None of the three "calls to worship" in God's house in Hebrews directly specifies to the community which house of God is in view nor its nature. But the nature of the house is indirectly suggested in Hebrews 10:19–22. This is because the house of God the community is encouraged to enter confidently in drawing near to God is the same one in which Jesus the high priest (10:21) serves. If this is the case, then the house of God in which the community has been called to worship is metaphysical in nature, since Jesus serves in God's house which is built by God himself (8:2). It is not of this creation (9:11). In other words, Jesus serves in God's house – in heaven itself (9:24). In Hebrews 12:22 the location and thus the nature of God's house are directly specified.

In the said passage (12:18–29), the author reveals to the community that they have drawn near (*proseléluthate*) to the heavenly (*epouranió*) Jerusalem, the city of God where Mt Zion is located, to pray and offer sacrifices. In contrast to earthly life, heaven here is not simply spatial, as in the sky above, which would mean that it is beyond the reach of the community of faith who live on the earth. Rather, it is a dimension of existence or life beyond the realms of ordinary human experience, where God's presence is experienced fully and God's will is done because his reign is experienced absolutely (Matt 5:34; 6:10). For this reason, Mt Sinai as God's past dwelling on earth is inferior to the heavenly Mt Zion. According to Hebrews, Mt Sinai was earthly, and the people of Israel were accompanied by fire, gloom, darkness, the sound of trumpets, and a voice, all of which brought fear and dread (Exod 19:16, 18; 20:18–19). In contrast, Mt Zion is heavenly, and the community of faith finds itself in the company of a myriad of angels, of just ones made perfect, and of Jesus, and of God, himself. Such a place and company bring forth joyous praise and gratitude.

The prophets prophesied of a transformative restoration of Mt Zion. In Hebrews this promised restoration has occurred and Mt Zion has been transformed into the heavenly Mt Zion. Hebrews calls the community of faith to worship at this mountain and not at the temple in earthly Jerusalem. In some real sense, then, in Christ this community is in God's heavenly house offering prayers and immaterial sacrifices as they are asked to do in Hebrews 13:15. However, their worship is part of the journey to being fully in God's presence when he restores his dwelling in the world and thereby realizes his purposes for it. Thus God's intent to live among the people of Israel on Mt Zion in order to dwell fully once again with human beings is now taking place through his presence with his people in Christ on Mt Zion above. The destiny of the heavenly Mt Zion and Jerusalem is the fullness of God's dwelling among human beings, as was to have been the destiny of the earthly Mt Zion (a destiny that would have been realized had it not been for Israel's disobedience).

This destiny of Mt Zion is supported in Hebrews' constellation of revelatory pronouncements which point to a future in the fullness of God's dwelling. These revelatory pronouncements mention the powers of an age to come (6:5), receiving the promised eternal inheritance (9:15), Christ appearing a second time to save those who believe in him (9:28; 10:35–39), better and abiding possessions beyond the earthly ones that are being plundered (10:32–39, the day of the Lord (10:25), and the city to come (11:10, 16; 13:14). This destiny is also seen in John's vision when he witnesses the heavenly Jerusalem come down and God dwelling fully with the redeemed (Rev 21:1–4).

As mentioned, God's house and reign are inseparable, hence God's throne in the tabernacle and temple. This inseparable relationship is clear in Hebrews. By being in God's heavenly house (12:18–24), the community of faith is before his throne (see 4:16). There, as priest in God's heavenly dwelling, Christ is seated at the right hand of the throne of God (1:3; 8:1; 12:2). The community is part of God's kingdom which cannot be shaken (12:27) and of whose fullness they will partake in the future. The destiny of the heavenly Mt Zion will simultaneously be the restoration of God's kingdom in the world, which results in the realization of God's purposes for God's creation.

Obedience to God in daily living is necessary. This is the other half of worship. Accordingly, Hebrews' audience is repeatedly warned against disobedience. In Hebrews 12:18–29 the relationship between worship in God's house and worship in daily living is most clear. The call to obedience in Hebrews 12:25 immediately follows the revelation that they have come to worship in God's heavenly house (12:18–24). God's people, Israel, rejected God who spoke from Mt Sinai by disobeying him in the desert, and they were punished for it. Now Hebrews warns the community of faith that they will not escape judgment if they reject God by disobeying him (12:25). Moreover, the revelation that their worship is in the heavenly court prompts the exhortation to obedience (12:12–17). To put it differently, their approach to God in the heavenly Mt Zion should be accompanied by their daily obedience. Such worship (*latreuōmen*) is pleasing (*heuarestōs*) to God (12:28). Other warnings against disobedience in Hebrews (including 2:1–4; 3:7–16; 4:1–11 and 12:1–2) should be viewed from this perspective.[37]

To sum up, Hebrews' ecclesiology is of a community approaching God, in Christ, in his heavenly dwelling, to offer him prayers and immaterial sacrifices. They live in obedience to him on the way to being in the fullness of his presence and kingdom, resulting in the realization of God's purposes for creation which we discussed earlier.

Conclusion: Hebrews Ecclesiology and African Christianity

Some years back I argued that the intersection of Africa's spiritual enchanted world and the Christian faith is what accounts for the character of Christianity in Africa.[38] African Christians believe and understand that the spiritual world is in constant interaction with the material world of humans and largely determines its fortunes. For this reason, African Christians, like the rest of the population, are alert to the spirit world, if not preoccupied with it. Thus, Hebrews ecclesiology, which has to do with a plane of existence not of the material kind, which those in Christ are now a part of, finds hospitable ground in Africa. In consequence, it would readily appeal to African Christians and help them understand in African terms the nature of the church and provide guidance for their faith practices, thus contributing to the formation of authentic African Christians.

In conclusion, Hebrews ecclesiology is not limited to informing the faith and practices of African Christians' understanding of the nature of the church. God's revelation in Scripture is offered to all those in Christ, wherever they may be. However, I have offered this ecclesiology in light of the observation that people's contexts and history will make certain biblical texts more meaningful and have a greater relevance to them

37. Indeed, Son (Kiwoog Son, *Hebrews 12:18–24 as a Hermeneutical Key to the Epistle* [Carlisle: Paternoster, 2005]) has argued that the content of Hebrews should be viewed through Hebrews 12:18–24.

38. Peter Nyende, "An Aspect of the Character of Christianity in Africa," *Journal of Theology for Southern Africa* 132 (2008): 38–52.

than they would to others. Therefore, although Hebrews' ecclesiology may be appreciated by Christians outside Africa, I think it is an ecclesiology that African Christians would more readily ponder and appreciate.

Further Reading

Chaillot, Christine. *The Ethiopian Orthodox Tewahedo Church Tradition: A Brief Introduction to Its Life and Spirituality.* Paris: Inter-Orthodox Dialogue, 2002.

Hendriks, H. Jurgens. *Studying Congregations in Africa.* Wellington: Lux Verbi BM, 2004.

Kitshoff, M. C., ed. *African Independent Churches Today: Kaleidoscope of Afro-Christianity.* African Studies 44. Lewiston, NY: Edwin Mellen, 1996.

Lowery, Stephanie A. *Identity and Ecclesiology: Their Relationship among Select African Theologians.* Eugene, OR: Pickwick, 2017.

Mugambi, Jesse N. K., and Laurenti Magesa, eds. *The Church in African Christianity: Innovative Essays in Ecclesiology.* Nairobi: Acton, 1998.

Nyamiti, Charles. *Studies in African Christian Theology*, Vol. 4: *Christ's Ancestral Mediation through the Church Understood as God's Family: An Essay on African Ecclesiology.* Nairobi: Catholic University of Eastern Africa, 2010.

Onwubiko, Oliver Alozie. *The Church in Mission in the Light of Ecclesia in Africa.* Nairobi: Paulines, 2001.

Orobator, A. E. *The Church As Family: African Ecclesiology in Its Social Context.* Nairobi: Hekima College, 2000.

Sundkler, Bengt, and Christopher Steed. *A History of the Church in Africa.* Cambridge: Cambridge University, 2000.

Tambwe, Richards M. *Towards an African Ecclesiology in Stones: A Theological Cry of An African Newborn Child.* Saarbrücken: VDM Verlag Dr. Müller, 2011.

Tanye, Gerald K. *The Church As Family and Ethnocentrism in Sub-Saharan Africa.* London: Transaction, 2010.

Thoresen, Frank-Ole. *A Reconciled Community of Suffering Disciples: Aspects of a Contextual Somali Ecclesiology.* Frankfurt: Peter Lang, 2014.

CHAPTER 8

Ecclesiology and the Theology of the Land: A Palestinian Christian Perspective

MUNTHER ISAAC

ABSTRACT

The theology of the land gives insight into our understanding of the meaning of *ekklesia* (church). This is because God, land, and community are always connected in the Bible. The church is always defined by a context, and that context is the people in a certain time and space. The particularity of the Palestinian church, being located in the biblical land, shapes the ways the Palestinian church understands itself and its identity.

The Palestinian church[1] takes its identity and theology from its natural and unbroken relationship with the biblical land. This is the land where Jesus was born, and where many of the Bible events took place. There is an existential relationship between Palestinian Christians and their land. Mitri Raheb, a Palestinian Christian pastor and theologian, puts it this way: "My identity was stamped by the fact that I was born in this particular place. I feel I have something like a special relationship to

---

1. I use the term "the Palestinian church" as a representation of all the churches and denominations in Palestine today. There are about 45,000 Christians in the West Bank (including East Jerusalem) and Gaza, and about 120,000 in Israel, the majority of whom are Greek Orthodox and Catholic, with a few Protestants. For more, see Rania al Qass Collings, Rifat Odeh Kassis, and Mitri Raheb, *Palestinian Christians in the West Bank: Facts, Figures and Trends* (Bethlehem: Diyar, 2012); and Johnny Mansour, *Arab Christians in Israel: Facts, Figures and Trends* (Bethlehem: Diyar, 2012).

David and to Christ – a relationship developed not only by way of the Bible, not only through faith, but also by way of land. I share my city and my land with David and Jesus. My self-understanding as a Christian Palestinian has a *territorial dimension*."[2] Even though this statement is made with the first person singular pronoun, one could easily replace the "I" with "we," as in "we the church in Palestine." In other words, the self-understanding of the Palestinian church has a territorial dimension.

Palestinian Christians have written a lot about the theology of the land. When Palestinian Christians speak of the land, they talk about their *homeland* and the homeland of their ancestors. The theology of the land for us is not simply an abstract academic study but a matter of existence and identity. This paper will focus on the interplay between land and church as it shapes the Palestinian Christian understanding of ecclesiology.

The first part will look at the land and ecclesiology from a biblical theological standpoint, and consider the question: How does the theology of the land shape our understanding of ecclesiology?[3] The second part will offer insights that are particular to the experience of the Palestinian church in the land today.

The Theology of the Land and Ecclesiology

The Land Belongs to God

Palestinian Christians believe and emphasize that the original promised land, like all other "lands" in the world, belonged to the creator God (Gen 1:1; Ps 24:1). And so, when God promised Israel the land, he made it clear that the land would remain *his land* nevertheless: "For the land is mine" (Lev 25:23 ESV). The former Latin Patriarch in Jerusalem Michel Sabbah comments: "Land has a particular status in the Bible. It belongs to God . . . Israel, therefore, could not become the absolute owner of the land: it was only God's guest. The worst possible thing that could befall Israel would be to forget this truth, to settle this land, and

---

2. Mitri Raheb, *I Am a Palestinian Christian* (Minneapolis: Fortress, 1995), 3. Emphasis added.

3. The arguments in this section are based on my work *From Land to Lands, From Eden to the Renewed Earth* (Carlisle: Langham Monographs, 2015).

to substitute it for God in its worship and values system."[4] Similarly, Palestinian Orthodox theologian Paul Tarazi argues regarding the allotment of the land: "It is an assigning of the tribes to certain parts of that earth, and not an allocation of land to each of the tribes as though each would become the owner."[5]

The claim "for the land is mine" comes in the context of the Jubilee laws (Lev 25). The importance of these laws in Leviticus 25 is that they are a reminder to Israel that it *does not own the land*, for the land belongs ultimately to God (25:23). Israel is not free to do with the land whatever it wants, or to claim eternal possession of it. These laws are a reminder that "land is not from Israel but is a gift to Israel, and that land is not fully given over to Israel's self-indulgence."[6] Such a way of administrating the land is a challenge to the "empire" concept, where the king owned and administrated the land and the people were mere servants or slaves (1 Sam 8:10–17).

Why a Land?

The theology of the land must begin by asking the question: Why a land? Why did God promise Abraham a land to begin with?

Why was a particular geography critical in God's plan for history? The significant role of this local geography is counter-intuitive, since the covenantal God of Abraham is the Creator of both heaven and earth who proclaims, "For all the earth is mine."[7]

Giving a land as part of the project of redemption highlights that God is committed to his created order and to the redemption of human society. Redemption in the Bible is not merely about individuals, personal piety, or spiritual existential experiences. It is about redeeming whole societies and communities on earth, who in turn make the church. It is ultimately about redeeming the whole of humanity.

---

4. Michel Sabbah, "Reading the Bible Today in the Land of the Bible," November 1993, Latin Patriarchate of Jerusalem, http://www.lpj.org/fourth-pastoral-letter-patriarch-sabbahreading-bible-today-land-bible-november-1993/, accessed 12 May 2017.

5. P. N. Tarazi, *Land and Covenant* (St. Paul: OCABS, 2009), 130.

6. Walter Brueggemann, *The Land: Place As Gift, Promise, and Challenge in Biblical Faith* (Minneapolis: Fortress, 2002), 59.

7. E. B. Korn, "Jewish Reflections on Richard Lux's 'The Land of Israel (*Eretz Yisrael*) in Jewish and Christian Understanding,'" *Studies in Christian–Jewish Relations* 3 (2009): 4.

The biblical storyline could have been different. God could have given Abraham moral commandments for himself and his family. He could have instructed him to wander around in the world proclaiming the worship of the one true God. Instead, he chose to bring Abraham to a place, to engage with humans in a certain history and a certain geography, and to create from Abraham's descendants a unique and distinct society – one that would reflect his image on earth in the midst of the nations: the church.

Finally, this pattern of choosing a nation and a land and dwelling in the midst of people underscores God's desire for fellowship with humanity. The Bible portrays God as a God who seeks to dwell among humanity and thus in the midst of communities. This is evident throughout biblical history, whether in the garden of Eden, the tabernacle, or the temple. It is in this sense that we could describe the faith of Israel as "incarnational."[8] The people of God always embodied the presence of God in their midst, and this becomes a part of their definition. The presence of God in the land was dependent to a certain degree on the presence of the Israelites in the land, for he dwells not merely in the land, but also in the midst of his people: "For I the LORD dwell in the midst of the people of Israel" (Num 35:34 ESV).

The Land Universalized: The Promised Earth

Palestinian theologians look to the land as more than just "Canaan," or modern-day Palestine and Israel. The descriptions of the boundaries of the land in the Old Testament are "fluid."[9] The outline in Genesis 15:18–21 speaks of universal dominion and not merely of a specific territory in the ancient Near East. This is confirmed by Paul's language in Romans 4:13 that Abraham was promised the "world."

---

8. See N. T. Wright, "Jerusalem in the New Testament," in *Jerusalem Past and Present in the Purposes of God*, ed. P. W. L. Walker (Carlisle: Paternoster, 1994), 58.

9. The boundaries of the land in the OT roughly make two maps: (1) the land of Canaan, and (2) a wider territory (from the river to the river) that includes most of the ancient Near East. We can speak of "micro borders" (Canaan) and "macro borders" (the Euphrates). In addition, in the different periods, the land had different shapes. The allotted land, for example, is different from the land during David's and then Solomon's reign, and in both cases the boundaries went beyond modern Israel and Palestine.

Furthermore, Palestinian theologian Yohanna Katanacho argues, from the well-known words in Genesis 12:1–3, that the "climax of the speech" comes in the statement that "through you all the families of the earth will find blessing." As such, "it seems that the land of Abraham is not going to have fixed borders. It will continue to expand . . . thus increasing in size both territorially and demographically. The land of Abraham will continue to extend until it is equal to the whole earth."[10]

In the New Testament the domain of this kingdom – its land – is the whole earth. The declaration of Jesus at the conclusion of Matthew's Gospel is perhaps one of the most important statements in the New Testament on the theology of the land: "All authority in heaven *and on earth* has been given to me. Go therefore and make disciples of *all nations*" (Matt 28:18–19 ESV). Jesus here receives *all the lands of the earth* as his inheritance. The "promised land" has been eclipsed by the breakthrough of what we may call the "promised earth." The land has been *universalized*. The kingdom of Israel is now a universal kingdom. It is not limited to one land or one people, because the king in this kingdom has authority over heaven and earth. This is indeed a fulfillment of the original vision regarding the kingdom of God in the Old Testament. Psalm 2:8 is now a reality: "You are my Son; today I have begotten you. Ask of me, and I will make the nations your heritage, and *the ends of the earth your possession.*" The risen Christ can now claim this psalm and make it his: he was appointed the "Son of God," the nations are his "heritage," and the "ends of the earth" are his "possession."

In short, the theology of the land has a universal thrust. We cannot simply speak about the theology of *the land*, but instead we should speak about the theology of *the earth*. The theology of the land is ultimately the theology of the earth, and this, in turn, will take us back to the creation (Ps 24:1).

This universalization of the land is by no means a negation of the role and importance of the land in Christian theology, but instead serves only to emphasize its importance. The universalization of the land takes shape in three ways: through expansion, through reproduction, and finally in the consummation.

---

10. Yohanna Katanacho, *The Land of Christ* (Bethlehem: Bethlehem Bible College, 2012), 80.

Universalization by Expansion

The coming of Jesus caused the borders of the land to expand. This is particularly evident in Acts 1:8: "you will be my witnesses in Jerusalem and in all Judea and Samaria, and to the ends of the earth." The image envisioned here is that of progression or expansion. As the gospel of the kingdom moved from Jerusalem into Judea, then Samaria, and to the ends of the earth, the borders of the land also shifted outwards to include these new places. In this image, the promised land grows until it reaches the ends of the earth. In other words, the "land" grows into the "earth." This has important consequences for our understanding of the church and its "universal" character.

This aspect of the universalization reminds us of the historical nature of Christianity. That is why the Jesus-event had to take place *in the land of promise*, and that is why the first church had to be a *Jerusalemite church*. The land plays an integral role in New Testament biblical theology. The reign and presence of God began expanding to the rest of the world *from the land*.

Because of this, the Palestinian church considers itself "the original church." Christianity started from Jerusalem, after all, and for Palestinian Christians this is a source of pride.

Universalization by Reproduction

Second, and more directly related to our discussion on ecclesiology, the land is universalized in that the mission of the church establishes new "holy places" in new lands. We can refer to this as *establishing new "land realities" in new lands*. As new communities of believers in new lands embody the presence and reign of God, taking responsibility for their territory, they recreate the story of Israel in new lands. In this process, Jerusalem no longer has to play a central role in relation to the other new locations, because Jesus is now the cornerstone – the center of the new Christian movement. The New Testament thus has a decentralized ecclesiology – but it is still territorial. Any place has the potential to become a "holy place." Any land has the potential to become a holy land. Any city has the potential to become a holy city or a city on a hill – as evident by the role of Antioch in the early stages of Christianity (Acts 11:25–30). As Burge explains: "The New Testament . . . brings an ecclesial alternative to the problem of Holy Land. Christians in other lands, lands deeply valued by God, bring with them the possibility of bearing the reality of Christ to these places. Which explains the fundamental basis of Christian mission. This is a divinely appointed task to bring that which the Temple and the land once held – the presence of God – into the nations of the world."[11]

This is not to deny that God is present everywhere and at all times. Nor is it a denial of the possibility of divine presence and encounters apart from the church. Yet it remains true that God is present in a "special" way in the midst of the church. The presence of God in a particular way in the midst of God's people is a biblical principle. In the Old Testament, the presence of God in the land depends to a certain degree on the presence of the Israelites in the land, for he dwells not merely in the land, but also in the midst of his people: "For I the LORD dwell in the midst of the people of Israel" (Num 35:34 ESV). Joosten even argues that God's dwelling in the land is "inseparably connected to the fact that he dwells in the midst of the Israelites."[12]

The church, however, brings more than just the "presence of God" to new lands. It speaks prophetically for God in new lands. It cares for neighbors and the sojourners in new lands. It promotes and embodies the kingdom ideals of justice and equality in new lands. In this way, it creates new land realities in new lands. *The land is universalized when Israel's model is Christified and replicated in new lands.* In addition, the new "land realities" function as a signpost and point forward to the time of consummation, when all the earth will be fully redeemed.

Universalization in the Consummation

Third, the universalization of the land is intended to point towards a time when the whole created order will be renewed in the form of a "new heavens and a new earth." This holistic and universal redemption serves to remind us of the goodness of creation. The land is part of God's good creation. The restoration of the land is an integral part of the

---

11. G. M. Burge, *Jesus and the Land: The New Testament Challenge to "Holy Land" Theology* (Grand Rapids: Baker Academic, 2010), 131.

12. J. Joosten, *People and Land in the Holiness Code: An Exegetical Study of the Ideational Framework of the Law in Leviticus 17–26* (Leiden; New York: Brill, 1996), 192.

restoration of the earth – a moment towards which history is moving. Until this happens, however, the lands continue to groan.

These three aspects of the universalization of the land together make a complete picture. The land is universalized as it expands beyond Jerusalem into new lands. This expansion includes an element of decentralization, which no longer necessitates the central role of Jerusalem in redemptive history. Rather, new land realities are created in new lands, as Israel's model is replicated in new places. This process culminates in a "new heavens and a new earth" when God intervenes in time and space – by bringing complete redemption to the universe.

The Cross as the Paradigm

It is crucial to underscore that declaring a territory as belonging to God and announcing Jesus as Lord over new lands is not done through military or political means. The church cannot rely on power or the secular authorities to implement the reign of God in new lands. The church in the past has erred in trying to enforce the kingdom of God over people and territory – evident, for example, on occasions in the Byzantine Empire, the Crusades, Calvin's Geneva, the Puritans, and colonial history. The role of the church cannot be confused with that of political rulers or civil authorities.

The church conquers the world not by weapons or force; the kingdom of God expands through preaching and evangelism in both words and deeds. *The non-violent and sacrificial approach of the Messiah determines the nature of his reign and the method and approach of his followers.* The kingdom, though violently resisted (Acts 14:22), is to expand non-violently – through sacrificial service and the power of the Spirit (1 Cor 2:3–5).

Embodying the Presence and Reign of God on Earth

The church must take seriously the theology of being made in God's image and of being entrusted with vice-regency. The community of believers, collectively, represent God on earth. The local church represents God in a particular village, or city, or land. The believers should take this responsibility seriously. God and the land demand holiness, and the covenant that God made with his people always demands the fruits of justice and righteousness.

The church in all its community-based activities creates, as it were, a sacred arena where God can be encountered. The church community is thus the natural medium of theophany today. The community, liturgy, and sacraments embody and manifest the presence of God within a particular land. The presence of God is a sanctifying presence: it transforms individuals, communities, societies, and lands. Again, this is not to deny the presence of God or divine activity beyond the realm of the church. General revelation cannot be denied (e.g. Acts 17; Rom 1).

The church should also take its priestly task seriously. The church not only represents God within a certain land, but also represents a certain land and the people of that land before the face of God. As such, it must continuously engage in prayers of intercession on behalf of the nation and the land (1 Tim 2:1–2).

A church must also recognize its identity as the "light" and "salt" of the land. Corrupted salt or a fading light is a recipe for the corruption and darkness of society and land. The church in a particular land must have a sense of accountability toward that land and the people and society of that land. With election comes responsibility.

Land, Community, and the Church[13]

The Christian experience today is always rooted in time and space. To be "in Christ" is to be with him *here* and *now* and this, at the same time, is a *community experience*. To be "in Christ" is to be in him with the community of believers – and this is directly related to the land of that community. The theology of the land emphasizes the role of the community. It is very important that the Christian life demands responsibilities from and to those within the community. The social dimension of the theology of the land helps reclaim this community element in redemption. Chris Wright further proposes that ancient Israel's mission in the land can become a model for the experience of being "in Christ" today. He calls this a "typological understanding of

---

13. This section is adapted from my book *From Land to Lands*, 366–367.

the significance of Israel's land":[14] "The typological interpretation of the land, which relates it to the person and work of Jesus the Messiah, does not come to a 'dead end' with Jesus himself. Rather, it carries the social and economic thrust of Old Testament ethics onwards into the ethics of practical relationships within New Testament Israel, the Messianic community. Citizenship of the kingdom of God most certainly has a social and economic dimension."[15]

Wright's contribution to the theology of the land is immensely important. He avoids any spiritualization or "heavenization" tendencies by anchoring the thesis "In Christ = In the Land" in the experience of the community of believers on earth and also by linking this to a Christian version of Israel's theology of the land. As such, the theology of the land continues to be an important category of faith in Christian theology – with an important role to play in defining the mission and identity of the church.

Land Matters

The biblical narrative is a story about land. Covenant, as Brueggemann stresses, never concerned only people and God, "*but the land is always present to the interaction and is very much a decisive factor.*"[16] In many Christian circles, the transition from the Old Testament to the New Testament resulted in two dissimilar versions of redemption: the covenant in the Old Testament between God, people, and land became in the New Testament a covenant between God and *individuals – with no reference to land or community.* However, a serious biblical theological approach to the Bible as a whole must, however, challenge such an approach – especially in light of the fact that the New Testament authors so clearly present the Jesus-event as the continuation and climax of the story of Israel.

In the biblical narrative the role of the community is emphasized alongside that of the individual – perhaps even above it. The biblical context of redemption is the community. In many Christian circles, salvation has become a private matter that is not related to land and

---

14. C. J. H. Wright, *Old Testament Ethics for the People of God* (Downers Grove: InterVarsity, 2004), 193.

15. Wright, *Old Testament Ethics*, 196.

16. Brueggemann, *The Land*, 200. Emphasis added.

community. The focus is on God's encounters with individuals and God is relevant only as he is involved in personal and private matters. But the theology of the land shows that the covenant has always been between *God, communities,* and *land.* As Brueggemann powerfully argues:

> It will not do to make the individual person the unit of decision-making because in both Testaments the land possessed or promised concerns the whole people. Radical decisions in obedience are of course the stuff of biblical faith, but now it cannot be radical obedience in a private world without brothers and sisters, without pasts and futures, without turf to be managed and cherished as a partner in the decisions. The unit of decision-making is the community and that always with reference to the land.[17]

God is the God of nations and lands, and not just the God of individuals. The focal point in biblical theology is the community and not the individual. This is not a denial of the need for individuals to make faith decisions. God is the one who meets individuals where they are. However, once an individual believes in the gospel of the reign of God through Christ, he or she becomes a member of a community – a family. He or she is accountable to the community just as the community is accountable to him or her. *Meaning, mission, and identity can only be defined in the context of the community.* This is the true definition of ecclesiology.

This is where the New Testament concept of fellowship comes into play. Fellowship is not merely a symbolic spiritual articulation of Christian unity in Christ. Rather, "the experience of *fellowship* – in its full, rich, concrete New Testament sense – fulfils analogous theological and ethical functions for the Christian as the possession of *land* did for Old Testament Israelites."[18] Christian fellowship, therefore, manifests itself in the socio-economic sphere and is interpreted in socio-economic actions, such as sharing possessions, meeting the needs of the community, and maintaining a system of equality among the members of the fellowship. The experience of the community is central to what it means to be a Christian.

17. Brueggemann, 199.
18. Wright, *Old Testament Ethics*, 195. Emphasis in the original.

The Church in Context: Territorial Ecclesiology

The church is always a church in a context. For Paul Tarazi, this understanding of territorial ecclesiology is rooted in the foundational relationship between the church and the world. The church, he argues, "is not a separate entity which stands vis-à-vis the world or even in the world." Rather, the church and world are two "faces of the same reality, which is the creation. The world is the first creation; the church is the new one."[19] However, the church and world are at the same time radically different faces of the same reality. While the world is the sinful and not-yet-redeemed creation, the church is that part of creation which has responded to and willingly accepted salvation by and in Jesus Christ.[20] Tarazi then concludes: "Orthodoxy has consistently taken the New Testament expression 'the church of God in such and such a place' to be a basic truth at the core of sound ecclesiology. There is no such thing as an ethereal church of God at large, but the same church of God taking different shades and colours according to its various dwelling places on this earth."[21]

This understanding of ecclesiology is extremely important. It emphasizes the rootedness of the church in the land. *A church in a particular land exists for the sake of that land and takes its mission agenda from it.* The church, in other words, derives much of its purpose from its locale. This is not simply a matter of contextualizing the Christian gospel and making it more "relevant." This has to do with the self-definition of the church. This requires that each church identifies its territory and claims this territory as the realm of its vice-regency. The mission of the church in the world is, after all, a declaration of the sovereignty of the Son of God over all the lands of the world. The local church needs to apply this global reign of Christ in its own distinctive locality. This declaration of sovereignty can only be done through sacrificial love and service. It cannot be imposed or forced. The biblical meaning of vice-regency is that of service of the other and selfless love of the neighbor. This is how God reigns!

---

19. Paul Nadim Tarazi, "Covenant, Land and City: Finding God's Will in Palestine," *The Reformed Journal* 29 (1979): 14.

20. Tarazi, "Covenant, Land and City," 14.

21. Tarazi, 14.

Churches today are defined more in terms of doctrine and beliefs than territory. Mission is defined in reference to individuals and people groups, not territory. Yet the biblical vision of holistic redemption and the paradigm of Israel together suggest a different way of doing church and mission. *The church in a particular land exists with the view that this land will one day become a new restored creation.* Therefore, the church of a particular land must embody, advocate, and implement God's agenda for that land. God's agenda for a particular land must then unify the churches that exist in a particular land toward fulfilling this agenda. *A missional theology of the land thinks territorially.*

The Particularity of the Palestinian Church

One Holy, Catholic, Apostolic Church

Palestinian Christians view themselves, naturally, as part of the "one holy, catholic, apostolic church," as the Nicene-Constantinopolitan Creed declares. In fact, the Jerusalem church was part of the first five original seats, though a small one, besides Alexandria, Antioch, Constantinople, and Rome.

Yet the unity of the "one church" has been jeopardized by the many divisions and conflicts Christians have had among themselves, but especially in conflicts that have taken place in the Holy Land itself. The Jerusalem seat has been coveted over the years, and everyone has wanted to have a foot in Jerusalem, the place where Jesus was crucified and rose from the dead. This resulted in the presence of many churches and bishops – even two Patriarchs – in Jerusalem.

So what do we make of the fact that the church looks different from one locality to another? And what do we make of the fact that these differences and conflicts have resulted in the presence of many churches in Jerusalem today? Tarazi answers:

> As to the oneness of the church, it is a delusion to think that either a centralized administration or a pseudo-theological justification of actual chaos can realize it. The church is one because the Holy Spirit is one. And it is precisely this colorful Holy Spirit who is responsible for the various shades the church takes in its different earthly dwell-

ings, thus making it a richly vested and beautifully adorned bride to the great joy and glory of the bridegroom, the Lord Jesus Christ.[22]

Interestingly, Palestinian Christians identify more in terms of their geo-political identity than their denominational one. We are "Palestinian Christians" first, and then Orthodox, Catholics, or Lutherans. The reason for this is twofold: first, the particularity of Palestine as the biblical land, and second, the historical developments and the sense of pride Palestinians feel in response to the Israeli occupation.

The Land as the Fifth Gospel

For Palestinian Christian theologians, the original promised land has lost its strictly *theological* and *salvific* significance. It is no longer a distinct "holy Land" or even a "promised land." The New Testament went beyond land to the whole earth, claiming that Jesus is the ultimate fulfillment of the Old Testament story, and that after his death and resurrection, the land has been universalized. In this sense, the land has lost its theological significance.[23]

However, once this critical point has been granted, we can readily acknowledge that the land continues to act as a witness to God's work in history. Sabbah argues that, according to the teachings of Jesus, the committed believer does not need to worship God in a particular place, be it Jerusalem or the promised land. True worship is in spirit and truth anywhere in the world. This, however, does not negate the importance of holy places for Christians as places of faith and prayer and destinations for pilgrimage. Rather, priority is given to faith over the place in which one practices one's faith.[24]

The land will always be the historical backdrop or scenery against which the biblical drama took place in actual time and space: the call

---

22. Tarazi, 14.

23. Some have suggested that the land could possibly be the theater of the final drama in salvation history, namely, the place where Christ will return. See R. L. Wilken, *The Land Called Holy: Palestine in Christian History and Thought* (New Haven: Yale University, 1992), 47. However, as we have seen, the focus in the final vision of the NT is on the new heavens and the new earth, and the new Jerusalem, not on the land.

24. M. Sabbah, *Sawtun Sarikhun Fil Barriya (A Voice Crying Out in the Wilderness)* (Arabic book; Jerusalem: Latin Seminary, 2008), 31.

of Abraham, the birth, death and resurrection of Christ, and the place where the church first began. So, in this sense, the land still has a special role that it can play within Christian faith – *as a witness*. This is why many have called the land "The Fifth Gospel." Palestinian theologian Naim Ateek comments: "St. Cyril of Jerusalem (c. 304–386) considered the various places of Palestine as bearing a true witness to Christ. Such sites . . . were for him an eloquent witness to Jesus Christ. What was true for St. Cyril, the archbishop of Jerusalem in the fourth century, is still true today in the experience of countless pilgrims. Palestine is a fifth Gospel to them."[25]

Palestinian Christians are proud that their church continues two thousand years of Christians witness in the land where it all started. The Jerusalem church is unique in that respect. Tarazi says:

> In digging further into their own background the [Christian] citizens of Jerusalem discover that the unique contribution of their city and their land lies in the holiness of them: Jerusalem is the Holy City and Palestine is the Holy Land. In fear and trembling we realize the weight of such a responsibility, knowing that holiness is God's attribute; still in humility and obedience we accept the fact that the same Holy God has anointed in a unique way Jerusalem and Palestine. In a way the Palestinian Orthodox have no choice, since even our own flesh and blood are products of that land: its dust, its climate, its air, its food, its water – which centuries ago produced the flesh and blood of our Savior and Lord Jesus Christ.[26]

The land today tells a story! It tells the story of a God who has chosen a people and land, and dwelt in their midst – eventually bringing from that people and that land a powerful redemption which can reach to all the families and the lands of the earth. It tells the story of a God who blesses but also demands holiness and justice.

It is in this sense that the land can be considered sacred, as British Anglican bishop Inge argues: "sacred places will be those which have been associated with sacred stories, places linked with divine

---

25. N. Ateek, *Justice and Only Justice: A Palestinian Theology of Liberation* (New York: Orbis, 1989), 114.

26. Tarazi, "Covenant, Land and City," 14.

disclosure."[27] The land gives a testimony to thousands of years of salvation history. It can, as such, become a place where God is encountered in a special way – especially by people who find themselves in places which they are familiar with from their reading of Scripture. The land functions as a stimulus for spiritual reflection, prayer, and fresh encounters with God. That is why over the centuries Christian pilgrims have visited this land, seeking a deeper encounter with God.[28]

However, we must warn against idolizing the land – something to which this very same land itself testifies. The land serves as a warning against idolizing the land! As Ateek says, "History teaches us that whoever concentrates heart and mind on the land will be cursed and vomited out of the land. This is what happened to the crusaders, Christians who fell into this trap. The land can, however, *become* holy to those who put their trust in the God of the whole universe, whose nature does not change – a God of justice for all, who desires goodness and mercy for all people living in this and every land."[29]

The Palestinian church constantly declares that *our connection is with the God of the land, the God whose story the land tells, and not with the land itself.* The Crusades and the Crimean War are two examples of how far Christians are willing to go when the land is absolutized over the God of the land. In addition, and as we have seen, there is no guarantee that a holy place will continue to be holy forever – as Jerusalem itself testifies.

The Living Stones – the Church – as the Sixth Gospel

Ateek says: "The Palestinian Christians of today are the descendants of those early Christians, yet this is no cause for *hubris*. With a humility that befits their Lord, they accept it as a privilege that carries with it a

---

27. J. Inge, "Towards a Theology of Place," *Modern Believing* 40 (1992): 47. Inge argued extensively for what he called an "Incarnational" theology of the land where a place in which God is experienced in a special way can become sacred. It is important to observe that for Inge, any place or land, like a cathedral, could become sacred, and not just the original land of promise. See also his book J. Inge, *A Christian Theology of Place* (Aldershot; Burlington: Ashgate, 2003).

28. See the book by Wilken, *The Land Called Holy*. See also P. W. L. Walker, *Holy City, Holy Places? Christian Attitudes to Jerusalem and the Holy Land in the Fourth Century* (Oxford: Oxford University, 1990).

29. Ateek, *Justice and Only Justice*, 111.

responsibility for service . . . They and their ancestors have maintained a living witness to Jesus and his Resurrection from the beginning of the Church, and they should see themselves dynamically continuing such a witness in the land."[30]

Christians must remember that the people of the land are as important as the land itself when it comes to narrating the biblical story and the story of the land over the centuries. Christians who visit the land must have a connection not just with old stones of old churches, but, more importantly, with the "living stones" of the land – the community of faith where God in reality dwells. The presence of God by his Holy Spirit in the midst of the community of faith in the land is what makes this land, as indeed any other land, holy. The people of the land are an integral part of the witness of the land. The testimony of the land apart from the people of the land is an empty testimony. If the land is the Fifth Gospel, then the people of God in the land are, according to Raheb, the "Sixth Gospel":[31] "The Palestinian people are an important continuum from the biblical times until today of the peoples of the land and their distinct cultures. Their understanding of the context is important to understand the text of the bible. They constitute another important hermeneutical key to the bible."[32]

The Land as a Model

For Palestinian Christians, the theology of the land has a missional role. The theology of the land of biblical Israel – modified in the Jesus-event – is a paradigm for Christian communities living in other lands. Naim Ateek argues:

The land that God has chosen at one particular time in history for one particular people is now perceived as a paradigm, a model, for God's concern for every people and every land. As God commanded

30. Ateek, 113.

31. See also M. Raheb, "Towards a New Hermeneutics of Liberation: A Palestinian Christian Perspective," in *The Biblical Text in the Context of Occupation: Towards a New Hermeneutics of Liberation*, ed. M. Raheb (Bethlehem: Diyar, 2012), 11–28.

32. Mitri Raheb, "Shaping Communities in Times of Crisis: Narratives of Land, Peoples and Identities" (unpublished conference paper; Bethlehem: International Center of Bethlehem, November 2005).

the Israelites to obey God's law in their life in the land, so God demands the same from all peoples in their lands . . . Every nation can say about its own country . . . "This is the Lord's land, and the Lord demands a life of righteousness and justice in our land."[33]

If this is true for any church in a land, then it is certainly true for the Palestinian church. It actually begins here – in Jerusalem. That is why Palestinian Christians believe that their land has a "universal mission." In 2009 Palestinian Christian lay leaders, theologians, pastors, and activists from all church backgrounds issued an important document called "The Kairos Palestinian Document." In it they said:

> We believe that our land has a universal mission. In this universality, the meaning of the promises, of the land, of the election, of the people of God open up to include all of humanity, starting from all the peoples of this land. In light of the teachings of the Holy Bible, the promise of the land has never been a political programme, but rather the prelude to complete universal salvation. It was the initiation of the fulfillment of the Kingdom of God on earth.[34]

Sharing the Land: The Land of Peace, Justice, and Reconciliation

Palestinian Christians emphasize that God's ultimate vision for "the land" is that it will be like "the garden of Eden," "a dwelling place for God with humanity, and a homeland for all the children of God."[35] That is why Palestinian Christians reject any exclusive claim to the land. The land belongs to God, and as such it is a land for all.

It is evident that the land is a place of hostility, strife, and division. The reality in the land is one of injustice. In 2017 we commemorate fifty years of the Israeli occupation of Palestinian land.[36] There are op-

33. Ateek, *Justice and Only Justice*, 108–109.

34. Kairos Palestine Document, section 2.3, http://www.kairospalestine.ps/index.php/about-us/kairos-palestine-document, accessed 12 May 2017.

35. Sabbah, *A Voice Crying Out*, 28.

36. For more on the history of the Palestinian–Israeli conflict, see B. White, *Israeli Apartheid: A Beginner's Guide* (London: Pluto, 2009).

pressors and there are the oppressed. In the State of Israel, not all the people of the land are equal.[37] There are laws that differentiate between ethnicities and religions – against the biblical vision of equality. The resources of the land are not shared equally. Theology has been used in Palestine to justify the occupation and injustice.[38]

In response, Palestinian Christians call for a theology of a *shared land*, which means that all the dwellers of the land share the land and its resources equally and have the same rights – regardless of their ethnicity or religion.

A shared-land theology emphasizes that there are no "second-class" citizens in this land. No one is marginalized in God's vision of the land. *A shared land is not simply an option; it is the only way forward.* This is the biblical vision and so it must be the prophetic vision of the church in Palestine and Israel. The reality on the ground is that of "walls," yet what is needed is a vision of "bridges." *Palestinians and Israelis must think collectively in terms of a common future in which they cooperate – not a divided future in which they separate.*[39]

Conclusion

For Palestinian Christians, land, ecclesiology, and identity are inter-related. Furthermore, Palestinian theology makes a strong connection between territory, ecclesiology, and mission. The church as a community of believers defines its identity and mission from its context.

---

37. For the inequality in the State of Israel, see B. White, *Palestinians in Israel: Segregation, Discrimination and Democracy* (London: Pluto, 2012).

38. See M. Raheb, *Faith in the Face of Empire: The Bible through Palestinian Eyes* (New York: Orbis, 2014).

39. Isaac, *From Land to Lands*, 380. Most of the political discussions today center around the idea of a "two states solution," in which Palestinians and Israelis divide the land. The practicality of this solution is now debated since it is becoming more and more impossible to define the borders of each side's territory as a result of the Israeli settlements. This is why many academics and activists today are calling for a "one state" solution, in which there is one country and one law, but two governments. I believe that the church must not get involved in suggesting political solutions. Rather, the message should be that regardless of which political solution is adopted and implemented, the vision and ideals of God, of justice and equality in the land – indeed any land – must be respected.

For Palestinian Christians, the context of conflict and occupation has important consequences for the self-understanding of the church. For them, no one can claim possession or ownership of any land. Human beings are only tenants in the land, and as such must share the blessings of the land with their neighbors. The Palestinian church emphasizes that the land is something to share, not to possess. It is given as a gift for the good of the society, and is shared equally among the members of the community. The principle of shared and inclusive land means that an ideal church and an ideal land are places where people of all ethnicities and social backgrounds are treated equally.

Finally, the Palestinian church makes every effort to be a place of peace, fellowship, and reconciliation; a place where enemies meet and are reconciled. The principle of recommissioning reminds us that the church should be a community of peacemakers. It must be engaged in active and sacrificial peacemaking in the land.

Further Reading

Isaac, Munther. *From Land to Lands, From Eden to the Renewed Earth.* Carlisle: Langham Monographs, 2015.

Katanacho, Yohanna. *The Land of Christ: A Palestinian Cry.* Eugene, OR: Pickwick, 2013.

Raheb, Mitri. *I Am a Palestinian Christian.* Minneapolis: Fortress, 1995.

Sabbah, Michel. "Reading the Bible Today in the Land of the Bible." November 1993. Latin Patriarchate of Jerusalem, http://www.lpj.org/fourth-pastoral-letter-patriarch-sabbahreading-bible-today-land-bible-november-1993/. Accessed 12 May 2017.

Tarazi, P. N. "Covenant, Land and City: Finding God's Will in Palestine." *The Reformed Journal* 29 (1979): 10–16.

———. *Land and Covenant.* St. Paul, MN: OCABS, 2009.

Contributors

Gene L. Green (PhD, University of Aberdeen) is the Academic Dean of NAIITS: An Indigenous Learning Community. Previously he was Professor of New Testament at Wheaton College in Illinois and served as Professor of New Testament, Academic Dean and also Rector of the Seminario ESEPA in San José, Costa Rica. He is the author of four Bible commentaries written in Spanish and English, co-author of *The New Testament in Antiquity* (Zondervan, 2009), and co-editor of *Global Theology in Evangelical Perspective* (IVP Academic, 2012). His current research focuses on the intersection of the Christian faith and cultures, both ancient and contemporary, and the theology of Peter.

Munther Isaac (PhD, Oxford Centre for Mission Studies) is a Palestinian Christian pastor and theologian. He now pastors Christmas Lutheran Church in Bethlehem, and is at the same time the Academic Dean of Bethlehem Bible College. He is also the director of the highly acclaimed and influential "Christ at the Checkpoint" conferences, and is a board member of Kairos Palestine. Munther is passionate about issues related to Palestinians and Palestinian Christians. He speaks locally and internationally on issues related to the theology of the land, Palestinian Christians, and Palestinian theology. He is the author of *From Land to Lands, From Eden to the Renewed Earth: A Christ-Centered Biblical Theology of the Promised Land* (Langham, 2015). Munther has earned a Master's in Biblical Studies from Westminster Theological Seminary, and a PhD from the Oxford Centre for Mission Studies. He is married to Rudaina, an architect, and together they have two boys: Karam and Zaid.

Veli-Matti Kärkkäinen (Dr Theol., Habil., University of Helsinki) is Professor of Systematic Theology at Fuller Theological Seminary and Docent of Ecumenics at the University of Helsinki. A native of Finland, he has also lived and taught theology in Thailand. An ordained Lutheran minister (ELCA – Evangelical Lutheran Church in America), he is also an expert in global Pentecostal–charismatic issues. A regular participant in theological, missiological, and ecumenical projects and consultations at a global level, he also participates in interfaith dialogues, most recently with Muslims. He is a prolific author with over twenty books written and edited; the latest include the five-volume series titled *A Constructive Christian Theology for the Pluralistic World* (Eerdmans, 2013–17), whose last volume, *Hope and Community*, sets forth a new vision for ecclesiology (and eschatology) in the pluralistic global world.

Stephanie A. Lowery (PhD, Wheaton College) is lecturer in Systematic Theology at Scott Christian University in Machakos, Kenya. She grew up in Kenya and returned to live there after completing her PhD. She has a book on ecclesiologies in Africa, *Identity and Ecclesiology* (Pickwick, 2017), as well as a forthcoming co-authored article on theological perspectives on identity and community. Her research interests include African theologies, African ecclesiologies, and the doctrine of the Trinity.

Wonsuk Ma (PhD, Fuller Theological Seminary) is a Korean Pentecostal serving as Distinguished Professor of Global Christianity and PhD Program Director at Oral Roberts University, Tulsa, OK, USA. He served as a missionary educator in the Philippines (1979–2006), where he launched *Asian Journal of Pentecostal Studies* and *Journal of Asian Mission*. He also served as Executive Director of the Oxford Centre for Mission Studies (2007–16), during which time he led the publication of the thirty-five-volume Regnum Edinburgh Centenary Series. He has also participated in various international mission and ecumenical functions, including the Reformed and Pentecostal (Theological) Dialogue (1997–2005), Edinburgh 2010, Lausanne meetings, and various ecumenical conferences including the World Council of Churches and the Global Christian Forum. He has also participated in networks for theological education, including Global Forum of Theological Educators. His research interests include Old Testament theology, Prophets, the Spirit of God in the Old Testament, contextual theology, Asian Pentecostalism, Pentecostal mission, and global Christianity. He has authored and edited thirteen books, in addition to numerous scholarly writings.

Peter Nyende (PhD, University of Edinburgh) is an associate professor of New Testament and the head of Biblical Studies at the School of Divinity of Uganda Christian University. He is also a priest and a Canon in the Anglican Church and a commissioned evangelist with the Church Army Society of Africa. His area of interest in scholarship is the interpretation of the Bible, with a special emphasis on the book of Hebrews, within various African contexts. To this end, he has published a number of articles in leading biblical journals, with the most recent in *Expository Times* (127, no. 17 [2016]) titled "Tested for Our Sake: The Temptations of Jesus in the Light of Hebrews."

Ruth Padilla DeBorst (PhD, Boston University) is a wife of one and mother of many, a theologian, missiologist, educator, and a story-teller. She has been involved in leadership development and theological education for integral mission in her native Latin America for several decades. She works with the Comunidad de Estudios Teológicos Interdisciplinarios (CETI), a learning community with Master's and Certificate level programs. She coordinates the Networking Team of INFEMIT (The International Fellowship for Mission as Transformation) and serves on the board of Arocha. She lives in Costa Rica with her husband, James, and fellow members of the Casa Adobe intentional Christian community. Her education includes a Bachelor's in Education (Argentina), an MA in Interdisciplinary Studies (Wheaton College), and a PhD in Missiology and Social Ethics from Boston University.

Carlos Sosa Siliezar (PhD, University of Edinburgh) is Assistant Professor of New Testament at Wheaton College, Illinois. He holds a PhD in New Testament Language, Literature and Theology from the University of Edinburgh, Scotland. He is the author of *Creation Imagery in the Gospel of John* (Bloomsbury T&T Clark, 2015) and *La condición divina de Jesús: Cristología y creación en el Evangelio de Juan* (Salamanca, 2016).

Xiaxia E. Xue (PhD, McMaster Divinity College) is an Assistant Professor of New Testament at the China Graduate School of Theology, Hong Kong. She was brought up in Fujian province in China and was involved in the youth ministry of her church in her early and college years. After receiving her Master's degree in Philosophy at RenMin University in Beijing, she was called to study theology. She earned her PhD in New Testament studies from McMaster Divinity College in Ontario, Canada. Xiaxia's teaching includes courses in New Testament Greek, biblical exegesis, Pauline letters, and classes in early Christian origins. She also participates in church ministry in Hong Kong, preaching sermons and teaching adult Sunday school. Her first book is entitled *Paul's Viewpoint on God, Israel, and the Gentiles in Romans 9–11: An Intertextual Thematic Analysis*, published in the Langham Monographs series (2016). She has also published several articles and presented several papers at international conferences, including the Society of Biblical Literature. She is one of the editors of the online journal *Dialogismos*.

Index of Names

Index of Subjects

Index of Scripture References

Old Testament

New Testament

Langham Literature and its imprints are a ministry of Langham Partnership.

Langham Partnership is a global fellowship working in pursuit of the vision God entrusted to its founder John Stott –

> *to facilitate the growth of the church in maturity and Christ-likeness through raising the standards of biblical preaching and teaching.*

Our vision is to see churches in the majority world equipped for mission and growing to maturity in Christ through the ministry of pastors and leaders who believe, teach and live by the Word of God.

Our mission is to strengthen the ministry of the Word of God through:
- nurturing national movements for biblical preaching
- fostering the creation and distribution of evangelical literature
- enhancing evangelical theological education

especially in countries where churches are under-resourced.

Our ministry

Langham Preaching partners with national leaders to nurture indigenous biblical preaching movements for pastors and lay preachers all around the world. With the support of a team of trainers from many countries, a multi-level programme of seminars provides practical training, and is followed by a programme for training local facilitators. Local preachers' groups and national and regional networks ensure continuity and ongoing development, seeking to build vigorous movements committed to Bible exposition.

Langham Literature provides majority world preachers, scholars and seminary libraries with evangelical books and electronic resources through publishing and distribution, grants and discounts. The programme also fosters the creation of indigenous evangelical books in many languages, through writer's grants, strengthening local evangelical publishing houses, and investment in major regional literature projects, such as one volume Bible commentaries like *The Africa Bible Commentary* and *The South Asia Bible Commentary.*

Langham Scholars provides financial support for evangelical doctoral students from the majority world so that, when they return home, they may train pastors and other Christian leaders with sound, biblical and theological teaching. This programme equips those who equip others. Langham Scholars also works in partnership with majority world seminaries in strengthening evangelical theological education. A growing number of Langham Scholars study in high quality doctoral programmes in the majority world itself. As well as teaching the next generation of pastors, graduated Langham Scholars exercise significant influence through their writing and leadership.

To learn more about Langham Partnership and the work we do visit **langham.org**

9 781783 684489